D1229947

WITHDRAWN

The Melville Archetype

The Melville Archetype

Martin Leonard Pops

The Kent State University Press

CALVIN T. RYAN LIBRARY
KEARNEY STATE COLLEGE
KEARNEY, NEBRASKA

Copyright © 1970 by Martin Leonard Pops.
All rights reserved.
ISBN 0-87338-093-2
Library of Congress Card Catalog Number 71-101699
Manufactured in the United States of America
at the Press of The Oberlin Printing Company.
First Edition.
Designed by Merald E. Wrolstad.

For my Mother and Father

Contents

Preface

This study is principally concerned with the quest for the Sacred, for the realization of soul, in the works of Herman Melville: first, because the quest is a major passion in the lives of his most important protagonists; and, second, because by approaching Melville as a religious artist one can best perceive that principle of order which affords his oeuvre a coherence and a unity. Melville was a heterodox Christian, and the quest carried his heroes outside the boundaries of formal worship, toward the sacramental modes of romanticism, primitivism, and, ultimately, that archetypal experience C. G. Jung called individuation. We must examine the texts in relation to these modes —although in concentrating on the quest for the Sacred, we must not overlook that other passional dominant of many of his personae, the quest for sexual fulfillment. In fact, these quests are often interdependent, and we shall not fully understand the structure of Melville's informal sacramentalism until we are aware of its sexual correlate.

For a study which explicates a principle of order a sequential analysis of the *Works* is perhaps more appropriate than a topical one, and after Chapter I, which is a preliminary and schematic presentation of themes, we analyze the canon in its chronological succession—the entire canon because everything Melville wrote impinges, to a greater or less degree, upon our subject. Individual books, however, do tend to group themselves into wholes, and our chapter-divisions are meant to reflect and acknowledge this tendency. In the appendix, taking a cue from Jay Leyda's *The Melville Log*, we resurrect a sketch long buried in *The Democratic Press and Lansingburgh Advertiser* which we can now, with every confidence, assign to Melville: entitled "The

Death Craft" (1839), it is, like the second of the "Fragments from a Writing Desk," filled with many of the proto-symbols Melville would elaborate in later years and, as such, provides us with another fascinating glimpse of the young pre-South Seas author.

The quest for the realization of soul is as rarely successful among artists as it is among laymen. Of all his major American contemporaries—Emerson, Thoreau, Whitman, Poe, Hawthorne, Dickinson— only Melville mounted through all the spires of psychologic form: birth, life, death, rebirth. At the end the rest either fail to create or they fail to mature; they either break down or they repeat themselves. Melville's quest is strongest in the novels, least strong in the short stories and poetry, but, at the end, as the ascendent Billy affirms, the quest is realized. And as the *oeuvre* is his macrocosm, *Moby-Dick* is his microcosm: the quest is strongest, of course, during the chase, least strong during the excursions into cetology, but in the creamy vortex Ishmael is granted a sacred, though transient, renewal. In reading *Moby-Dick* we can never fully participate in the transactions of spirit until we penetrate the matter of whales and whaling; in reading the *oeuvre* we can never fully understand how Ishmael, who intuits the divine presence, prefigures Billy, who incarnates it, until we understand the literature between them. This is why I have spent more time on the short stories and poetry than they would perhaps deserve were they studied apart from the canon.

Ishmael's Epilogue expresses Melville's last vision of earthly transcendence; *Pierre*, which follows, his first metaphysical descent, into fire; the stories, which follow *Pierre*, the resistance of souls to their season in hell. But these tales could not forestall a still deeper progress, into the spiritual dryness of *The Confidence-Man*. And then for a while Melville stopped writing altogether, for his world had perished twice: first, as the outraged Pierre charges the indifferent walls, with a bang; then, as the Con Man leads his nearly senile victim away, with a whimper.

In *Moby-Dick* Melville suggests the density and bulk of the Whale by the very density and bulk of the cetological passages; the encyclopedic reality of barely transformed fact recreates the narrative sense. In *Pierre* Melville again uses a non-narrative vehicle to convey

his meaning and renders life at Saddle Meadows by a calculated sub-
version of style. But in *The Confidence-Man*, through a labyrinthine
and ambiguous prose, Melville comes to depend as much upon his
medium as upon his narrative, and the logic of this progression implies that when there is nothingness to express, Silence, like the Voice
of Pierre's God, will be his only speech. Without an integrative vision
of this world and the next, Melville's prose becomes a silent instrument, and his Long Quietus will not end until *Billy Budd* grants what
The Confidence-Man had denied. Hence one significance of the poetry. For unlike the stories which seek to check a terrible descent, the
poems are a purgatorial medium through which Melville rediscovered
his original dialectic and which allowed him to celebrate Billy's Ascension in his most authentic voice.

I should like to acknowledge my gratitude to Professors Lewis
Leary of the University of North Carolina, Robert Gorham Davis of
Columbia University, Howard Vincent of Kent State University, and
my colleagues at the State University of New York at Buffalo, Leslie
Fiedler and Jerome Mazzaro, for their advice and encouragement. I
should like to acknowledge a particular debt to Professor Michael
Wood of Columbia University for his valuable critique of my manuscript. Finally I should like to thank the Committee on the Allocation
of Support Funds for a grant allowing me clerical assistance in the
preparation of my manuscript, and the Arts and Letters Committee on
Institutional Funds for a grant making possible the publication of this
book.

MARTIN LEONARD POPS

State University of New York at Buffalo

1. *Reverence for the Archetype*

Introductory

Man is the shuttle, to whose winding quest
   And passage through these looms
God ordered motion, but ordained no rest.
Henry Vaughn, "Man"

Allan Melville was so humbled by the power of God that he
spelled His name with three capitals; his son, Herman, could so doubt
that power that he wondered if even one wasn't "a slight dash of
flunkeyism."[1] Allan's attitude suggests the intensest humility, Herman's that inflation of personality which is a sickness of soul, but
both are rooted in the same spiritual condition: the absence of symbolic mediation between man and God, the desacramentalized faith of
their ancestors. For Protestantism, as James Baird describes it in his
brilliant book on Melville, "shows a willful and consistent process of
discarding sacramental forms, where sacramentalism itself is a distinguishing property of the human imagination in its symbol-making
power."[2] Furthermore, "the impoverishment of Protestant symbolism" leads directly to a condition of "cultural failure" which Baird
defines as "the loss of a regnant and commanding authority in religious symbolism, since religion is here understood as the ultimately
effective symbolic authority in the total culture of a race."[3] Melville's
fullest expression of this collapse of symbolic authority is *Pierre*, perhaps the bitterest of all American novels (see Chapter III). But long
before he came to articulate his despair and rage—indeed, long before he came to understand the meaning of "cultural failure"—he
was already intuitively questing for a new sacramentalism. For this is
the real importance of the second of those two amateurish "Fragments

1

from a Writing Desk," with which, at twenty, he inaugurated his career.

Although Allan Melville was a devout Unitarian, his idea of God hardly rivalled the inscrutably transcendent, "just, rigorous, angry, but also merciful,"[4] vision of his wife's Calvinism. And certainly after Allan's death (if not before), it was her vision that their young son inherited. But Maria's God could not quench Herman's thirst for the Sacred, and herein lies one of the most important facts about Melville as man and artist: that this thirst of his is intense and lifelong and that it finds expression in virtually every book he ever wrote—even in those where the quest appears to be an intellectual pursuit and the goal of the quest a metaphysical abstraction (Final Truth, Essence). Beneath Ahab's rational demeanor burns a subterranean fire, and, therefore, whenever the quest fails, the result is not really a "tragedy of mind," a failure to read the unreadable, but a tragedy of being, in large part a failure to appease the demands of *homo religiosus.*

Melville could neither rest easily in his nominal Protestantism— "Cut off, cut off! While all the depths of Being moan . . ."—nor could he accept the authority of Catholicism, although in his long poem *Clarel,* from which this *cri de coeur* is taken, he speaks of the Roman Church with the greatest sympathy and in his last book, *Billy Budd,* describes a version of the Incarnation. Nor could he accept those substitutes for Christian sacrament which solaced some of his predecessors and contemporaries. For example, in the wake of Newton, John Locke wrote in the *Reasonableness of Christianity* that "the works of nature in every part of them sufficiently evidence a Deity," and Alexander Pope observed in *An Essay on Man* that nature was "a mighty maze! but not without a plan."[5] Melville's own response to the argument from design and the Watchmaker God was hardly calculated to inspire a similar confidence: "The reason the mass of men fear God, and at bottom dislike Him [he once told Hawthorne], is because they rather distrust His heart, and fancy Him all brain like a watch."[6]

Still, as Melville rejected these commonplaces of eighteenth century logic, he found as little refuge in certain discoveries of nineteenth century intuition. Wordsworth, for instance, may have experienced God through Nature, in that "sense sublime/Of something far more deeply interfused,"[7] but Melville doubted the natural world was divine or, as Coleridge supposed, could be divinized by the recreating imagination. In fact, Melville most often posits the sensationalist universe Coleridge abhorred: an "inanimate cold world" in which "objects (*as* objects) are essentially fixed and dead,"[8] the best example of which is the "dead blind wall" face of the White Whale. Melville was as unsatisfied by the current secular mythologies as he was by the dogmatically religious ones, and yet he could not live with any sense of well-being in a desacramentalized world.

James Baird was the first critic to recognize Melville's "exit from crisis" as an essentially primitivist act. "Authentic primitivism is a mode of sentience, a creed springing inevitably from a state of cultural failure. It represents one attempt of Western man to restore the symbolism of human existence," and Baird carefully distinguishes between this "existential" primitivism which he defines "as sentient expression of religious emotion conceptualized (as art, symbolic of primitive feeling)" and the "academic" primitivism of Rousseau which is defined "as an idea (as art, referential to exterior states of the primitive)." Melville's "symbols of primitivism," then, "are formed in answer to the basic human need for sacrament, when previously authoritative forms of sacrament have become powerless."[9]

> Modulations in the symbolic structure of literature, as new symbols are substituted for old, initially compel regression to primordial, as opposed to 'civilized,' forms. The material for the symbol of the new key is taken from a state of human existence which is prototypic, unsophisticated, and, in some respects, universal for man. . . . The symbolist's awareness of cultural failure becomes atavism . . . the reversion of the creating mind to an earlier state of man's cultural (religious) history. . . . In recent primitivism, atavism discards the symbolic structures of Christian tradition and permits . . . the re-emergence of archetypes. This amounts to saying that the I-You relationship of the Protestant condition eludes the authority of traditional dogma perpetuated in Christian symbols and reverts to archetypal patterns which were always there in the unconscious, but earlier 'controlled' or 'obscured' by traditional symbols.[10]

The "decadence of Protestantism, as Jung saw it, enables man to 'rediscover the gods as psychic factors,' " and Baird argues—though I cannot here do justice to the complexity of his argument—that occidental primitivists like Melville naturally employ their experience of the Orient in the creation of new symbols of deity because for Westerners "the Orient is the imagined return to the source of religion." "If the symbols inherited will not fascinate and overpower, if they will not command, and get, allegiance, the 'fresh strangeness' of Eastern symbols offers a possibility of escape."[11] The central section of Baird's book is devoted to an analysis of six such symbols of deity, but I would point out that there is an even more extensive substrate of sacramental symbolism in Melville, non-oriental in character, one that finds its first rude expression *before* his voyage to Oceania, in the second of the "Fragments from a Writing Desk"; and that this substrate, since it is so primal and extensive, is perhaps the fundamental pattern upon which Melville's primitivist quest for sacrament is based.

In Melville's pattern Sacred Reality is spatially manifest as an area enclosed and central (often, but not always, circular) within a boundary of some denseness; and, less frequently, as an acentric area beyond. In addition, in the manner of mythological motifs, the Sacred is often represented by gold, treasure, a secret, or a virgin maiden, and it is often associated with absolute silence and the imagery of sexual generation, particularly of the womblike enclosure. However, the quest for sexual fulfillment, whatever its symbolic elaboration or disguise, is not just a metaphor of the quest for sacrament as it is in the late poetry of Hopkins; on the contrary, it is often the correlative of that quest, a central principle, as in the poetry of union in Shelley.[12] Melville explored the permutations of love to an extent unparalleled in nineteenth century American literature, portraying at one time or another, the heterosexual, the bisexual, the auto-erotic, the incestuous, the lustful, the sterile, the sexless, *et al*. These characterizations are not, of course, self-portraits—except in that imaginative sense which is, more properly, the concern of the speculative biographer than the literary critic—and they do not interest us for any confessional insights they may afford. Rather they interest us for their analogic truth: because the history of the quester's sexuality is directly related to his history in seeking the holy.

Most, though not all, of Melville's protagonists are questers, and although those who do quest are obviously individualized, almost all of them, consciously or unconsciously, seek a manifestation of the Sacred Reality and a version of sexual fulfillment. And since these two quests are collateral and since they are frequently unsuccessful, we should not be surprised that the questers bear common scars, common punishments for failure. On one hand, madness is the wound to the mind for those who hubristically seek God, and this is why at least ten questers—Captain Ahab is the foremost example—are mad, or rave, or are temporarily aberrant. It must be realized, however, that as Melville grew older, his protagonists grow saner; that is, with age, he came to realize that, despite the real nobility of questing, there was something fundamentally unhealthy about it as well, a sickness in seeking the impossible. His last protagonist, Billy Budd, who neither quests nor fears the death which must be, is, theoretically, the sanest of all.

As madness is the wound to the mind, so sexual injury is the corresponding wound to the body: again Ahab is the supreme example. But, once more, as Melville matured, this quest also grows less and less exacerbated until Billy forgoes sex entirely and becomes the incarnate god. Melville's choice of maiming, like his choice of madness, is terribly ironic, yet vastly appropriate, and I allude not merely to his easily documented concern for his own sanity or, according to Freud, man's immemorial fear of castration.[13] The context of irony is subtler still: if man seeks the Ideal, he must wrestle it from the gods, must risk and ultimately sacrifice his own thin humanity to a degree commensurate with his megalomania. And if his commitment to the quest be total, as Ahab's is, the wound to his mind and body is equivalently total—death, beyond madness or castration.

Between the quester and Sacred Reality lies the phenomenal, deanimate, desacramentalized universe which encircles the Sacred or stands, barrier-fashion, before it. The quester's object is to overcome that encirclement or barrier, to scale, undermine, or (most frequently) pierce through those emblems of Secular Reality: mountain, wall, hill, pyramid, chimney, stone, underbrush, or reef; tent, glass, veil, garment, mask, face (as of a man, woman, or whale); maze, catacomb, or labyrinth. This notion of a double world is obviously not original with Melville, and in fact it may be traced at least as far back as Plato, "the first great Romantic," and to his "romantic" conception of an ideal world concealed behind the visible, his "city laid up in heaven."[14] But Melville surely did not go to historical sources to discover the legacy of disaffiliation quite familiar to his contemporaries wrought by three centuries of burgeoning scientism. Here, for instance is how the popularizer James Murdock described the "rationale of post-Kantian philosophy":

> The chief aim of most of these systems was, to penetrate into the *terra incognita* of Kant, that is, into the region of *noumena* and of *supersensible* things. The authors were unwilling to believe we can know so little, as Kant had represented. They therefore attempted to rend the *vail* [sic], which conceals the unknowable; or to bridge the *unpassable gulf* of Kant, which separates between phenomena and noumena in the material world, and between ideas and the object of them in the world of thought.[15]

One can also observe this relation of Secular to Sacred Reality in a host of important English and American writers of the period: Shelley, Coleridge, Emerson, Holmes, and Emily Dickinson—to select a representative group.[16] In short, the geography of Melville's double world was a Romantic *donnée*, and we should be surprised if he had not accepted it.

Melville's desire to thrust beyond the Secular defines, in fact, an essential aspect of romanticism—that aspect, in David Perkins' phrase, dedicated to the "quest for permanence"—a desire which suggests, as Hoxie Fairchild has said, that romanticism is "at its deepest and most intense . . . essentially a religious experience";[17] or, as he says in another place:

> Romanticism is the endeavor, in the face of growing factual obstacles, to achieve, to retain, or to justify that illusioned view of the universe and of human life which is produced by an imaginative fusion of the familiar and the strange, the known

and the unknown, the real and the ideal, the finite and the
infinite, the material and the spiritual, the natural and the super-
natural. . . . From the viewpoint here suggested, romanticism is
the quest of an illusion. That illusion may be sought in super-
naturalized nature. . . . [It] may be sought in man's own
imagination, the true abiding place of the power to make dreams
real and the real a dream.[18]

What Melville did was to dramatize this search by projecting it upon
a riddlingly naturalistic background, although, by so doing, he was
eventually forced to acknowledge "the barrenness of [his] . . . illusion"[19]—which accounts, in part, for the nihilism of *The Confidence-
Man* (1857). Astonishingly, however, (although it did take thirty
years and more), Melville was able to reinstate the "illusioned view"
—for this is how some would characterize the miracle of *Billy Budd*
(completed 1891).

As Melville's quest for the Beyond undeniably owes something to
romanticism, the much more powerful quest for the Sacred Center,
the quest Within, is an essential aspect of primitivism. The geograph-
ical analogues of the enclosed Biblical Garden and the *locus amoenus*,
that recurring, even conventional *topos* of classical and medieval literature,[20] suggest an ancient tradition, and *Rasselas*, perhaps, furnished Melville with a modern clue. Furthermore, Melville's vision
of an encapsulated area recalls the Transcendental theory of organic
symbolism, for, as Charles Feidelson has perceived,[21] "the topography
of *Typee* [Melville's first novel] is metaphoric. . . . *Typee* shadows
forth the pattern of Melville's world, which is remarkably like the
spherical universe of Emerson." "Line in nature is not found," quotes
Feidelson; "unit and universe are round." And, in fact, Melville constantly describes his Polynesian isle in terms of circles and semi-circles.
We should also notice that, as early as *Typee*, Melville was already
beginning to exploit an image he derived from Egyptology, of bur-
rowing into the heart of a pyramid, using it, in Dorothee Metlitsky
Finkelstein's phrase,[22] for "the archetypal search for one's own soul."

In his study, James Baird investigates Melville's primitivist symbols
of sacrament as they reconstitute the archetypal reality of the Sacred
Center. What we must do now is investigate the Sacred Center itself

in its affiliation with historical primitivism, and, to do this, we shall turn to one of its chief modern expositors, Mircea Eliade. Our contention is that an historian of primitive religion will illuminate Melville insofar as Melville's own quest for sacrament is "primitive"; that is, insofar as the condition of sacramental failure in his culture (and ours) demanded the activation of that aspect of archaic man still resident in the modern psyche, the archetypes of the collective unconscious. These "pre-existent pathways which man has received with his brain are awakened to new life,"[23] and therefore, just as "to be able to understand his patients it is . . . necessary for the doctor to study the life of primitive peoples as expressed in the old rites and myths," so it is similarly necessary for the critic to study the ontological mode of primitivism if he would understand Melville's sacramentalism of the Center.

> For religious man [writes Eliade], space is not homogeneous;
> he experiences interruptions, breaks in it; some parts of space
> are qualitatively different from others. 'Draw not nigh hither,'
> says the Lord to Moses; 'put off thy shoes from off thy feet,
> for the place whereon thou standest is holy ground' (Exodus
> 3:5). There is, then, a sacred space and hence a strong, significant
> space; there are other spaces that are not sacred and so are without
> structure or consistency, amorphous. Nor is this all. For religious
> man, this spatial nonhomogeneity finds expression in the ex-
> perience of an opposition between space that is sacred—the only
> *real* and *real-ly* existing space—and all other space, the formless
> expanse surrounding it.[24]

The difference between secular and sacred space, in short, is the difference between Chaos and Cosmos. For the primitive (whom Eliade calls "religious") or for the man in whom primitive feelings are stirred, "the *sacred* is equivalent to a *power*, and, in the last analysis, to *reality*. The sacred is saturated with *being*." And "the center . . . is pre-eminently the zone of the sacred, the zone of absolute reality. Similarly, all the other symbols of absolute reality (trees of life and immortality, Fountain of Youth, etc.) are also situated at a center."[25]

But the center is not only associated with the sacred; it is associated with the sexual too, for, in the ontology of primitive man, the sacred and the sexual are intimately related: "fertility, above all, is an attribute of the 'centre,' and emblems of it are often sexual":

> Indeed one of the major differences separating the people of the early cultures from people to-day is precisely the utter incapacity of the latter to live their organic life (particularly as regards sex and nutrition) as a sacrament. . . . For the modern they are simply physiological acts, whereas for primitive man they were sacraments, ceremonies by means of which he communicated with the *force* which stood for Life itself.[26]

By that informal alliance of the sacramental and the sexual throughout his books, Melville was responding to the vibrations of this primitive modality.

Now, in the literature of the mythological quest,

> The road leading to the center is a 'difficult road' . . . and this is verified at every level of reality: pilgrimages to sacred places (Mecca, Hardwar, Jerusalem); danger-ridden voyages of the heroic expeditions in search of the Golden Fleece, the Golden Apples, the Herb of Life [cf. Ahab's quest for the 'center' of the Whale]; wanderings in labyrinths; difficulties of the seeker [cf. Ishmael] for the road to the self, to the 'center' of his being, and so on. The road is arduous, fraught with perils, because it is, in fact, a rite of the passage from the profane to the sacred, from death to life, from man to the divinity. Attaining the center is equivalent to a consecration, an initiation; yesterday's profane and illusory existence gives place to a new, to a life that is real, enduring, and effective.[27]

Moby-Dick, in other words, is a paradigmatic book of the quest, and Ahab and Ishmael paradigmatic questers. We might do well to consider this assertion a little more closely. First of all,

> Those who have chosen the Quest, the road that leads to the Center, must abandon any kind of family [cf. Ahab's wife and child] and social situation [cf. Ishmael's schoolteaching], any 'nest,' and devote themselves wholly to 'walking' toward the supreme truth, which, in highly evolved religions, is synonymous with the Hidden God, the *Deus Absconditus*.

But the quest for spiritual values, for the Center and the symbols of

Absolute Reality therein is, as we have observed, difficult to consummate:

> Heroes [like Ahab], initiates [like Ishmael, who seeks the Whale
> for the first time] descend into the depths to confront marine
> monsters; this is a typical initiatory ordeal. To be sure, variants
> abound in the history of religions: sometimes dragons mount
> guard over a treasure, sensory image of the sacred, of absolute
> reality; the ritual (=initiatory) victory over the guardian
> monster is equivalent to a conquest of immortality.[28]

"Water animals," writes Eliade in another place,[29] "particularly fish
(which also serve as erotic symbols) and sea monsters, become emblems of the sacred because they stand for *absolute reality*, concentrated in water." The White Whale is the sea monster who guards the
sanctum of Absolute Reality within himself, which the heroes would
penetrate, and their battle with the monster is a venerable mythological motif found in many literatures around the world. Scholars have
considered the American variant in relation to analogues found in
Old English (Beowulf: Grendel's Dam), in Babylonian (Bel-Merodach: Tiamat), in Persian (Rustam: the White Demon); and one
Melvillean, Bruce Franklin, shows how Melville "partly shapes *Moby-Dick*" by using the Egyptian analogue (Osiris: Typhon).[30]

No one of course conquers the White Whale, but, in the waters
where the *Pequod* meets her final destiny, Ishmael attains the creamy
heart of the whirling vortex, the Sacred Center. And only then is he
ejected out of the sea onto his life-buoy, his thirst for Being, for Cosmos, for real existence momentarily satisfied. Ahab, on the other hand,
disappears into the depths, into Chaos, torn away into profane space
where only death awaits: ". . . immersion in water," says Eliade,[31]
"signifies regression to the preformal, reincorporation into the undifferentiated mode of pre-existence. Emersion repeats the cosmogonic
act of formal manifestation; *im*mersion is equivalent to a dissolution
of forms. This is why the symbolism of the waters implies both death
and rebirth." Immersion for Ahab, but emersion for Ishmael . . . Melville's own intimation of immortality.

Since Ishmael's "emersion repeats the cosmogonic act of formal
manifestation," since, in other words, it repeats "a primeval action ac-

complished at the beginning of time by a divine being, or mythical figure," it is meaningful. For the primitive or for the man of primitive sensibility, an act is sanctified only insofar as it imitates a transcendent model,[32] and this is why we say that Ishmael momentarily participates in the divine (if he is not divine himself). Melville's unformulated vision of the sacred to some degree, then, externalizes Coleridge's romantic concept of the imagination—"a repetition in the finite mind of the eternal act of creation in the infinite I AM."

Melville's questers exist in two historical dimensions: one, personal or ontogenetic (in which they are obviously differentiated); the other, transpersonal or phylogenetic (in which they are secretly connected). In his ontogenetic dimension each quester bears no interpsychic relation to any other; his birthdate, deathdate, and history are unique unto himself. A dominating aspect of his development is the quest for sexual gratification, and since the psychologist who is preeminently concerned with the sexuality of modern man is Sigmund Freud, we should not be surprised that those sexual symbols which abound in Melville's work are precisely those which Freud was to explicate. Even a sampling of them—and I select only those which appear in Melville's books and which are specifically mentioned in *The Interpretation of Dreams* (3rd English ed., 1931)—argues the powerfully sexual drive of the Melvillean quester and of the usefulness of psychoanalysis in understanding him. Thus one may discover in both Melville and Freud identical symbols of the male genitalia (such pointed or penetrating weapons or objects as the knife, the pistol, and the key—as well as such other symbols as the snake, the lizard, the gravity-defying balloon, the hand, the tree, elaborate machinery, and the idea of threeness); the female genitalia (such containing or enclosing objects as the house with frontal projections, the room, the ship, and the cave—as well as such other symbols as the landscape, the valley, and the spatially central area); the pubic hair (woods and thickets); sexual intercourse (such a rhythmical activity as dancing); onanism (playing musical instruments); castration (blinding or haircutting); and defloration (plucking flowers).

In his phylogenetic character, however, each of the questers bears to one another an intimate interpsychic kinship; that is, their histories are inextricably linked in the psychological and spiritual evolution of one Quester who incorporates them all; who is born in the first book and reborn in the last. The dominating aspect of his development is a thirst for self-realization, and since the psychologist who is pre-eminently occupied with modern man in search of a soul is C.G. Jung, we should not be surprised that the road to sacrament intuitively taken by Melville, over the course of his long career, should be precisely the one Jung was to demarcate: we speak of the archetypal road to indi-viduation, which we shall presently discuss. Hence the necessity for studying the entire *oeuvre* and for studying it in strict chronological sequence.

Although it is true that Freud and Jung disagree about certain fundamentals of their science, the methodological objection to using them both in a single study of Melville (or any artist) is not well-founded. For the difference between them is finally more mythologi-cal than scientific: a difference in the vision of what Man is and how he should be studied. To speak roughly, Freud is chiefly concerned with the life of ontogenetic man, from conception to bodily death; Jung, with phylogenetic man, from ancestral unconsciousness to the Assumption of New Life. One does not ask then, "Freud or Jung?" One attends them both as their complementary visions illuminate complementary aspects of Melville's work. Nevertheless, I do not mean that other comprehensive psychologies are inadmissible or in-valid tools for examining literature in general or Melville in particu-lar—for example, an Adlerian study of the questers' will to (and weapons of) power would certainly be fruitful. But given the nature of Melville's work, the systems of Freud and Jung seem the most, if not the only, appropriate approaches: Freud's because we must expli-cate an insistently powerful sexual impulse; Jung's because we must explicate the growth and progress of a psyche in a religious context.

Now the transpersonal Quester exists at an unconscious or virtually unconscious level, and, therefore, he is a far more accurate reflection of the author's own psychic life than the more consciously shaped figures who populate the surface of the texts. In fact, if we were at-tempting an interior biography of Melville, now that Leon Howard and Jay Leyda have provided us with exterior ones—and we are attempting no more than the outline of that biography here—we should surely focus on the transpersonal Quester. In order to describe his evolution, we have borrowed a technique used by the Jungian psychologist Erich Neumann in his study of mythological heroes: that is, we shall trace the gradual emancipation of the Quester's ego consciousness as it emerges "from the overpowering embrace of the unconscious. . . ."[33]

> In the beginning is perfection, wholeness . . . [one symbol of which] is the circle. Allied to it are the sphere, the egg . . . [and] the circular snake, the primal dragon of the beginning that bites its own tail, the self-begetting . . . [uroboros]. . . .
> This round and this existence in the round, existence in the uroboros, is the symbolic self-representation of the dawn state, showing the infancy both of mankind and of the child. . . . [T]he 'round' of mythology is also called the womb and uterus, though this place of origin should not be taken concretely. In fact, all mythology says over and over again that this womb is an image, the woman's womb being only a partial aspect of the primordial symbol of the place of origin from whence we come. This primordial symbol means many things at once: it is not just *one* cosmic region where many contents hide and have their essential abode. "The Mothers" are not *a* mother.
> Anything deep—abyss, valley, ground, also the sea and the bottom of the sea, fountains, lakes and pools, the earth . . . the underworld, the cave, the house, and the city—all are parts of this archetype. Anything big and embracing which contains, surrounds, enwraps, shelters, preserves, and nourishes anything small belongs to the primordial matriarchal realm.[34]

Obviously, then, those texts which describe symbolized or unsymbolized relationships between man and man are not relevant to our present purpose: *Redburn*, *White-Jacket*, *Israel Potter*, almost all of the short stories, *The Confidence-Man* and *Billy Budd*. It is only in those books which concern relationships between man and woman that the stages of ego development in the Quester are discernible: the second "Fragment," "The Death Craft,"[35] *Typee*, *Mardi*, *Moby-Dick*, *Pierre*, "America" from *Battle-Pieces*, *Clarel*, and "The Enviable Isles" and "The Maldive Shark" from *John Marr*. Insofar as the first

stage is concerned, we may say that intra-uterine existence is symbolized in the second "Fragment."

As consciousness develops and the ego emerges from its primordial
abode into "the lower world of reality, full of dangers and discom-
fits," it

> becomes aware of pleasure-pain qualities, and from them it ex-
> periences its own pleasure and pain. Consequently the world
> becomes ambivalent. . . .
>
> This growing ambivalence gives rise to an equally ambivalent
> attitude on the part of the ego towards the archetype in whose
> power it lies.

For the just-emerging ego, like the newborn child, is as yet "a tiny,
defenseless speck, enveloped and helplessly dependent, a little island
floating on the vast expanse of the primal ocean"—the metaphor is
particularly apt for a study of Melville's questers. The archetypal
"round" in this next stage of the ego's development is symbolized by
the Great Mother who is, at once, the "wicked, devouring mother and
the good mother lavishing affection. . . ." The Quester's birth from
the "round," from the Great Mother in her doubleness, is finally ac-
complished in *Typee*, a partially fictitious tale of a "man who lived
among [and had to escape from] the cannibals"! The Quester then
battles this archetypal antagonist in *Mardi, Moby-Dick*, and *Pierre*,
and, to be sure, loses each time. But during the struggle and because
of it (particularly in the latter two books) his ego is solidified by the
assimilation in consciousness of unconscious contents, and that is why
he is finally able, in *Pierre*, to conquer the Mother (although at the
cost of Pierre's life). Still, this is a considerable feat, and "The growth
of self-consciousness and the strengthening of masculinity thrust the
image of the Great Mother into the background; the patriarchal society [which, historically, supersedes the matriarchal one] splits it up,
and while only the picture of the Good Mother is retained in consciousness, her terrible aspect is relegated to the unconscious."[36] Indeed, in the stories and novels which follow *Pierre* the Great Mother
is notably absent and when she does finally return, after an absence
of fourteen years, in *Battle-Pieces* (1866), she is split in two: her
conscious aspect is as the Good Mother, America at peace; her aspect

"relegated to the unconscious" is as the Terrible Mother, America at war. Thus in *Battle-Pieces* this Devouring Female is finally pacified (that is, the Quester has gained power over her, not she over him), and in *Clarel* this pacification is wellnigh completed.

The last stage of ego consciousness in the Quester marks the last stage in the psychologic development of modern man, a stage represented in Melville's latest work by "The Maldive Shark" and "The Enviable Isles." The struggle of the ego with the realm of the Mothers, the unconscious, is over, and a new harmony between them is achieved. At this time "ego development is replaced by the development of the self, or individuation."[37] This term refers of course to the way of psychological maturation described by C. G. Jung, and it may be said, in fact, that Melville's transpersonal Quester—indeed, it may be said that Melville himself—develops in accordance with it. Obviously, then, the way of individuation can proceed not only "artificially, through analysis," but also normally, "through the archetypal situation," that is, through the ego's confrontation with the symbolic figures of the unconscious during the course of one's life.[38] Melville naturally took the second route, and we must retrace his steps because it is through the process of individuation that his quest for the Sacred is ultimately assured.

Not everyone, however, is able to confront his unconscious, for the way of the archetypes is not dependent upon "the will or the mind but of the total staking of the whole of one's life, and this is at the same time a natural process of separation: 'But under all circumstances only those people attain a higher degree of differentiation who are called and destined from the very beginning, that is, who have an urge and a capacity for higher differentiation, wherein, as is well known people are extremely varied. . . . Nature is aristocratic.' "[39] Melville was blessed with this "urge towards self-realization," for he was, as the Hawthornes knew perhaps better than anyone else, one of Nature's noblemen. He was a man, said Sophia,

> with a true, warm heart, and a soul and an intellect,—with life
> to his finger-tips; earnest, sincere, and reverent; very tender and
> *modest*. And I am not sure that he is not a very great man; but
> I have not quite decided upon my own opinion. I should say, I am

not quite sure that *I do not think him* a very great man; for
my opinion is, of course, as far as possible from settling the matter.
He has very keen perceptive power; but what astonishes me is,
that his eyes are not large and deep. He seems to see everything
very accurately; and how he can do so with his small eyes, I
cannot tell. They are not keen eyes, either, but quite undistin-
guished in any way. His nose is straight and rather handsome, his
mouth expressive of sensibility and emotion. He is tall and
erect, with an air free, grave, and manly. When conversing, he is
full of gesture and force, and loses himself in his subject. There
is no grace nor polish. Once in a while, his animation gives place
to a singularly quiet expression, out of those eyes to which I have
objected; an indrawn, dim look, but which at the same time makes
you feel that he is at that instant taking deepest note of what is
before him. It is a strange, lazy glance, but with a power in it
quite unique. It does not seem to penetrate through you, but to
take you into himself.[40]

And her husband confided to his journal six years later, in 1856,
about this man who would stake the whole of his life:

He stayed with us from Tuesday till Thursday; and, on the
intervening day, we took a pretty long walk together, and sat
down in a hollow among the sand hills (sheltering ourself from
the high, cool wind) and smoked a cigar. Melville, as he always
does, began to reason of Providence and futurity, and of everything that lies beyond human ken, and informed me that he had
'pretty much made up his mind to be annihilated'; but still he
does not seem to rest in that anticipation; and, I think, will never
rest until he gets hold of a definite belief. It is strange how he
persists—and has persisted ever since I knew him, and probably
long before—in wandering to-and-fro over these deserts, as
dismal and monotonous as the sand hills amid which we were
sitting. He can neither believe, nor be comfortable in his unbelief;
and he is too honest and courageous not to try to do one or the
other. If he were a religious man [Hawthorne means, I think, an
orthodox religionist], he would be one of most truly religious
and reverential; he has a very high and noble nature, and better
worth immortality than most of us.[41]

What I propose to do now is nominate the main stages of the individuation process as they pertain to Melville's Quester. First, though, a definition:

Individuation means becoming a single, homogeneous being, and, in so far as 'individuality' embraces our innermost, last, and incomparable uniqueness, it also implies becoming one's own self. We could therefore translate individuation as 'coming to selfhood' or 'self-realization.'

It is not to be confused with individualism, which

means deliberately stressing and giving prominence to some supposed peculiarity, rather than to collective considerations and obligations. . . . Individuation, therefore, can only mean a process of psychological development that fulfills the individual qualities given; in other words, it is a process by which a man becomes the definite, unique being he in fact is. In so doing he does not become 'selfish' in the ordinary sense of the word, but is merely fulfilling the peculiarity of his nature, and this . . . is vastly different from egotism and individualism.[42]

Since it is my contention that the transpersonal Quester advances toward individuation, we may expect to find in the works "those symbolic figures that are characteristic of the principal stages of the process." This is of course exactly what we do find, and in the order Jung's researches indicate we should find them. Through the activation of the contents of the unconscious, Melville's conscious mind first came into contact with and assimilated a content of the personal unconscious (the Shadow); second, at a deeper level, a content of the collective unconscious (the Anima); and last, in the condition of selfhood, achieved the "union of both partial systems—consciousness and the unconscious" at the new "centre of the psychic totality" (the Self). Let us recapitulate this process.

The shadow stands, so to speak, on the threshold of the way to the 'Mothers,' to the collective unconscious. It is the real counterpart of our conscious ego, the not or not sufficiently lived side of our psyche. It bars the way to the creative depths of the unconscious with the dark mass of that stuff of experience we have never admitted into our life.[43]

.   .   .   .

> If the repressed tendencies, the shadow . . . were decidedly
> evil, there would be no problem whatever. But the shadow is merely
> what is inferior, primitive, unadapted, and awkward, not wholly
> bad. It contains inferior, childish, or primitive qualities that
> would in a way vitalize and even embellish human existence. . . .[44]

In Melville's early books the quester is thrown into contact with but
refuses to confront the Shadow; at the end of *Typee*, Tommo (the
just emergent ego) flees terrified from Mow-Mow and, similarly, at
the end of *Mardi*, Taji flees from the spectral sons of Aleema. Psychologically, the ego is not yet able to assimilate the unconscious content and thereby reduce the tension of opposites between itself and
the unconscious. As a result both books end with the quester thrown
into a state of great anxiety. But in *Moby-Dick* the figure who was
Taji is split into Ishamel and Ahab. Both questers have Shadows,
the primitive Queequeg and the child Pip, but only Ishmael's Shadow
is incorporated. Nevertheless, this still represents a major psychological advance not only because Ishmael's life is vitalized and embellished
but also because it opens the way to the next stage in the career of the
Quester, the assimilation of the Anima-figure, who first appears in
Melville's succeeding book, *Pierre*. I allude of course to Isabel. (I do
not mean, however, that the Shadow-figure never reappears in Melville's work, for he does at least twice more: Pierre's Shadow is Glen
Stanly and Billy Budd's is John Claggart. On both occasions the protagonist kills rather than assimilates an aspect of his unconscious and
suffers the fate of the homicide whose victim, psychologically, is himself.)

Although it is true that Isabel has many antecedents in the Melville
canon, none of them is a genuine Anima-figure because all of them,
as we shall see, are "captives" of the Great Mother. Isabel is the first
Melville heroine to disengage herself, a process in Jungian psychology
called the "crystallization of the anima from the mother archetype,"[45]
and Pierre's meeting with her constitutes the next vital step in the
way of individuation:

> The archetypal figure of the soul-image [the Anima in the man]

stands for the respective contrasexual portion of the psyche, showing partly how our personal relation thereto is constituted, partly the precipitate of all human experience pertaining to the opposite sex. In other words, it is the image of the other sex that we carry in us, both as individuals and as representatives of a species.

. . . .

Union with the opposite sex in the first half of life has as its aim, above all, physical union, in order to bring the 'bodily child' into being as a fruit and continuation, whereas in the second half of life the goal is above all the psychic 'coniunctio', a union with the contrasexual both within one's own inner world and with its image-bearer in the outer, in order that the 'spiritual child' may be born. The meeting with the soul-image regularly signifies that the first half of life with its necessary adjustment of consciousness outwards is ended, and now the most important step in inward adjustment, the confrontation with one's own contrasexual component, must begin. The activation of the archetype of the soul-image is therefore an event of fateful significance, for it is the unmistakable sign that the second half of life has begun.[46]

According to Jung the second half of life begins gradually between the ages of thirty-five and forty[47]—by thirty-six Melville's four children were already born—and although, chronologically, he was but thirty-one at the writing of *Moby-Dick*, he felt that he had already "come to the inmost leaf of the bulb, and that shortly the flower must fall to the mould."[48] With the completion of *Pierre* and the activation of the Anima a year later, the flower fell for all to see; his friends and acquaintances, as Newton Arvin reminds us, substantiated his gloomy prediction:

It had taken him a little more than a year to write *Moby Dick*, yet in every sense but the literal one it was as if half a lifetime had passed. In the months before he had begun the book, and even at times while he was at work on it, Melville must have struck those who encountered him as still essentially a young man. This is what his London journal suggests to us, and there is much of the same impression of youth and high spirits in some of the glimpses we have of him at Pittsfield and Lenox. After *Moby Dick* we virtually never have that impression again; already it is a middle-aged man who looks out at us from the letters or memories of people who saw him in these years. . . .[49]

But the great struggle of *Pierre* was not fought in vain, for

As the making conscious of the shadow makes possible the knowledge of our other, dark aspect, so does the making conscious of the soul-image enable us to gain knowledge of the contrasexual in our psyche. When this image is recognized and revealed, then it ceases to work from out of the unconscious and allows us finally to differentiate this contrasexual component and to incorporate it into our conscious orientation, through which an extraordinary enrichment of the contents belonging to our consciousness and therewith a broadening of our personality is attained.[50]

With the continuing expansion of ego consciousness, a less embattled relationship between the ego and the unconscious begins to unfold, as the poem "America" from *Battle-Pieces* and *Clarel* indicate. Nevertheless, the Self—"the centre of the psychic totality, as the ego is the centre of consciousness"[51]—has not yet been born. Jung carefully distinguishes between the ego and the Self and insists that the Self is "a construct that serves to express an unknowable essence which we cannot grasp as such, since by definition it transcends our powers of comprehension." "Sensing the self as something irrational, as an indefinable existent, to which the ego is neither opposed nor subjected, but merely attached, and about which it revolves very much as the earth revolves round the sun—thus we come to the goal of individuation."[52] The Self is represented by a "unifying symbol," which expresses its "transcending function, i.e., of the unification of the different pairs of opposites in the psyche in a higher synthesis."[53] In a phrase, says Jung, the Self "might equally well be called the 'God within us.' "[54] One feels, for instance, that Ishmael, in his moment of highest holiness, at the Sacred Center of the whale armada, momentarily intuits his sacred Self:

And thus, though surrounded by circle upon circle of consternations and affrights, did these inscrutable creatures at the centre freely and fearlessly indulge in all peaceful concernments; yea, serenely revelled in dalliance and delight. But even so, amid the tornadoed Atlantic of my being, do I myself still for ever centrally disport in mute calm; and while ponderous planets of unwaning woe revolve round me, deep down and deep inland there I still bathe me in eternal mildness of joy.[55]

Although Jung praised *Moby-Dick* as "the greatest American novel,"[56] there is no evidence that he borrowed the astronomical imagery by which he expresses the relation of the ego to the Self from Melville, whose unacademic language neatly expresses and, as it were, independently underscores, Jung's perception.

The "unifying symbol" by which Melville represents the intuition of Self is one which Jung will make much of in this context—the mandala, the wheeling, magic circle with a center, about which we shall have more to say later. Now we should only note that the sense of wholeness Ishmael experiences is a temporary sensation, not a permanent condition. For Melville himself had not yet experienced any more than this intimation of selfhood, and he would not experience a genuine birth of the Self until after *Clarel*, and probably not until the mid-1880's. For that was the time, as he said, of his "spontaneous after-growth" (after, long before, having fallen "to the mould"), and one may take his words in both a psychological and a literary sense. Melville not only had begun to write again, but he also seems to have undergone that ultimate "centreing of personality" indicative of individuation. Not only do "The Enviable Isles" and "The Maldive Shark" mark a new harmony between the ego and the unconscious, but two archetypal symbols of the Self also appear in his latest work.

First, in the titular figure of the prose sketch "Daniel Orme" (and again in the Dansker of *Billy Budd*) Melville represents the "masculine half" of the Self by the archetype of the Old Wise Man, "the personification of the spiritual principle."[57] Thus Orme bears on his chest and on the side of his heart crossed scars which form a crucifix, representing, as James Baird tells us,[58] "pagan acceptance through the connotations of tattooing, the Christian promise of the Redemption, and this promise slashed by the co-existing forces of violence and evil." In Jungian terms, "the center of gravity of [Orme's] . . . total personality" has shifted from the ego to the Self, and, as a result,

> a personality develops that suffers only in the lower stories, so to speak, but in the upper stories is singularly detached from painful as well as joyful events.

> .   .   .   .

> [An attitude of mind develops] which is out of reach of intense emotional involvement and therefore safe from absolute shock; . . . a consciousness detached from the world. I have reason for believing that this sets in after the middle of life and is actually a natural preparation for death.[59]

Thus Daniel Orme, the Westerner with the wisdom of Queequeg, sits alone by the sea and calmly accepts death, safe from absolute shock.

William Braswell has suggested[60] that the name "Orme"—or me —contains a pun on the author himself, and Braswell is surely right, for Melville not only identifies himself with the aging sailor but also the Biblical wise man: not, as in youth, with rootless Ishmael or tempestuous Ahab, but now, in age and with unerring intuition, with Daniel, who learned somehow to live unscathed among lions.

In "Daniel Orme" the phylogenetic Quester, in the penultimate guise of the Old Wise Man, dies; in *Billy Budd* he is reborn as the Divine Child, as "Baby" Billy. Melville's progress is as crucial as his consummation is rare, for as Orme represents only the masculine half of the Self, so Billy represents the synthesis of an individuated psyche, a synthesis which, says Erich Neumann, "is frequently accompanied by symbols representing the new unity of opposites, such as the symbol of the hermaphrodite."[61] But Billy is not only hermaphroditic but divine and symbolizes "in biological terms—the coexistence of contraries, of cosmological principles (male and female) within the heart of divinity." "The *coincidentia oppositorum*," adds Eliade, "is one of the most primitive ways of expressing the paradox of divine reality."[62]

We recognize Billy as a "unifying symbol" not only from the biological but also from the sacramental point of view. For, as Jung tells us,[63] "in the world of Christian ideas Christ undoubtedly represents the self," and, therefore, insofar as Billy participates in His Reality, he too is such a symbol. Christ, says Jung,

> is the still living myth of our culture. He is our culture hero, who, regardless of his historical existence, embodies the myth of the divine Primordial Man, the mystic Adam. It is he who occupies the center of the Christian *mandala*, who is the Lord of the Tetramorph, i.e., the four symbols of the evangelists, which are like the four columns of his throne. He is in us and we in him. His kingdom is the pearl of great price, the treasure buried in the field, the grain of mustard seed which will become a great tree, and the heavenly city. As Christ is in us, so also is his heavenly kingdom.
>
> These few familiar references should be sufficient to make the psychological position of the Christ symbol quite clear. *Christ exemplifies the archetype of the self.*

Thus as the Self is the "God within us"—for "the spontaneous symbols of the self, or of wholeness, cannot in practice be distinguished from a God-image"[64]—so Christ, so Billy, is Melville's embodiment of the final archetype in the way of individuation.

Melville's own interior life, then, will itself reward analysis and study, for, as it traverses a path from the birth of the ego to the birth of the Self, it too aspires to the condition of art. And if we may say, with profound regard for the individuated man, that "the art of life is the most distinguished and rarest of all the arts,"[65] then I would suggest that Melville's life, as it transcends tragedy, approaches the most distinguished of all art-forms, the divine comedy. One recalls the strictures of Maud Bodkin:

> [T]he archetypal pattern corresponding to tragedy . . . the character of its essential theme—reflects the conflict within the nature of any self-conscious individual between his assertion of his separate individuality and his craving for oneness with the group—family or community—of which he is a part. . . .
>
> The theme of the conflict between the generations . . . as corresponding to an ambivalent attitude toward a parent figure—is plainly related to this more general theme and pattern. . . .[66]

Miss Bodkin's chief examples are Hamlet and Orestes, but one may, I think, relate this pattern to Melville's life as well as it is *phylogentically reflected* through the characters of Captain Ahab and Billy Budd. At the central point of his creative life is Ahab who would slay the Parent, the Great Whale, and arrogantly assert his separate individuality: "In the midst of the personified impersonal, a personality stands here."[67] "But," says Miss Bodkin, "with the emotionally predetermined fall of the hero goes a predetermined resurrection. The life-force which, in one manifestation, perishes, renews itself in another." Renews itself in Billy who loves the Father, Captain Vere, and humbly submits to the authority of the group. "So the tragic lament passes into exaltation," the New Life that mitigates death.[68] Billy cries "God bless Captain Vere!" and Captain Vere, who answers "Billy Budd, Billy Budd" on his own deathbed but "not [in] the accents of remorse," *is* blessed.[69] And so too was their reconciler, Herman Melville, the shuttle to whom rest was finally ordained.

In other words, we must affirm Mrs. Hawthorne's intuition: Herman Melville was "a very great man" and for the very reason she implies—not because, as artist, he was greatly endowed but because, as man, he was greatly souled; because he was "called and urged from the very beginning," because he had that essential "urge . . . and capacity for higher differentiation," because, as Mr. Hawthorne knew, his spiritual life was staked on behalf of that differentiation. Melville's is a genius of soul—as rare, surely, as genius of hand or intellect—and such genius demands investigation. The problem, of course, is how to investigate it, for everyone knows that drawing conclusions about an author on the basis of his work is especially hazardous—and Melville, as several notorious analyses indicate, seems to be an especial temptation! But Melville also provides us with an opportunity few other authors do, the opportunity of charting the birth, life, death, and rebirth of a phylogenetic character—the key to it all—as he is unconsciously projected throughout an *oeuvre* which itself took over half a century to complete and, therefore, could not have been premeditated.

We do not mean to sound dogmatic about the *consummatum est* of *Billy Budd* nor deny its strain of ironic, even hostile, ambiguity.

Nor would we disregard a central postulate about the process of individuation: that although it

> is an event spread over the whole of life, [it] is never completed.
> It is always an unending approximation to which death provides
> the ultimate limitation. Yet though there is an existential lim-
> itation in time, the extent is unlimited, since there is always the
> addition of the personality factors, arising from the unconscious,
> to which no boundaries can be ascribed [an argument which
> helps account for the emergence of the Shadow figure and for the
> ambiguously deceitful Old Wise Man in *Billy Budd*].[70]

And therefore, as Jolande Jacobi admits to never having found "anywhere a *fully* individuated being"—indeed, as shrewd Ishmael observes: "any human thing supposed to be complete, must for that very
reason infallibly be faulty"[71]—so we may speak of only the *primary*
effect of *Billy Budd* as redemptive. (Italics added.) But that, after all,
is the major effect, and our conclusion necessarily follows: that with
Billy Budd Melville won through to his sacred Self, the immanently
numinous, and could then go gentle into that good night.

2. *Typee-Truant*

"Fragments from a Writing Desk"
through *White-Jacket*

> Idealism is a hypothesis to account for nature by other
> principles than those of carpentry and chemistry. Yet, if it
> only deny the existence of matter, it does not satisfy the
> demands of the spirit. It leaves God out of me. It leaves me
> in the splendid labyrinth of my perceptions, to wander
> without end.
>
> R. W. Emerson, "Nature"

On 4 and 18 May 1839 Herman Melville published two "Fragments from a Writing Desk" in *The Democratic Press and Lansingburgh Advertiser*, a local and inauspicious New York State newspaper; both pieces—his earliest fiction—are patently juvenile and without literary merit, but the second is of great importance nonetheless, for in it are buried certain thematic and symbolic charges which will reverberate throughout the Melville canon. Our present study, then, must begin with this second "Fragment."

Its protagonist is a young man very much like Pierre, the titular hero of Melville's seventh novel (1852), who moons about Saddle Meadows "lost in revery, and up to the lips in sentiment" (265).[1] One evening, while "lying upon the grassy turf," the Youth is approached by a cloaked figure who drops a note at his feet, just as Pierre, en route to the home of his fiancée, Lucy, one night, is secretly handed a note by a hooded figure.

'Certes!' cried I, springing up, 'here is a spice of the marvelous!'
and stooping down, I picked up an elegant little, rose-coloured,

26

lavender-scented billet-doux, and hurriedly breaking the seal (a heart, transfixed with an arrow) I read by the light of the moon, the following:

'Gentle Sir—

If my fancy has painted you in genuine colours, you will on the receipt of this, incontinently follow the bearer where she will lead you.

INAMORATA.' (265)

When, therefore, we recoil at the exaggerations of *Pierre*—this notorious passage particularly[2]—

Love is both Creator's and Saviour's gospel to mankind; a volume bound in rose-leaves, clasped with violets, and by the beaks of humming-birds printed with peach-juice on the leaves of lilies— [IX, 45]

we must remember that Melville was engaging not merely in the parody of popular fiction but in the cruelest sort of self-parody as well.

Like Pierre, who is not certain whether he will open Isabel's message for fear—and the fear is well-taken—that "in some way the reading of it [will] irretrievably entangle his fate," so the Youth at first refuses to follow, as he is bidden: " 'The deuce I will' exclaimed I.—'But soft!' " (266) and unburdening himself of his mantle and beaver but retaining his cane, he follows his "conductress"—although, however fast he runs or walks after her, she keeps, as if by magic, a certain distance between them. She is Melville's first portrait of the tantalizing *femme fatale* who, after a series of literary transformations, eventuates in the seductive Isabel who fatally arouses Pierre. And like Pierre's, the nature of the Youth's frustration is clearly set forth:

. . . descrying me plunging ahead like an infuriated steed, she gave a slightly audible scream of surprise, and once more fled, as though helped forward by invisible wings. (266)

Melville will use an identical steed image in "The Tartarus of Maids" (1855) to symbolize the orgastic intrusion of the seedsman into the Black Notch.

Recovering himself, the Youth continues to follow as his guide, "plunging into a neighboring grove, pursued her way with augmented speed, till we arrived at a spot . . . [of] singular and grotesque beauty. . . ." (267); Pierre, similarly, must leave Saddle Meadows and cross an adjoining wood in order to reach Isabel's home: and in both instances, as in *The Scarlet Letter*, entrance into the wood symbolizes a return to a more primitive condition, a return which evokes man's primal emotions. Thus, as the Youth remarks, "even amidst the agitating occurrences of the evening I could not refrain from observing" that

> A circular space of about a dozen acres in extent had been cleared in the very heart of the grove: leaving, however, two parallel rows of lofty trees, which at the distance of about twenty paces, and intersected in the center by two similar ranges, traversed the whole diameter of the circle. These noble plants shooting their enormous trunks to an amazing height, bore their verdant honors far aloft, throwing their gigantic limbs abroad and embracing each other with their rugged arms. This fanciful union of their sturdy boughs formed a magnificent arch. . . . I caught the diminutive figure of my guide, who, standing at the entrance of the arched way . . . was making the most extravagant gestures of impatience at my delay.—Reminded at once of the situation . . . I replied to her summons by immediately throwing myself forward, and we soon entered the Atlantian arbor, in whose umbrageous shades we were completely hid.
>
> Lost in conjecture, during the whole of this eccentric ramble, as to its probable termination—the sombre gloom of these ancestral trees, gave a darkening hue to the imaginings, and I began to repent the inconsiderate haste which had hurried me on, in an expedition, so peculiar and suspicious. . . . [M]y mind was . . . haunted with ghostly images . . . an agony of apprehension. . . .
> (267–68) [Note the imagery of the circle and the center.]

The sexual fantasy of this passage is, I think, incontestable; the Youth enters the uterine passage, and he is afraid.

When Pierre reaches the edge of the wood, he too is stricken with fear—although he is not greeted by a giant womb symbol, but by symbolic phalli:

In front [of Isabel's house], three straight, gigantic lindens stood guardians of this verdant spot. A long way up, almost to the ridgepole of the house, they showed little foliage; but, then, suddenly, as three huge green balloons, they poised their three vast, inverted, rounded cones of verdure in the air.

Soon as Pierre's eye rested on the place, a tremor shook him. [IX, 154].

Isabel lives in a simple cottage, but the Youth is led out of the arched trees to a "country villa" (albeit "unpretending"). Pierre gains admittance without difficulty, but the Youth, after advancing through "a small postern" in a garden wall, confronts an "edifice" without doors and with "well-defended windows . . . sufficiently high from the ground, as effectually to baffle the prying curiosity of the inquisitive stranger" (269). Thus, for the first time, the quester confronts the eternal barrier, the symbol of Secular Reality. His problem, which he bequeaths to all of Melville's subsequent questers, is the penetrating of the wall:

As my imagination, ever alert on such an occasion, was busily occupied in assigning some fearful motive for such unusual precautions; my leader suddenly halted beneath a lofty window, and making a low call, I perceived slowly descending therefrom, a thick silken cord, attached to an ample basket, which was silently deposited at our feet. (269)

The Youth is drawn through a window, and

My fellow voyager was quickly beside me, and again enjoining silence with her finger, she seized the lamp and bidding me follow, conducted me through a long corridor, till we reached a low door concealed behind some old tapestry, which opening to the touch, disclosed a spectacle as beautiful and enchanting as any described in the Arabian Nights. (269)

That is to say, the uterine canal fantasy is repeated, but this time the quester enters the symbolic womb proper, and it is a room of "Eastern splendor . . . redolent of the most delicious perfumes" (269):

The walls were hung round with the most elegant draperies, waving in graceful folds, on which were delineated scenes of Arcadian beauty. The floor was covered with a carpet of the finest texture, in which were wrought with exquisite skill the most striking events in ancient mythology. Attached to the wall by cords composed of alternate threads of crimson silk and gold, were several magnificent pictures illustrative of the loves of Jupiter and Semele, Psyche before the tribunal of Venus, and a variety of other scenes, limned all with felicitous grace. Disposed around the room, were luxurious couches, covered with the finest damask, on which were likewise executed after the Italian fashion the early fables of Greece and Rome. Tripods, designed to represent the Graces bearing aloft vases, richly chiseled in the classic taste, were distributed in the angles of the room, and exhaled an intoxicating fragrance.

Chandeliers of the most fanciful description, suspended from the lofty ceiling by rods of silver, shed over this voluptuous scene a soft and tempered light, and imparted to the whole, that dreamy beauty, which must be seen in order to be duly appreciated. Mirrors of unusual magnitude, multiplying in all directions the gorgeous objects, deceived the eye by their reflections, and mocked the vision with long perspective. (270)

William Gilman cites[3] various parallels between this room and Aladdin's Palace in *Redburn*, but he does not emphasize their essential difference: here the pictured love scenes are not salacious and pornographic, as they are in the later novel; for the quester now enters the Sacred Center, as Redburn will enter a patent perversion and caricature of it, more like Hautia's Bower in *Mardi* than any sacred place.

"Reclining upon an ottoman," lute in hand, within her magnificent shrine, is Inamorata; "with a queenly wave of the hand," she motions the conductress from the room. The gesture, the instrument, and, as we shall see, her sexual magnetism all indicate that Melville's first incarnation of the Sacred Reality resembles Isabel who is, to a substantial degree, a temptress. But Inamorata combines this aspect of woman with its opposite, for, like the innocent and modest Lucy (also of *Pierre*), she is dressed in "a flowing robe of the purest white," her "zone . . . of pink satin, on which were broidered figures of Cupid in the act of drawing his bow. . . ." (270). As her name and the symbol-

ism of her realm indicate, she is a Goddess of Love. And so the Youth
addresses her:

> 'Here do I prostrate myself, thou sweet Divinity, and kneel at the
> shrine of thy peerless charms!' (271)

just as Pierre will Lucy: " 'Ah! thou holy angel, Lucy! . . . thou height
of all delight' " [IX, 54] and will regard *her* bedchamber as a
"shrine" [IX, 53].

Approaching the damsel, the Youth falls instantly in love: the
"fires" of her eyes "kindled . . . [his] soul in flames!" (271). At once
he forswears another (as Pierre forswears Lucy on first being sexually
attracted by Isabel), and, in imagery reminiscent now of Taji's first
encounter with Yillah in *Mardi* (see below, p. ——), the Youth per-
forms a symbolic intercourse:

> The silken threads were snapped asunder; the golden cords had
> parted! A new dominion was creeping o'er my soul, and I fell,
> bound at the feet of my fair enchantress. A moment of unutterable
> interest passed, while I met the gaze of this glorious being with
> a look as ardent, as burning, as steadfast as her own. . . . *'Fair
> mortal!'* I exclaimed, *'I feel my passion is requited. . . .'* (271)
> (Italics added.)

Sexual love has requited his passion—for who can doubt what that
"moment of unutterable interest" is?—but it has also demythologized
the maiden: before, she was a "divinity"; now, a "mortal." A passage
in *Pierre* aptly annotates Melville's meaning:

> Now, crossing the magic silence of . . . [Lucy's] empty cham-
> ber . . . [Pierre] caught the snow-white bed reflected in the
> toilet-glass. This rooted him. For one swift instant, he seemed to
> see in that one glance the two separate beds—the real one and
> the reflected one—and an unbidden, most miserable presentiment
> thereupon stole into him—[IX, 53]

the tragic discrepancy between divine love and human. And, therefore, despite sexual fulfillment, the Youth has still not achieved the
highest happiness. He begs assurance that he is loved as he loves, but
the maiden does not answer his frantic plea; although her lips move,

no sound is forthcoming, and the "Fragment" concludes on this wildly melodramatic note:

> I flung her from me, even though she clung to my vesture, and with a wild cry of agony I burst from the apartment!—She was dumb! Great God, she was dumb! DUMB AND DEAF! (271)

William Gilman quite rightly observes that

> Of profound significance is the fact that the "Fragment" tells the story of a frustrated quest. The pattern of this adolescent experiment with the marvelous is the essential pattern of *Mardi*, *Moby-Dick*, and *Pierre*. Here Melville's hero pursues the trivial end of sensuous perfection. At the very end he is suddenly disappointed. . . . The ending of the second "Fragment" shows that as early as his twentieth year Melville's mind had formulated, however crudely, the concept that pursuit of the ideal is foredoomed to disillusion and defeat.[4]

In addition, three other remarks are relevant: first, it is very important to realize that Melville's formulation of the dualistic cosmos, the worlds of the Secular and the Sacred, derives ultimately from the primitive quest for the Center and from the symbolism of sexuality. In the "Fragment" this formulation clearly reveals its archaic and originally unconscious character. Second, the pervading silence that attends Inamorata, however much it may be a part of Melville's *Arabian Nights* source and however well it may define the passivity of the female, is, more significantly, the first of many instances in which the Sacred is represented by Silence: the unanswering god, Moa Artua, of *Typee*; Babbalanja's remark in *Mardi* that "the final wisdom is dumb"; the silent Whale; and Melville's observation in *Pierre* that "Silence is the only Voice of our God." Third, we might notice that the "Fragment" ends with the quester still in the house, presumably in the corridor. That is, he has not yet effected his escape.

Thus the ontogenetic history of Melville's first quester. But the Youth exists in two temporal dimensions, not just one, for he also initiates the Quester's phylogenetic history. In this second "Fragment," as again in *Typee* and *Mardi*, we recognize the presence of two "women"—one of whom, following the terminology of Erich Neumann, we shall call the Mother, the other the virginal Captive. In all cases, the questers may free themselves only by overcoming the former and marrying the latter. In the "Fragment," as we have seen, the Youth retreats into the Mother (as symbolized by the cord, corridor, and the house itself), momentarily possesses the Captive (Inamorata) but, as the tale ends, has not yet been able to disengage himself from the womb of prenatal existence. Psychologically, that is, the piece *is* a fragment.

The Youth's problem, of course, is to be born, to descend by the umbilical cord, thick and silken, and cut it. In order to cut his own cord (although he had other reasons as well), Melville left his mother's home at twenty-one, buried himself in the South Seas, and did not return to America, by his own account, until his symbolic birth four years later. "From my twenty-fifth year," he subsequently told Hawthorne, "I date my life." From his twenty-sixth year dates his first novel.

T ypee (1846) is, first and most memorably, a travelogue tale of adventure and love: of cliff-hanging descents and hairbreadth escapes, of the somnolent Valley and the gentle Fayaway; a tale told by a very young man. *Typee* is this, first and best, but it is also of deeper implication, for it contains many Melville motifs in embryo. Here, inchoate, is the symbolism of land and sea; unexplored, the conflict between conscious and unselfconscious love; dimly adumbrated, the choice a Westerner must make between civilization and primitivism. Here for the first time is Appearance distinguished from Reality; is Evil caused by those who would do Good; and here Melville again suggests the quester's confrontation with Secular Reality.

After Tommo and Toby desert the *Dolly*, they strike out for the Nukuhevan interior, the paradisiacal Happar Valley. But access is not easy: to attain the island's center, they must thrust through unyielding underbrush, suffer the effects of hunger and thirst, expend every last ounce of stamina, nerve, and physical courage. Melville first describes their hardships in realistic detail and then delivers himself through comparison: "Belzoni, worming . . . through the subterranean passages of the Egyptian catacombs, could not have met with greater impediments than those we here encountered" [I, 77]. There is never any attempt to amplify or extend this rudimentary conceit —in fact, Melville seems and undoubtedly is totally unaware of its symbolic possibilities—but there is no doubt that, in his comparison of dense underbrush with masonry surfaces, his protagonists are confronting Secular Reality. That the catacombs are specifically "Egyptian" emphasizes their time-forgotten origin and the perpetual presence of the external world, just as the ancient stone monuments of Nukuheva, which, according to Kory-Kory, are coeval with the creation of the world, are likened to the Pyramid of Cheops. Melville is also reminded of the Druids, for in the Typeean jungle, as in Egypt and at Stonehenge, primitive religionists once observed their sacred rites. In short, Melville is awestruck at Man's attempt to communicate with and know God, and later, when his heroes quest for Him, the pyramid will become one of the symbolic obstacles they must conquer.

Tommo and Toby thread the catacombs and attain the center, but the Happar Valley turns out to be the dreaded Typee Valley (which, in turn, after *Rasselas*, Tommo ironically renames the Happy Valley): ironical because his confinement there—he is under a kind of house arrest—is hardly Edenic. He suffers and endures a painfully wounded leg, the seeming desertion of Toby, a lack of privacy, the absence of intellectual companionship, the fear of cannibalism and tattooing. For Fayaway, there is Mow-Mow: prelapsarian innocence and barbarism conjoined. In other words, Tommo exchanges the problems and anxieties of a sophisticated society for those of a primeval one before discovering (surely to his surprise, if not disillusion) that the earthly Paradise is a fiction; and that the world within is merely different in degree, not kind, from the world without.

Fayaway, Melville's second heroine, is young, beautiful, passive, innocent—as if she were Eve in the Garden before the Fall. But Melville is not merely intent upon idealizing her; he would, in fact, make her the whole, the perfect, woman, and this is why—as hindsight reveals—he describes her face as "singularly expressive of intelligence and humanity" [I, 144]. He means, despite the crudity of his shorthand, that she combines the conscious intellect of a Western woman with the unselfconscious heart of a Polynesian, the best, so to speak, of both possible worlds. To suggest her moral perfection, Melville intimates her faithfulness in love: just as Tommo eschews the company of other women—and is particularly disgusted by sailor promiscuity [I, 18]—so she eschews the company of other men, an attitude unexpectedly puritan in an island maiden. Nevertheless, it is because of—not despite—such unrealism that love prospers. "*I* was a child and *she* was a child," Tommo might have sung, for his affection is also not only pure but puerile, a commitment to the pleasures of the lover and a refusal to the responsibilities of the husband. And, as in "Annabel Lee," it is a love destined to die, a fantasy love that cannot thrive except in the imagination, where Melville soon installs it—a constant reminder that heterosexual love is never a final satisfaction.

Nevertheless, even as Tommo possesses Fayaway (and appreciates the domesticity of the maternal Tinor), he often escapes the company of women by retreating to the bachelor grove of Ti, the tabooed sanctuary. Not, of course, that he seeks homosexual contact, and, in fact, it is possible that the fear of such contact is one of the reasons he jumps ship in the first place: for Tommo is haunted, Melville tells us, by the prospect of sailing indefinitely in a world without women, tacking near Buggerry Island or the Devil's Tail Peak [I, 28]. In the end, Tommo mediates his desires and "marries" a man, first Toby with whom he "weds" palms [I, 42], and then, in the continuation of his adventures in *Omoo*, the congenial Dr. Long Ghost. But like all solutions in Melville, this one too is partial.

A harder reconciliation, however, still awaits the hero: balancing the claims of Society against the opposing claims of Ego. There are many reasons why Tommo wants to leave Typee—loneliness in an alien land, love of home and family, desire to revitalize the intellect —but none so significant as the feeling, conscious or otherwise, that, despite himself, he is slowly assimilating into the Typeean society; that, as he forms intimate relationships with her men and women, he must necessarily give up questing. His mysteriously wounded leg is indeed symbolic: of that castrating injury which results whenever the claim of the quest challenges the claim of the tribe—any tribe, primitive or modern, it does not matter. One is reminded of Ahab, for he too suffers a wound in the leg (when his ivory pierces him near the groin), a wound that is of the same symbolic consequence as Tommo's, for it too expresses the irreconcilable conflict of society and the quester. Ahab's is the punishment he must suffer for renouncing the quest in the communal interest (by taking a wife and fathering a child) and, then, renouncing that communal claim (by desecrating the marriage vow and deserting his family) for the quest. The conflict, in short, quite unmans a man, and Melville expresses the resultant wound in sexual terms, a natural metaphor for the loss of power and energy. In *Omoo*, as the sailors sign onto the whaler and thereby re-enter society, their beards are cut off, and in *White-Jacket*, this ritual act, called "shear[ing] off my manhood," [VI, 455], this symbolic castration, is perpetrated on the sailors before they are permitted to leave the *Neversink*. In *Pierre* we learn that Pierre's father had whiskers when he was a gay bachelor [VIII, 93] but that after marrying Mrs. Glendinning, he shaved them off. Perhaps in rebellion or assertion, or perhaps for no reason at all, Melville himself sported a large and bushy beard.

Tommo's symbolic descent into the Typee Valley (where the first people he sees are near-naked lovers and where he lives as one)—in short, his return to unconsciousness and the womb—parallels his penetration of the "catacomb": initially a grand success, each conquest diminishes in value until only a complete reversal of positions—a flight from rather than toward—can satisfy the quester. Thus as he has conquered the walls once, Tommo must now do it again, albeit from a different direction. And when he succeeds, his wounded leg heals, for he is escaping from society to momentary freedom, the delinquency of the wanderer or *omoo*. (That freedom in vagabondage is illusory and that questing itself is, if not properly moderated, an intolerable confinement, Tommo never contemplates.) Driven by intense, if obscure, impulses, he can only take immediate relief in shattering his prison: he never understands his own inner contradictions and, therefore, can never reorder his life. Indeed, he just barely survives, although that he does at all is still, as Donald Houghton asserts, "incredible":[5] Tommo seems at once able and unable to leave

Typee, and the final sequence of events is jumbled in a way very strange for a novelist who had such a powerful grip on facts. The confusion is not merely because Tommo cannot decide whether he wants to exchange primitive life for civilized, but also, at a more profound level, whether he wants to die in the Typeean womb or be born, for *Typee* is, as D. H. Lawrence intuited many years ago, "a bit of birth-myth, or re-birth myth. . . ."⁶ Tommo finally chooses life, not death, but not wholeheartedly, and, in fact, he narrowly escapes the final assault of the ferocious Mow-Mow who would capsize his canoe.

Nevertheless, as the transpersonal Quester, Tommo makes some progress toward emancipation. Like the Youth, he retreats into the realm of the Mother, the enclosed valley; and, again, like the Youth, he momentarily possesses the Captive, Fayaway; but, as the novel ends, only Tommo smashes his way into the beginnings of ego consciousness. His birth, to be sure, is hardly clean, but he survives because he is young, strong, and buoyed irresistibly by animal spirits.

With the success of *Typee*, Melville drifted into a landside career and into the world of books, for the literatus Evert Duyckinck opened his library to the young author, introduced him to literary New York and encouraged him to mine the vein he had opened. Melville responded with *Omoo* (1847), but, in one very important sense, this charmingly picaresque novel is not the sequel of *Typee*, as Lawrence properly implied when he wrote that here, as nowhere else, Melville really "takes life as it comes. . . . [He eats] the world like a snipe, dirt and all baked into one *bonne bouche*."⁷ That is, in *Omoo*, Melville immerses himself in unordered phenomena without trying to impress them with structure and symbolic meaning. For once, he is almost completely content to remain within one world without formulating and questing for another. For once he jettisons his intellectual apparatus, relaxes his Calvinist conscience, exults in the life of the senses and meanders without purpose. And, therefore, the one moment of questing in *Omoo* (or, better, quasi-questing) is truly half-hearted, for the wanderer and the quester are diametrically opposed.

That one moment comes when Typee (formerly Tommo) and Dr. Long Ghost seek the "solitary inland village" [II, 278] of Tamai, which, they have heard, is renowned for the beauty and unsophistication of her women—no longer an infantile wish for the womb, but an adolescent dream of free love. As in *Typee*, the search once more is for Eden, but now it is more a matter of curiosity than dedication. At their leisure they reach "the very heart of the island" [II, 281], the inmost center, where, after descending into a valley, they begin to climb "a steep mountain opposite" [II, 282]. This mountain, the obstacle of Secular Reality, is, like the Typeean underbrush, another unrealized symbol of unconscious design. But now the travelers proceed without urgency and experience no really arduous passage; halfway up the mountain they stop to eat, smoke, and nap, and when they reach the top, there, before them, is Tamai. They linger for a few days—and discover, to Typee's amusement and the Doctor's chagrin that the girls are not so unsophisticated after all—before fleeing from certain newcomers who would threaten their freedom. The earthly Eden, that is, again proves illusory. But, lest we misinterpret, Typee's departure is not called an Expulsion but a Hegira, and it is a flight Melville himself felt regretfully constrained to make. And, therefore, when Ishmael warns us about casting off from the "one insular Tahiti," we may be sure that he is alluding neither to South Seas life in general nor to anxiety-ridden Typee life in particular, but to the irresponsible wonderings of the Tahitian *omoo*, whose existence Melville himself momentarily enjoyed in Polynesia and which he never dared enjoy again.

In these first two novels we meet one typical Melvillean quester, the mild-mannered youth who is eager to learn and unwilling to offend; but, in *Omoo*, we also meet Melville's first manic quester whose presence is worth remarking because of his resemblance to Ahab. Bembo is a New Zealander who passionately desires to slay a certain whale and who, in desperation, finally leaps upon the whale's back in order to plunge in his harpoon, although, like Moby Dick, the whale escapes. Bembo is dark, moody, taciturn, demoniac; his hatred is fierce, and, on one occasion, he tries to scuttle a ship in order to avenge an insult. Eventually he is put into chains (one remembers how Ahab is confined after being dismasted), and his fate is undetermined. Although he lacks Ahab's rhetoric and the overlay of his Westernism, Bembo is indubitably the prototype of those later heroes who will risk all to achieve all.

For just as Melville realized that he could not forever indulge the sybaritic existence without, in Lawrence's words, his soul decomposing, so he also knew that he could not continue to write *Typee*s and *Omoo*s, pleasant books with pleasant heroes, without seriously suppressing his artistic impulses. Furthermore, at Duyckinck's direction, he was beginning to discover philosophy and metaphysics; and, as his mind began to grow and question, he found that he was formed for stories deeper than mere adventure and romance. Finally, during this same period, in August 1847, Melville married Elizabeth Shaw, the daughter of Lemuel Shaw, Chief Justice of Massachusetts and since the death of Herman's father in 1832 a Melville family benefactor. And marriage too would profoundly influence the direction of his forthcoming work. Although he had become a moderately lionized author, his own taste and that of his audience would not long coincide.

Mardi (1849), Melville's third book, is an explosion of "heart" and an exploration of mind, an enormously complicated work, which begins as narrative but sheers into allegory; whose author willingly entertains questions of ethics and metaphysics, politics and culture, sin and guilt, *inter alia*; and whose protagonists consciously seek the beautiful white Yillah, who, in the course of the book, becomes the symbolic embodiment of the Sacred Reality. As a multiplex symbol, she, like the White Whale, means different things to different men, although to Taji she embodies sacramental and sexual fulfillment and to Babbalanja, Melville's second closest projection of self, Final Truth.[8]

The crucial moment of Taji's career is when he stabs Aleema, Yillah's protector, in order to rescue the maiden who is confined within a tented sanctuary and whom Aleema intends to sacrifice. Like Yil-

lah, the priest also functions symbolically: standing *between* the
quester and his goal, he is Secular Reality incarnate:

> The old priest, like a scroll of old parchment, covered all over
> with hieroglyphical devices, harder to interpret, I'll warrant, than
> any old Sancrit manuscript [*sic*]. And upon his broad brow,
> deepgraven in wrinkles, were characters still more mysterious,
> which no Champollion nor gypsy could have deciphered. He
> looked as old as the elderly hills; eyes sunken, though bright;
> and head white as the summit of Mount Blanc. [III, 151]

We are at once reminded of identical symbols of the natural world
in other books: Moby Dick's broad, wrinkled brow described with
hieroglyphs no Champollion can decipher; the hills and mountains of
Pierre; and the face of Plotinus Plinlimmon whose delineation and
function in *Pierre* in part parallel Aleema's but who is drawn with
full consciousness of symbolic overtone.

But having penetrated Secular Reality once by stabbing the priest,
Taji must penetrate it again to attain his end, although now, as he
pierces Yillah's tent, enters the sacred enclosure, and retrieves the
maiden, the character of his act is distinctly sexual. Despite the gigan-
tism of Melville's images (as in the womb vision of the second "Fragment"), his allegory needs little explication:

> By means of thin spaces between the braids of matting, the
> place [note "place," a deliberately vague usage] was open to the
> air, but not to view. There was also *a round opening* on one
> side, only large enough, however, to admit the arm; but this aper-
> ture was *partially closed from within. In front, a deep-dyed rug
> of osiers, covering the entrance way*, was intricately laced to the
> standing part of the tent. As I divided this lacing with my *cutlass*
> [observe the pun: cut lass], there arose an outburst of voices
> from the Islanders. . . .
> Before me crouched a beautiful girl. [III, 158] (Italics added.)

Taji, then, divides the braids and attains the Sacred Reality, but his
victory—like the Youth's before whom the cords part and the threads
sunder—is momentary and ominously pyrrhic; he suffers immediate
remorse, and Aleema's spectral sons who haunt him throughout the
book, as the Furies Orestes, effectively symbolize that tormenting con-

sciousness of guilt he can neither escape nor expiate. Furthermore, soon after her defloration, Yillah, no longer virginal, naturally disappears. In the company of Babbalanja a philosopher, Yoomy a poet, Mohi an historian, and Media a king, Taji searches the island archipelago for her, but, of course, she is never found. For just as Paradise is never inviolable in Melville, so is it, once lost, never regained.

If Fayaway is sketched directly from life (although idealized in the process), Yillah is the product of a much purer fantasy. Like her predecessor, she too is beautiful, ethereal, innocent, submissive, and unconscious of her sexual attraction. But Yillah is also saintly [III, 158]—her first home was Oroolia (Paradise)—and although, like Fayaway, she has lived most of her mortal life in a glen, it is not in the Typee Valley but in the Vale of Ardair [III, 179], a mythicized place reminiscent of Shakespeare's Arden and Poe's Aidenn. But perhaps the most remarkable difference between them is that Yillah is white-skinned, not olive. Two explanations for this variance are offered— two ways, that is, of explaining Yillah's origin—and that the reader should accept one while rejecting the other is vital to Melville's strategy. Yillah may be an albino Polynesian, but she is, almost surely, the naturally white daughter of white parents slain in the South Seas. Read "the values of the Western World" for "white parents"; in other words, Yillah possesses not only "intelligence," like Fayaway, but also a genetic and cultural heritage, however dormant. Thus— and it is a rather heavy hint—she enjoys being spoken to in English, a language she cannot understand but which she can readily repeat, a talent none of the Polynesians has [III, 177]. Yillah is Melville's third attempt at the perfect female.

So much, however, is sex and love bound up with guilt and fear that even this absolutely docile virgin can be won only through murder, and possessed only through deception. For Taji does deceive her, telling her that he too is of Oroolia and that he would restore their other-worldly happiness, the happiness they enjoyed frolicking in their "arbour, where the green vines grew over the great ribs of the stranded whale" [III, 166]. Taji conjures an image of the Bower of the Arsacides, a Paradise, as *Moby-Dick* confirms, that proves false. But Yillah, in her innocence, succumbs to his blandishments. "We lived and we loved" [III, 185]: again the lovers live together unwed, as man and mistress. Thus in the untrammeling of his fantasy Melville creates and Taji comes to possess a truly improbable woman: White-Western yet sexually unselfconscious. And so is their love contradictory—ascetically sexual, as if anything but the purest touch will corrupt the fragile Yillah. As indeed it will! As indeed it does! Sex destroys Yillah, and sexual love again provides but temporary delight.

But Taji's idea of perfect love has also begun to change. For despite her Western heritage, Yillah remains innocent—as Taji does not—and the love of a pure maiden becomes finally as unsatisfying to him as it will to Pierre. But at the outset of the later novel Isabel clearly displaces Lucy in Pierre's imagination, and the displacement of the one and the emergence of the other are aptly related as effect and cause. In *Mardi*, however, Yillah is never overtly denied, for the quester has not yet become disenchanted with the asexual ideal, nor with the perpetual avoidance of sex which the pursuit of Yillah demands. Therefore, Hautia, the temptress, simply appears after Yillah vanishes (much as Inamorata succeeds the "conductress"), and the one event seems to have no causal relation to the other, as, of course, it does. I do not mean that Yillah and Hautia are identical with Lucy and Isabel—they are not, although they do share some similar characteristics—but that as *Mardi* is a relatively crude, so *Pierre* is a highly complex, rendering of essentially the same love story—of a man trapped between two women—retold with much greater subtlety and nuance, a sophisticated psychologizing, and a surer narrative technique. In any event, Hautia suddenly appears, and she is a woman of such devious quality that she conducts her affairs incognito or through emissaries who communicate in an artificial language, that of flower symbolism. Yillah, by her absence, offers Taji the quest; Hautia, by her presence, sex and society. Melville calls her sinful, and, to the extent that she "kills aspiration . . . by emphasizing only the animality of the natural senses,"[9] she is. Yet it is as wrong to regard her as exclusively evil, as it is to regard Yillah as exclusively beneficial—and, in fact, Melville contradicts himself on just how evil Hautia is anyway, for she offers Taji "beauty, health, wealth, long life, and the last lost hope of man" [IV, 396]. She begs him for love, wants to marry him, and suffers sexual frustration upon his refusal. F. O. Matthiessen's remark is precisely to the point: ". . . Taji's rejection of the dark girl's advances . . . involve[s] a denial of mature passion."[10] At times, Hautia is more victim than victimizer.

As in *Pierre*, where the quester burns his father's picture and then runs off with Isabel, Taji's original sins also suggest parricide and, as Richard Chase observes,[11] incest (although in *Mardi* these relationships are not clearly expressed). James E. Miller's biographical hypothesis is not without point in this connection:

> Lemuel Shaw had been in love with Nancy Melville, sister to
> Herman's father Allan, and after her early death, had continued
> his close association with the Melville family, advising and aid-
> ing the widow after Allan Melville's death. Herman's sense
> of gratitude was very strong, and in fact he dedicated his first
> book, *Typee*, to Lemuel Shaw. If it is possible that in marrying
> Elizabeth Shaw, Melville felt a sense of duty in the fulfilment of
> an obligation [although he was obviously in love as well], he
> may also have felt, below the levels of consciousness, a sense of
> guilt in the commitment of an incestuous sin. For if Lemuel
> Shaw acted like a father, Elizabeth must at times have seemed a
> sister.[12]

Now I am not about to suggest an identification between the Chief Justice and Aleema (or, for that matter, between Herman and Taji or Elizabeth and Yillah), but I would point out two things: first, that in cognizance of the many Melvillean puns on proper names scattered throughout the canon, "A*leema*" may well be a distortion of "*Lem*uel" and, second, as Dorothee Metlitsky Finkelstein has noted,[13] the Arabic connotation of the name "Aleema" suggests " 'a man of science or learning . . . a term more particularly given to a doctor of the law,' " Lemuel Shaw's profession!

Only by succumbing to the sons of Aleema can Taji expiate the murder of the father-figure and only by succumbing to Hautia and the maturer sexuality she symbolizes can Taji disavow (and, therefore, to some degree, expiate) his guilt in seizing Aleema's ward. But Taji chooses to bear both burdens and to follow Yillah, a flight which, however heroic, is also foolish and, more to the point, sinful, escap-

ist, and cowardly—a flight from justice, society, and sex. And, therefore, Aleema's sons, those unexorcised spectres of Taji's sin-ridden
conscience, must continue to pursue, to plague him for avoiding simple justice and the maturity of marriage, and for clinging childishly
to a lost innocence.

Nevertheless, the transpersonal Quester—as embodied in this instance by Taji—does make slight progress toward maturity; at least
he reaches adolescence. Again, after momentarily possessing the Captive (Yillah, who is first the prisoner of Aleema and then of Hautia),
Taji loses her and must overcome the maturer woman, the "Mother,"
in order to regain her; and he can overcome Hautia only by remaining in her cave (first house, then valley, now cave) and by yielding
to the temptation she represents—that is, by committing "incest."
Now I have already said, in concurrence with Matthiessen and others,
that by eschewing Hautia, Taji eschews maturity. But how, one may
ask, may the commission of incest signify maturity? Erich Neumann
asserts that in the development of ego consciousness in the transpersonal Hero:

> Victory over the mother, frequently taking the form of actual
> entry into her, *i.e.* incest, brings about a rebirth. The incest pro-
> duces a transformation of personality which alone makes the
> hero a hero, that is, a higher and ideal representative of man-
> kind. . . . [For] what distinguishes the hero is an active incest, the
> deliberate, conscious exposure of himself to the dangerous in-
> fluence of the female, and the overcoming of man's immemorial
> fear of woman.[14]

Taji, in fact, is titillated in the extreme by Hautia but finally flees in
fear; that is, the Quester is not yet ready to engage the Mother in
single combat, and, therefore, Taji denies himself the "regenerative"
incest, choosing rather the fruitless pursuit of what he mistakenly assumes is the Ideal.

Indeed, only in this pathetic sense is his flight heroic—and since
he also believes that sex will tempt him from the quest, he resists
Hautia at all costs. Wedlock, he says on one occasion, is suicide, and
he reminds us, on another, that Bardianna, the mythic wiseman, remained a bachelor, although Pesti [sic] tried to marry him. Melville

shows us how Annatoo, perhaps the caricature of the married woman, is ugly and noxious and tells us that King Uhia grew stronger after giving up sex. Such leaden jibes—American *kitsch* humor at its worst—are deplorable, even if Melville was a newlywed, but the sexual plight of Donjalolo is not comic at all, and Melville approaches it without laughter.

Donjalolo rules the island of Juam from Willamilla, a glen accessible only through "a subterranean tunnel, dimly lighted by a span of white day at the end" [II, 253]. Within is a green valley; the circumference, impassable mountains. (One is, of course, reminded of the Typeean terrain.) Donjalolo's private residence, within this womblike world, is a labyrinthine structure, and he sleeps at its innermost center:

> Traversing the central arbour, and fancying it will soon lead you to open ground, you suddenly come upon the most private retreat of the prince; a square structure; plain as a pyramid; and without, as inscrutable. Down to the very ground, its walls are thatched; but on the farther side a passage-way opens, which you enter. But not yet are you within. Scarce a yard distant, stands an inner thatched wall, blank as the first. Passing along the intervening corridor, lighted by narrow apertures, you reach the opposite side, and a second opening is revealed. This entering, another corridor; lighted as the first, but more dim, and a third blank wall. And thus, three times three, you worm round and round, the twilight lessening as you proceed; until at last, you enter the citadel itself: the innermost arbour of a nest; whereof, each has its roof, distinct from the rest. [III, 278]

In *Moby-Dick* Melville will describe the Whale, the vault of Sacred Reality, in similar terms: as a pyramid, a citadel, a wall, blank and inscrutable. But whereas Ahab is outside the whale trying to pierce within, Donjalolo, like Bartleby, is encapsulated within the donjon of Secular Reality trying to get out.[15] But Donjalolo can neither, figuratively, escape the labyrinth, nor, literally, circumvent the mountains. Melville's purpose in interchanging the position of the quester with that of the Sacred Reality is double: to discredit the notion of an exaltedly terrestrial inner world and to expose the intolerability of innocence. He would not necessarily suppose, as he had in *Typee*, that Eden was inland or that the Center was sacred.

Through certain familial circumstances, Donjalolo is forced to a Hobson's choice between becoming king and never leaving the glen or leaving the glen and never becoming king: Society or the Individual, the responsibilities of office or the quest. Donjalolo chooses kingship (and its attendant rewards, which include thirty mistresses), but his desires to quest will not down, and the unresolved conflict unmans him quite; he becomes sickly, moody, reliant upon alcohol, subject to spells, spectre-ridden, mad, and sterile. Nothing—neither his harem nor his intoxicants—can assuage his misery, for he had wanted, more than anything else, to know the outer world, and he is well aware that by renouncing freedom he has accepted "servitude." Obliged to stay within, Donjalolo, a would-be quester with a Westerner's sensibility, suffers the fate Tommo would have suffered had he failed to escape his imprisonment, a perpetual immaturity, a death in the womb.

But *Mardi*, for all its relevance to *Typee*, looks forward, not backward, and the figure in the Melville canon whom Donjalolo most resembles is not Tommo but Pierre (Pierre *Glen*dinning: Donjalolo of the *Glen* of Willamilla). Each is first revealed to us as a handsome innocent living within the confines of a valley; each is of royal or aristocratic lineage and is or is about to become lord of this inland demesne, which is surrounded by mountains of Titanic proportion. Each, too, would know, and is disillusioned by the futile quest for Final Truth: Donjalolo sends emissaries into Mardi, but when they submit widely differing reports of the same phenomenon, he ruefully concludes that Truth is not unitary but complex, not absolute but relative; and is finally unknowable. As for Pierre, his personal misadventures are so disillusioning that he finally and bitterly concludes that Virtue is "trash" and Truth nonexistent. But perhaps the major difference between them is that Donjalolo declines to leave Willamilla whereas Pierre plunges forth from Saddle Meadows. Ironically, however, the results of their decisions are virtually identical: each suffers mental and emotional disability, and, as Pierre becomes "neuter" [IX, 503], so Donjalolo, despite his thirty mistresses, fathers no chil-

dren, and is, apparently, sterile, a sterility which correlates exactly
with his incapacity to overcome the surrounding mountains. Most
fearful of all, each is damned to choose and damned to suffer his
choice—within the walls or without them.

Pierre, however, is not just the extrapolation of Donjalolo, but of
Taji as well, for he too is committed to the double quest: for sacramental Truth and pure love. We speak here of Taji at the end of the
book, for at the outset and even after he begins his search for Yillah,
he exhibits little of the questing mania. Indeed, it is one of the flaws
of *Mardi* that the decent youth we first meet—and who is undeveloped
during the long middle section of the book in which he almost disappears from view because he is so silent—should perpetuate the quest.
This long silence, according to Lawrance Thompson,[16] is the result
of "psychological fragmentation," in which Taji's various cerebral
functions—reason, memory, imagination—are embodied by his colleagues, Babbalanja, Mohi, and Yoomy respectively. Nevertheless, as
in the case of Bembo, it is also possible that Taji's increasing silence
is symptomatic of his growing mania, although it is equally possible
that his silence, like Clarel's, indicates nothing more than the absence
of learning and the consequent submission before his intellectual
superiors. In any event, Taji's ultimate setting forth over desperate
seas is not really in character; he becomes an Ahab-type quite unexpectedly, and we are unprepared for his transformation.

In their travels through Mardi, the expedition arrives at Maramma
where Mt. Ofo's lower reaches symbolize Secular Reality and its
cloudcovered, inaccessible peak the Sacred; and where Pani, a blind
man led by a child, is the island's physical and spiritual guide. Pani,
who doubts the purity of his soul, espouses a religious orthodoxy for
selfish as well as selfless reasons. On one hand, he feels obliged to
protect society by concealing his own uncertainty; but, on the other,
he preaches charity and solicits gifts; and, in his hypocrisy, is clearly
an ancestor of Plotinus Plinlimmon who solicits a case of claret from
an admirer, rejecting the gift of a library. Plotinus, however, is hardened beyond redemption: he can help Pierre, but remains silent,
whereas Pani genuinely believes that he cannot help the pilgrims
except by remaining silent and leaving them to their illusions. Both

men have apparently considered the quest for Truth and moved beyond it to a position of spiritual paralysis.

In soliloquy Pani broods:

> Have we angelic spirits? . . . I am dumb with doubt; yet, 'tis not
> doubt, but worse: I doubt my doubt. Oh, ye all-wise spirits
> in the air, how can ye witness all this woe, and give no sign?
> [IV, 21]

Pierre, who would also determine whether his soul is divine by addressing the spirits in the air, goes mad, surely in part because he
receives no sign. Melville too wrestled with this problem and in 1856
told Hawthorne that he had "pretty much made up his mind to be
annihilated";[17] that is, that he had more or less concluded that his
soul was not angelic and that, in consequence, he could not anticipate
an afterlife. His decision, to be sure, did not render him mad, but perhaps it did in part render him dumb, for the publication of *The Confidence-Man* in 1857 signals the end of his career as a novelist. Like
sightless Pani, "thread[ing] the labyrinthine wilds of Maramma"
[IV, 6], Melville too was left wandering, "dumb with doubt" in the
labyrinth of his perceptions.

The Supreme Pontiff of Maramma is Hivohitee, God's Papal Emis-
sary, and he too dwells in the "interior" [IV, 35]. But now, even as
Melville consciously relates the realm of Sacred Reality to Secular—

> the mystery that lieth beyond . . . that which is beneath the
> seeming; the precious pearl within the shaggy oyster. . . [the]
> circle's center—[IV, 36]

he agains mocks his own configurations, desecrating the world within
and blaspheming its divine inhabitant. For Hivohitee lives in a waste-
land where the air is miasmal, the waters are polluted, and hawks
and crows populate the trees: the *locus amoenus* contraverted.

On visiting Hivohitee's tower, Yoomy sees only "darkness" and
"The dim gleaming . . . of [his] gorget" [IV, 46] although earlier
he had been described as "an old, old man; with steel-gray eyes, hair
and beard, and a horrible necklace of jaw bones" [IV, 45]. (Similarly, one is reminded that Yillah, a White Goddess to the Mardians,
is, in fact, the naturally white daughter of Western parents.) But how

can the questers have misconstrued the nature of God's legate so badly? Babbalanja explains that "the shadows of things are greater than themselves; and the more exaggerated the shadows, the more unlike to the substance":

> This Great Mogul of a personage, then; this woundy Ahasuerus; this man of men; this same Hivohitee, whose name rumbled among the mountains like a peal of thunder, had been seen face to face, and taken for naught but a bearded old hermit, or, at best, some equivocal conjuror. [IV, 48]

Melville here initiates his quarrel with God, a quarrel which will continue until Conjur Man becomes Confidence Man.

Halfway around the world, the questers near the shores of California and, at this point, Melville introduces the image of gold (or treasure) to symbolize the Sacred Reality, an image which possibly derives from and is shorthand for the resplendent room of the second "Fragment"; in effect, the symbol of a symbol. On no occasion in Melville's mature work, however, is the gold substantial, because the Ideal can never be realized. (Hence the gold may also symbolize, quite tangentially, the Commercial Success Melville sought but never attained.) This symbol is used frequently throughout the canon, as I shall have occasion to note, but never before Taji and his friends encounter the "gold-hunters" (who appear again aboard the *Fidèle* in *The Confidence-Man*):

> Fast to the Promised Land we fly;
>   Where in deep mines,
> Or down in beds of golden streams,
> The gold-flakes glance in golden gleams!
>   How we long to sift,
>   That yellow drift!
> Rivers! Rivers! cease your going!
>   Sand-bars! rise, and stay the tide;
> 'Till we've gained the golden flowing;
>   And in the golden haven ride! [IV, 265]

Moved by this song, the impulsive Yoomy would join the contemporaneous Gold Rush, "and from the golden waters where she lies, our

Yillah may emerge" [IV, 265]—hence the conjunction of Yillah
with Gold, as Inamorata had been affiliated with the splendrous room.
Wise Babbalanja dissuades Yoomy from vain pursuit, remarking that
a man who mines for gold digs his doom (as well as reefing on "vulgar shoals"), and Yoomy, learning his lesson well, recants and eventually moderates his idealism.

Taji circumnavigates the globe in quest of Yillah and then, in desperation, plunges through the "circumvallating reef" into an outer
ocean; and the reef, as Tyrus Hillway suggests,[18] may well be "a picturesque and effective symbol for the borderline between life and
death," or, perhaps, since Taji is doomed to sail endlessly, between
life and death-in-life. Thus the impossible pursuit of an ideal woman
and for a fulfilling heterosexual love—begun resolutely in the second
"Fragment" and advanced tentatively in *Typee*—receives in *Mardi*
its first decisive check.

A s Melville finished *Mardi*, Elizabeth gave birth to the first of their
four children, and thus with a wife and child to support and with
Mardi a financial disaster, Melville had to make money and make it
quickly. *Redburn* (1849), in other words, was calculated to sell—
and it did. But it also earned the author his own contempt, for Melville knew he was doing what he could do easily rather than chancing
what he could not. Nevertheless, *Redburn* is a solid comic achievement, better and fuller than he knew or cared to admit and certainly
not the insubstantial "beggarly" fare he would have us believe. In
writing *Redburn*, Melville may have had other motives than the pecuniary one: the hope of still becoming a popular author, popularly
received; and perhaps the desire, conscious or otherwise, of restoring
some inner balance by writing in a lighter vein. (This same consideration may have motivated the writing of "Bartleby" in a serio-comic
spirit after the wracked *Pierre*.) But speculating on why Melville
did not write the kind of book he cared most about—the saga of the
quest composed, as he says in *Mardi*, to relieve "a full heart" [IV,
322]—conducts us to the fringe of literature, the psychology of au-

thorship; and it is not enough to speculate why *Redburn* is not about questing, but to describe how it is not.

Soon after we meet our Young Man from the Provinces, Wellingborough Redburn embarks on his first adventure, a steamer trip from Albany to New York.[19] Ill-at-ease and poorly clad, he suffers the humiliating stares of his fellow passengers until he is unable to stand them any longer:

> I then turned to . . . [one], and clicking my gunlock, deliberately presented the piece at him.
> Upon this, he overset his seat in his eagerness to get beyond my range, for I had him point blank. . . . [V, 14–15]

Later, in a Liverpool street, Redburn reports that "I was stared at . . . to be sure; but what of that? We must give and take on such occasions" [V, 258]. Conjoining these two incidents illustrates a fundamental truth about the book and its hero; that as certain events repeat themselves, Redburn's responses change—in accordance with his progression from innocence to maturity. Thus, before Wellingborough sails for England, he is cheated by a pawnbroker into selling his fowling piece at a reduced sum. "In vain I expostulated" [V, 26], he says before accepting the unfair, if not illegal, terms. As the book ends, he is cheated once more, this time of his wages, by Captain Riga; and again the letter, but not the spirit, of the law, is on the cheater's side. But now Wellingborough realizes that he has no recourse, and, therefore, without word or whimper, "turned to go" [V, 396].

Redburn is also present at two hiring scenes, his own and Harry Bolton's. At the first he imagines that the Captain will recognize his fine qualities and pamper him, but at the second, he realizes that the Captain's smiles and jokes are those of a "gallant, gay deceiver" [V, 282]. Differentiating Reality from Appearance is, of course, a major Melvillean motif; and although in his more serious work this problem of perception is compounded by the observer's faulty vision (figuratively as well as literally in *Pierre*), the ambiguity of the world outside the observer (*The Confidence-Man*), or a combination of both ("Benito Cereno"), in *Redburn* there are no such intricacies, for in his "nursery tale" Melville coats the philosophic pill.

Surely the most important double incident in the book concerns
Redburn's confrontation with depravity. In the prior instance, he is
thoroughly shocked by the sight of a mother and her three children
dying helplessly in a Liverpool alley. In search of aid he entreats the
neighboring ragpickers (they say the woman is unmarried); a police-
man (he says it is not his beat); Handsome Mary of the *Baltimore
Clipper* (she says she gives to beggars in her own district); the Dock
Police (they say it is not within their jurisdiction). Sadly disillusioned,
Redburn cries in despair, "What right [has] . . . anybody in the wide
world to smile and be glad, when sights like this [are] . . . to be seen"
[V, 232]? And timidly acting the idealist's role, he steals a few crumbs
and procures a little free water for the victims. On the passage home,
however, Redburn sees the diseased and dying aboard the *Highlander*
but now merely excoriates society for her ruthlessness. He neither engages in the slightest personal charity, nor seeks help from his fellow
crew-members, for he has become one of the nameless "we" and his
remedies are legislative. By becoming a little more stoic and a little
less heroic, by tacitly accepting what he knows he cannot change,
Redburn refuses the quester's mantle.

His changing attitude toward the villainous Jackson also reflects
the manner of his maturation. Jackson is Melville's first admitted
atheist, and his denial of God is seconded only by his hatred of Man.
Like Ahab, he is a scarred Cain afloat, although, again like Ahab, he
is not without his "humanities": as Pip elicits tenderness from Ahab,
so the stowaway child evokes it in Jackson. On the passage out Redburn is terrified by the very presence of this moral leper but also—
because he seems more woeful than wicked—feels for him a "secret
sympathy." Indeed, responding to his opposite, Redburn sees the possibility of becoming that opposite, and perhaps it is not unreasonable
to assume that Jackson was once himself a believer, and that Redburn,
sensing this, senses too the ghastlines of innocence corrupted. But on
the return trip Redburn is neither terror-stricken nor sympathetic:
neither terrified by evil nor attracted by woe. For, in the way of the
Liverpool and London worlds, he has lost the capacity for such simple-
hearted reactions. Hardened and purged of his innocence, he has

learned to accommodate himself to evil, to become righteously—but not maniacally—indignant in the presence of the unalterable.

As a child (if not truly as an adult) Redburn displays the quester's mania—for this is the real meaning of the incident of the glass ship in the glass case. Wellingborough is fascinated by the ship which "more than anything else, converted . . . [his] vague dreamings and longings into a definite purpose of seeking . . . [his] fortune on the sea. . . ." "And well did it repay the long and curious examinations . . . [he is] accustomed to give it."

> She carried two tiers of black guns all along her two decks; and often I used to try to peep in at the portholes, to see what else was inside; but the holes were so small, and it looked so very dark indoors, that I could discover little or nothing; though, when I was very little, I made no doubt, that if I could but once pry open the hull, and break the glass all to pieces, I would infallibly light upon something wonderful, perhaps some gold guineas, of which I have always been in want, ever since I could remember. And often I used to feel a sort of insane desire to be the death of the glass ship, case, and all, in order to come at the plunder; and one day, throwing out some hint of the kind to my sisters, they ran to my mother in a great clamor; and after that, the ship was placed on the mantle-piece for a time, beyond my reach, and until I should recover my reason.
>
> I do not know how to account for this temporary madness of mine, unless it was, that I had been reading in a storybook about Captain Kidd's ship, that lay somewhere at the bottom of the Hudson near the Highlands, full of gold as it could be; and that a company of men were trying to dive down and get the treasure out of the hold, which no one had ever thought of doing before, though there she had lain for almost a hundred years. [V, 7–8]

Several significant motifs are rather playfully located here. First, the quester would strike through a barrier, the symbol of Secular Reality. Second, he purposes to uncover hidden gold, the symbol of Sacred Reality. Third, as a kid, Redburn is a voyeur *manqué*. And fourth, Redburn as quester—but only as quester—is mad, and, therefore, only as a child is he a deep diver for gold guineas. His aberration is "temporary" because his is a comic tale, but in Melville's more serious work the maddened quester (like the monomaniac Ahab) never recovers his sanity.

In this tale of Innocence and Experience Melville opposes pure autoeroticism to corrupt heterosexuality and effeminacy, and introduces all of it in a somewhat disguised manner. Carlo, a lad of fifteen, derives great pleasure in playing his musical instrument, his hand organ [V, 320]; the pun is inescapable, and, in several other instances, as we shall see, Melville also uses musical instruments to symbolize genitalia. Carlo is a dreamy lad, virtually hermaphroditic, just as the name of his instrument is sexually ambiguous even if its description—it is hollow and expandable—is not. As Carlo plays, Redburn becomes sexually excited, and when Carlo finishes a particularly martial air, Redburn tells us that "I droop" [V, 323]. One is reminded of how Pierre undergoes a similar sympathetic ecstasy as Isabel plays her guitar—also, symbolically, the womb according to Dr. Murray (see below, pp. 107-8)—and how, at the conclusion of her playing, we are told that the music "drooped" [I,X 149]. Both Carlo and Isabel also claim that their instruments "sing" to them.[20] A second musician in *Redburn* is Billy the tailor, but he plays because he is frustrated, not happy: when his wife will have nothing to do with him, Billy plays his fiddle, and he will not put it down until she wins him back [V, 343–44].

Redburn quests for realms of gold, but Harry Bolton, like the "gold-hunters" in *Mardi*, is after the precious metal. Hoping, like them, "to snatch at Happiness," Harry takes Wellingborough to an ornately decorated gambling den, into a kind of antechamber and then, at a prearranged signal, through a

passage, toward a staircase lighted by three marble Graces, unitedly holding a broad candelabra, like an elk's antlers, over the landing.

We rambled up the long, winding slope of those aristocratic stairs, every step of which, covered with Turkey rugs, looked gorgeous as the hammercloth of the Lord Mayor's coach; and Harry hied straight to a rosewood door, which, on magical hinges, sprang softly open to his touch.

As we entered the room, methought I was slowly sinking in

some reluctant, sedgy sea; so thick and elastic the Persian carpeting, *mimicking* parterres of tulips, and roses, and jonquils, *like a bower in Babylon.*

Long lounges lay carelessly disposed, whose fine damask was interwoven, like the Gobelin tapestry, with pictorial tales of tilt and tourney. And oriental ottomans, whose *cunning* warp and woof were wrought into plaited *serpents*, undulating beneath beds of leaves, from which, here and there, they flashed out sudden splendors of green scales and gold. [V, 297] (Italics added.)

On the walls of this room

... were such pictures as the high-priests, for a bribe, showed to Alexander in *the innermost shrine* of the white temple in the Libyan oasis: such pictures as the pontiff of the sun strove to hide from Cortez, when, sword in hand, he burst open *the sanctorum of the pryamid-fane* at Cholula: such pictures as you may still see, perhaps, in *the central alcove* of the excavated mansion of Pansa, in Pompeii—in that part of it called by Varro *the hollow of the house*: such pictures as Martial and Suetonius mention as being found in the private cabinet of the Emperor Tiberius: such pictures as are delineated on the bronze medals, to this day dug up on the ancient island of Capreae: such pictures as you might have beheld in *an arched recess*, leading from the left hand of the secret side-gallery of *the temple of Aphrodite* in Corinth. [V, 297–98] (Italics added except for "*the hollow of the house*," which is Melville's.)

The paintings in this deceptively decorated, hidden, interior room are certainly pornographic in content. Melville intimates that after winding through the labyrinthine Palace of Aladdin, Harry leads Wellingborough into the realm of a fake Sacred Reality, a cunningly wrought "bower in Babylon," in spirit not unlike the elaborately furnished study in which Glendinning Stanly presides and into which the unfashionable Pierre bursts. And, like Pierre, "spite of the metropolitan magnificence" (not Glen's New York, but Harry's London), Redburn is horrified. "... I was mysteriously alive to a dreadful feeling, which I had never before felt, except when penetrating into the lowest and most squalid haunts of sailor iniquity. ..." [V, 303]. For

our Innocent Abroad has stumbled not into Inamorata's voluptuously
pure womb-chamber but into a brothel, extravagantly erotic.

Harry Bolton, on the other hand, is thoroughly familiar with sin;
and debauchery (idleness and gambling, if not sex) seems to have
effeminized him. After losing heavily at the tables, Harry contemplates suicide, asks Redburn to hold his knife, but then, "snatching
it from . . . [Redburn's] hand, he flung down an empty purse, and with
a terrific stab, nailed it fast with the dirk to the table" [V, 304]. It is
as if Harry, furiously angry with himself for losing his money, in self-
despite leaves his sex (if not his life) behind him, in a symbolic act
that explains his real condition. On another occasion, Harry, faking
a masculinity he does not possess, dons sham whiskers and mustache;
much as Jack Blunt, one of Redburn's shipmates, hoping to maintain
whatever blunted sexuality he does have, uses hair restoratives three
times daily. Only Max the Dutchman needn't worry: he has one wife
in New York, another in Liverpool, real red whiskers, and is, in all,
"the most combustible looking man . . . [Redburn] ever saw" [V, 101].

As for Redburn himself, he is never involved in a sexual relationship, just as he is not involved in a quest; in fact, he is rather unsexual
to begin with. The nearest he comes to a liaison (and even then he is
light-years away) is when he acquaints himself with three pretty sisters in the English countryside (but under the watchful eye of their
mama). Redburn is plainly nervous and acts with an exaggerated
courtesy just as, in *Omoo*, when a beautiful native girl visits the Cala-
booza Beretanee, where Typee and his comrades are being kept prison-
ers, Typee self-consciously casts himself into the most graceful posture he can devise [II, 152]. *Redburn*, then, does not reconcile sexual
Innocence with Maturity in either a homoerotic or heterosexual way;
as it eschews the quest, it simply avoids the problem of sex entirely.

The relationship between Redburn and Harry Bolton, however,
should not go unobserved, for it is fascinating. Redburn, who thrives,
does not quest, and Harry, who quests, does not thrive. Whereas Redburn, in "temporary madness," would smash the glass ship (but is
restrained), Harry, in a fit of "insanity," signs aboard a whaleship—
and is ingloriously crushed between a whale and the ship. But Harry
takes to whaling—that is, to questing—only after Redburn, despite

many kind words, abandons him in New York. Redburn, however, cannot forget his former friend (and, perhaps, cannot forgive himself), for when he learns that Harry may be dead, he exhibits so much emotion that he is taken for Harry's "brother." And, in a very real (*i.e.* psychological) sense, he is, for Harry is his Shadow, the foreign, the unlived, side of his being. (In Melville—it is a profoundly intuitive stroke—the Shadow-figures are always primitive, foreign-born or trained: Mow-Mow, the sons of Aleema, Harry, Queequeg, Pip, Glen Stanly, John Claggart.) Tommo and Taji flee their Shadows in terror; Ishmael embraces his in love. But in between *Mardi* and *Moby-Dick*, between outright rejection and love, falls *Redburn*, whose protagonist follows a median route of mixed emotion: for Redburn deserts Harry with remorse and remembers him with affection.

Despite its considerable charm, *Redburn* did not pull Melville to solvency, and, therefore, during New York's cholera epidemic in the summer of 1849, he sat down to *White-Jacket* (1850), a sequel of sorts in that it too eschews the manic quester and concentrates on the novitiate and his development. Although this novel was also written for money, and is, in part, straightforward, anti-flogging propaganda, Melville was simply incapable of purely realistic discourse. Symbol and allegory were his natural modes of expression, and, willy-nilly, he could not avoid them. Consequently, as is well-known, the titular hero's fall from the mast and the loss of his jacket symbolize, at the very least, his movement from Innocence and Otherness, just as the *Neversink* allegorically represents the natural world moving toward her final destination.

What is not recognized is White Jacket's kinship to Donjalolo. In order "to shelter [himself] from the boisterous weather," the influence, that is, of the outer world, White Jacket dons "a strange-looking coat," which is "white as a shroud," full of patches and quilts, "pockets and passageways."

> The principal apartments, two in number, were placed in the skirts, with a wide, hospitable entrance from the inside; two

more, of smaller capacity, were planted in each breast, with fold-
ing-doors communicating, so that in case of emergency, to accommodate any bulky articles, the two pockets in each breast could
be thrown into one. There were, also, several unseen recesses
behind the arras; insomuch, that my jacket, like an old castle, was
full of winding stairs, and mysterious closets, crypts, and cabinets;
and like a confidential writing-desk, abandoned in snug little
out-of-the-way lairs and hiding-places, for the storage of valuables.
[VI, 44]

In short, White Jacket figuratively enters the labyrinthine structure
of Secular Reality just as Donjalolo literally confines himself at Juam.
But since such a coat leaves him an easy target for thieves, White
Jacket sews up his pockets, just as the Kings of Willamilla tradition-
ally blockade the sole entrance to their Glen.   White Jacket says, "I
masoned up my lockers and pantries" [VI, 46]. Soon realizing, however, that complete isolation exiles, as well as protects, him from
other men, White Jacket, again like Donjololo, yearns to be free.
Finally, of course, he escapes the labyrinth, shucks off the pod of his
protective Ego, and purges himself of his innocence, for, in his trau-
matic Fall, his near death by water and rebirth therein, he is able to
rip through his encasement and enter the larger world. The strait-
jacket, floating free, is taken for a shark and harpooned—reminding
us of how Ahab, who also tries to pierce the metaphoric white wall
of Secular Reality, fails (literally) with his harpoon and fails (figuratively) to solve the "maze." But White Jacket's brave new world
without is the labyrinthine catacomb of the man-o-war, the natural
world of the *Neversink*, to be prized no more highly than the world
within:

> Through low arches in the bulkhead beyond, you peep in upon
> distant vaults and catacombs, obscurely lighted in the far end,
> and showing immense coils of new ropes, and other bulky articles,
> stowed in tiers, all savouring of tar. [VI, 155]

Howard Vincent regards *White-Jacket* as "a symbolical account of
spiritual growth,"[21] which it undoubtedly is; but it is also a symbolic
account of psychological growth. Melville spent the birthday from
which he dated his life aboard the *United States* en route to America,

and *White-Jacket*, wherein that voyage is fictionalized, recounts how his quasi-autobiographical hero falls into the sea, nearly drowns, but then is triumphantly catapulted forth. We may, then, by closely observing the books from *Typee* to *White-Jacket* discern some remarkable sea-changes in the evolution of the Quester. Tommo is born upon the high seas; Taji quests upon the high seas; Harry Bolton dies upon the high seas; and White Jacket, the latest representative of the transpersonal Quester, is reborn upon the high seas. The first part of Melville's career as a novelist, in other words, is complete.

We may reasonably characterize this early work as apprentice and cautious: apprentice because Melville first discovers the symbolic *schema* into which he has divided the world and the quester's role in relation to that world; because he becomes conscious of his images and symbols for Sacred and Secular Reality and of his power to convert the quester's passage into a symbolic act; and because he begins to experiment with variations on the theme of the quest (mythical, metaphysical, societal, sexual). Furthermore, Melville has learned that the sacred geography does not exist in the natural world; his questers may hope to discover it there, but they quest without guarantee. Nevertheless, Tommo and White Jacket, questers who do achieve limited goals, are not perceptibly disillusioned by their discoveries, and even Taji, who seeks much more and attains much less, does not suffer the final torments of Ahab and Pierre: maiming and death. In other words, the novels of this first phase are basically cautious, and even *Mardi*, the boldest of the early books, reflects a hesitant treatment of characters, events, and ideas. How else can one explain the fact that the quest is finally repudiated by all the major characters (except Taji) and the Babbalanja, the respected philosopher, undergirds their decision by quoting Bardianna: ". . . the plain [not the mountain] alone was intended for man" [IV, 2]? In *Pierre*, Melville will regard with contempt the similar conclusion of that other Bible for the Judicious, the "Chronometricals and Horologicals" of Plotinus Plinlimmon.

Melville's cautiousness in *Mardi* is evident from other points of view as well. Culturally, he dwells, in an almost Irvingesque manner, on America's cherished English heritage—a far cry from his review of Hawthorne's *Mosses*, which contains as radical a statement of literary nationalism as we shall find and a blatant attack on the English. In political, social, and religious matters Babbalanja's conservatism carries the day time and again. He voices the antidemocratic notion that monarchies are, in certain instances, better for their people than republics, insisting that he would not "cross spears" to save the Southern slaves": Better present woes for some, than future woes for all" [IV, 250]. And he proclaims that "The searcher of the cores of all hearts well knoweth that atheists there are none" [IV, 125]; although Jackson, in Melville's next book, is an atheist, Ahab is sometimes an unbeliever, and Pierre dies in doubt. But one incident illuminates Melville's caution in *Mardi* best of all: a handsome youth who would climb Mt. Ofo in order to reach God (instead of staying on the plain of institutionalized religion) is dragged away and condemned to death by a society that will not condone the maverick individualism of questing. King Media refuses to save him although it is in his power, and only Captain Vere similarly finds it in his heart to sentence an innocent in order, presumably, to protect the tribe.

But it is not for cautiousness that *Mardi* fails as literature (although caution is perhaps symptomatic of its failure). It fails, first, because Melville clearly knew too little about the myth, metaphor, and symbolism of the quest to go as far or as well as he later would; and, second, because, as the confrontation with Aleema (wherein the father-substitute is slain and the daughter, in effect, raped), Taji's refusal of Hautia (wherein a marital sexuality is rejected), and the scarifying dreamlike image which ends the book (of the guilty pursuer pursued), all indicate, the act of writing *Mardi* unleashed those demonic impulses of hatred, guilt, frustration, and terror that are relatively dormant in Melville's less serious work but that riot uncontrollably in *Mardi* and determine its final effect. The trouble was that Melville recklessly indulged his unconscious faculties. Describing Lombardo's *Koztanza* (read Melville's *Mardi*), Babbalanja tells us how the author "was not his own master . . . [but was rather] a mere amanuensis writing by dictation" [IV, 327] and how the book owes its final shape to the "one autocrat within—. . . [the] crowned and sceptred instinct" [IV, 328]. In *Moby-Dick* Melville would split the flawed figure of Taji, who uneasily combines within himself aspects of the manic and non-manic questers, embody these components in Ahab and Ishmael, and exorcise his demonic impulses by destroying Ahab. But in *Mardi* the exorcism of demons is never realized, for Taji remains unsplit.

As Taji is finally more Ahab than Ishmael, so Babbalanja is finally more Ishmael than Ahab. For if, like Ahab, Babbalanja quests for Final Truth, like Ishmael, he is willing to accept the Serenian compromise—Man's inevitable limitation. And if, like Ishmael who is subject to fits of depression and misanthropy during which he would make Ahab's "quenchless feud" his own, so Babbalanja is occasionally overcome by Azzageddi, his torrentially-talkative inner demon. In both men, however, the fits are transient: Babbalanja's expend themselves; Ishmael controls his by going to sea.

In sum, *Mardi* is notes to a great novel, not that novel itself. Nor could anyone have anticipated *Moby-Dick*, and, apparently, only Melville himself, as he intimates in *Mardi*, knew he had the "genius" [IV, 86] to create it. But if we cannot explain the ripening of Melville's genius, we can, at least, recognize some of the catalyzing circumstances that attended it. First of all, as Leslie Fiedler perceives, there is the importance of his trip to London in 1849.[22] Melville's ostensible reason was to bargain with a publisher over *White-Jacket*, but his deeper motive was to reestablish his connection with Ocean. Indeed, through conscious or unconscious design, he organized his life around her. Six times he sailed: in 1839 to Liverpool; from 1841 to 1844 to the Pacific and the South Seas; now in 1849; in 1856 to the Mediterranean and the Near East; in 1860 to California; and in 1888 to Bermuda. As Thoreau, like Antaeus, gained strength and rejuvenation from the land, so did Melville from the sea. And this was true even in the Custom House years (1866–1885) when he was unable to sail. That he could have forgotten Hawthorne's premonitory portrayal of Custom House life in *The Scarlet Letter*—its intellectual atrophy and spiritual decay—is unlikely. But Melville knew or divined what he was about; as for those he described in *Moby-Dick* who "of a dreamy Sabbath afternoon . . . stand thousands upon thousands . . . fixed in ocean reveries," the presence of ocean helped keep him psychically whole. And when he returned to America in 1850, intellectually restored and viscerally recharged, he was prepared to begin his masterpiece.

Nevertheless, Melville did not originally intend to write the book we now know but, as George Stewart discovered,[23] a comic narrative about the sea fishery without metaphysical implications. Several circumstances, however, redirected its course: Melville's meeting with and reading of Hawthorne, the only man in America whose literary excursions into the blackness of darkness could have encouraged him in his own deepest desires; and his rereading of Shakespeare whose glorious language and dark characters became his formidable example. But perhaps the most important condition of all for the creation of *Moby-Dick*—without which these external influences could have become neither operative nor causative—was a psychological one: Melville again felt, as he had during the composition of *Mardi*, filled to the brim and in need of discharge: as his "full heart"—he writes in *Mardi*—is "brimful, bubbling, sparkling; and running over . . ." [IV, 322], so, during the composition of *Moby-Dick*, does he request Evert Duyckinck to send him "about fifty fast-writing youths . . . because since I have been here [at Arrowhead] I have planned about that number of future works & cant [*sic*] find enough time to think about them separately."[24] And, in *Moby-Dick*, he wishes his inkwell were Vesuvius' crater and his pen a condor's quill he has so much to write. As before, this surging toward expression unleashed his deepest impulses, and, therefore, like Taji, Ahab too is an embodiment of those self-destructive demons of hatred and frustration. But if Melville could not destroy Taji without himself becoming a symbolic suicide, he can destroy Ahab without running a similar risk because, unlike Taji who bears seeds of the Tommo-type protagonist, Ahab is completely manic. He can—in fact, must—die in violent collision with the material world so that, through the resultant dispersal of demonic energy, his half-brother, Ishmael, may achieve a momentary purification. Taji, that is, is split, and as Ahab dies, Ishmael is cleansed. "I have written a wicked book," Melville wrote Hawthorne, "and feel spotless as the lamb."[25]

As in the case of *Mardi*, we have Melville's own testimony about the unconscious bases of *Moby-Dick*: he writes, for instance, in a well-known letter to Sophia Hawthorne that

> . . . your allusion . . . to the "Spirit Spout" first showed to me that there was a subtile [*sic*] significance in that thing—but I did not, in that case, *mean* it. I had some vague idea while writing it, that the whole book was susceptible of an allegoric construction, & also the *parts* of it were—but the speciality of many of the particular subordinate allegories, were first revealed to me, after reading Mr. Hawthorne's letter, which, without citing any particular examples, yet intimated the part-&-parcel allegoricalness of the whole.[26]

But—and this is the big truly inexplicable difference—in *Moby-Dick*, Melville was not only not betrayed by his unconscious faculties, but he was their master. And there is no better evidence of this mastery than in the creation of the principal characters in *Moby-Dick* and in their relation to *Mardi* where they are seminally presented: just as Ahab and Ishmael are splintered from Taji, so the White Whale is surely the unconscious coalescence of Aleema and Yillah—but more of that later. One cannot but marvel at this aspect of Melville's art, its seeming necessity, rightness, and design.

Besides a common compulsiveness, motivation, and a common utilization of the unconscious, *Mardi* and *Moby-Dick* also parallel one another in two other significant respects: each is preceded by two shorter, easier-to-write novels; and each begins as narrative realism and is rewritten as metaphysical symbolism. Of course, even in *Mardi* Melville well knew that the quest was futile: wise Babbalanja argued this very point of view. But Melville evidently could not rest until he had satisfied himself fictionally, not just dialectically, until he could feel with his heart what he believed with his mind. He could not find even the peace of exhaustion until his heroes had exorcised themselves by confronting or colliding with the material world. And, consequently, he would not concede that the walls of the splendid labyrinth were, indeed, impenetrable until he had vicariously partici-

pated in the fates of Ahab, Pierre, and Bartleby. In this sense, everything that precedes *Moby-Dick* is prologue to and preparation for this
finest moment, and everything that follows "Bartleby" is commentary.

3. *In the Splendid Labyrinth*

Moby-Dick through "Bartleby"

A. MOBY-DICK

If the greatness of *Moby-Dick* (1851) is now beyond dispute, the meaning of Moby Dick is still fiercely debated, as an ever-increasing bibliography testifies; and only by grouping those critics and scholars who share similar premises and convictions (at the risk of obscuring individual differences) can we clear a path through this thicket of scholarship. Accordingly, let us divide Melvilleans into "Ahabs" and "Ishmaels," those who stress that the Whale is, at least in part, specifically nameable (and thus to some degree knowable) and their colleagues who stress that he is, in whole, neither nameable nor knowable.[1] Critics of the former persuasion have variously interpreted the Whale as the symbol for Evil, the Energies of Existence, Phallic Being, the Freudian Super-Ego, the Parent, Life itself, and God (as Good, Evil, and Indifferent)—our list does not pretend to exhaust the possibilities.[2] Critics of the latter group, perhaps casting a wary eye at this varied speculation, emphasize that the proper approach to the Whale is finally rather like Pip's to the doubloon: "I look, you look, he looks; we look, ye look, they look." Thus, although they themselves are not in absolute congruence with one another, the spectrum of their opinion is much narrower. Moby Dick is "endlessly suggestive of meanings," "seems to be either the totality or essential of all meanings," remains "an irreducible symbol," or is an ineluctable "convincement . . . that there is a God beyond the powers of man to plumb."[3]

The fact is, however, that both approaches are valid and, indeed, complementary angles of vision: for as the proliferation of meanings for Moby Dick (some mutually exclusive) argues that no specific identification can account for his symbolic value, so certain individual meanings are patent and illuminating even if none of them corresponds with the whole. The point is that the Whale is both knowable and unknowable, nameable and unnameable at the same time; and that the contradiction in the criticism merely mirrors the contradiction inherent in the beast. Our first task, then, is to investigate the origin of his dichotomous nature, and, therefore, we must return to *Mardi*.

It is from Aleema that the Whale derives the knowable characteristics of Secular Reality: like the white-haired priest, Moby Dick is also masculine, malicious, and terrifying in his whiteness; both are described in mountain imagery, and both have broad, wrinkled, hieroglyphed brows no Champollion can decipher. But the White Whale is profoundly ambiguous because he seems to inherit as much from Yillah, the incarnation of Sacred Reality, as from her protector. Like her, Moby Dick is also a "phantom" of pure (not just terrifying) whiteness; is mild and beautiful (as in the "Spirit Spout" chapter); is feminine; and is described as a sanctuary (450), not just a protective shield. In *Mardi*, of course, the barrier to Yillah is penetrated, and she is revealed behind, but in *Moby-Dick* one may well ask whether the Absolute really exists; we cannot know definitely until the Whale's surface is penetrated. Furthermore, in *Mardi* we know that Yillah possesses certain individualizing characteristics unshared by Aleema, whereas in *Moby-Dick* Melville merges these two cardboard figures—a crude, dualistic formulation—into one vastly complex and believable Whale, and, in so doing, seemingly compounds their attributes. May not the Whale, then, be all Surface and no Substance, "nothing but superinduced superficies," as Pierre says in a similar context?

A passage in Melville's review "Hawthorne and His Mosses" speaks of man, the visible world as mask, and Essence beyond in similar terms: "Tormented into desperation, Lear, the frantic king, tears off the mask, and speaks the sane madness of vital truth." The passage is curiously ambiguous, but the less obvious interpretation should not go unnoticed: that the mask is not on Lear but is visible reality (as in the term "pasteboard mask") and that "speaks" does not mean that Lear is talking the Truth but that (as in the nautical language Melville uses in *Moby-Dick* and, of course, elsewhere), he is confronting it. Thus as Lear "tears off," so Ahab would "thrust through" the mask of Appearance. In other words, if we would learn the Whale's final secret, we must quest with Ahab as our chief representative, for, like us, Ahab is also perplexed by his seeming duality and, unlike us, is willing to sacrifice his life to know the final answer:

> All visible objects, man, are but as pasteboard masks. But in each event—in the living act, the undoubted deed—there, some unknown but still reasoning thing puts forth the mouldings of its features from behind the unreasoning mask. If man will strike, strike through the mask! How can the prisoner reach outside except by thrusting through the wall? To me, the white whale is that wall, shoved near to me. Sometimes I think there's naught beyond. But 'tis enough. He tasks me; he heaps me; I see in him outrageous strength, with an inscrutable malice sinewing it. That inscrutable thing is chiefly what I hate; and be the white whale agent, or be the white whale principal, I will wreak that hate upon him. (221)

His external aspects—his deadwall face, his spout, his sickle jaw, his flukes—are sensorily known, but an interior Essence may or may not exist. According to Ahab, the Whale is a wall behind which he is a prisoner, and the only way for him to reach what he sometimes believes is the "still reasoning thing," "the inscrutable thing," within the Whale-wall is by thrusting into it. Ahab's task is, to say the least, formidable, for "the front of the Sperm Whale's head is a dead, blind wall, without a single organ or tender prominence of any sort whatsoever" (436), and his brain, twenty feet from his forehead, is "hidden away behind its vast outworks, like the innermost citadel within the amplified fortifications of Quebec" (450). In short, Ahab must proceed from the realm of Fact and Matter to the realm of Spirit and Mind, two discrete worlds connected, according to the Melville metaphor, by a common, but impenetrable, barrier; but Ahab, who some of the time accepts the notion of direct correspondence, is not without hope. His fullest expression of this theory comes soon after he apostrophizes the Sphynx-like whale to reveal his inmost secret:

'O Nature, and O soul of man! how far beyond all utterance are
your liked analogies! not the smallest atom stirs or lives on matter,
but has its cunning duplicate in mind.' (406)

But at other times, he expects to confront nothing; for "sometimes I
think there's naught beyond," words reminiscent of Melville's own
reflection, "and perhaps, after all, there is *no* secret." And even the
fact that Melville again uses hidden gold to symbolize Essence is more
tantalizing than helpful, for it is the Essence of ordinary whales
only that the gold symbolizes, never Moby Dick:[4]

. . . Stubb slowly churned his long sharp lance into the fish, and
kept it there, carefully churning and churning, as if cautiously
seeking to feel after some gold watch that the whale might have
swallowed, and which he was fearful of breaking ere he could
hook it out. But that gold watch he sought was the innermost life
of the fish. (377–78)

In sum, when Ahab does believe that intelligence lies beyond Appearance, he is convinced that it is Evil: his purpose, then, is to thrust
through the wall of Appearance into the coordinate of that intelligence and slay the deliberately malicious whale, slay God; however,
when doubting the existence of reason in Moby Dick, simply to slay
the whale (now as "principal" not "agent") who has accidentally dismasted him. Ahab is a skeptic who is determined to prove whether
Absolute Reality—Evil as he would have it—really exists beyond surfaces. His scheme—the penetration of Nature by logic (for that is
the weapon of intellectual proof) in order to know God—is of course
a perversion of the transcendental theory of intuition, but one aptly
suited to the monomaniacal Ahab. His quest for knowledge of Essence is stymied, however, because his creator, unlike the Emersonians,
simply did not believe that Nature is the conduit to the Oversoul and
that knowledge of the former necessarily heralds knowledge of the
latter.

Another salient difference between Ahab and Melville is that Melville never considered Essence exclusively evil and never believed
that the "still reasoning thing," intelligence, was presumptive evidence of purposeful malice. These are Ahab's typically extreme and

irrational opinions, and to approach Melville's understanding of Essence, as he wrote in *Moby-Dick*, we shall have to consult Ishmael, his nearest surrogate, who interprets the Whale's whiteness as ambiguously symbolic: ". . . at once the most meaning symbol of spiritual things, nay, the very veil of the Christian's Deity; and yet . . . the intensifying agent in things the most appalling to mankind" (263). As Ahab regards Moby Dick as a personification to be slain, Ishmael regards him, in the words of R. E. Watters, "as a symbol of what might be called a metaphysical hypothesis" to be understood. Watters continues:

> [Ishmael] . . . is attempting to see the whale not partially, as a
> personified malignancy, a natural peril, a challenge, or a monetary
> value, but omnisciently, as a possibly intelligible microcosm in
> a possibly intelligible cosmos. The meaning of the white whale,
> for Ishmael, seems to be either the totality or essential of all mean-
> ings—in a word, attainable only by omniscience.[5]

Thus even as Ishmael supposes the Whale represents Final Truth, lacking onmiscience, he cannot fully comprehend him: Ishmael may inquire but not indisputably know. Is the whale "intelligent"? That is, in Ahab's terms, is there a "reasoning thing" behind the mask? Again the answer, "possibly." And, therefore, as a way of symbolizing his own uncertainty and that of his characters—and it is a brilliantly intuitive stroke—Melville reformulated the relationship between Aleema and Yillah; made Moby Dick part known, like the outside of a wall, and part unknown, like that which the wall conceals. As Ishmael observes, it remains for Ahab to try to thrust through one in order to determine the other. His bid, of course, fails, and therefore, at the center of the detailed and explicated cosmos which is *Moby-Dick*, that cosmos which Ishmael spends so much time elucidating, the White Whale remains as inscrutable as ever; just as at the center of life for this deeply religious artist are the "Powers" about whom much is supposed but nothing definitely known except that they are there. Melville, as Geoffrey Stone remarks,

> . . . was clearly one of those persons whose religious difficulties
> are less concerned with the question of God's existence than
> with what one's personal relationship with Him is to be.[6]

The wall as symbol for Secular Reality is further elaborated in
Pierre and given final articulation in "Bartleby," whereas the whale,
literally present in *Moby-Dick*, is a disguised motif in these later works.
And as, in these later works, Melville describes the metaphors for the
whale in Egyptian imagery, thus in *Moby-Dick* does he describe the
actual Leviathan:

> It was a black and hooded head; and hanging there in the
> midst of so intense a calm, it seemed the Sphynx's in the desert.
> (405) . . . [I]t was not so much his uncommon bulk that so much
> distinguished him from other sperm whales, but, as was else-
> where thrown out—a peculiar snow-white wrinkled forehead,
> and a high, pyramidal white hump. (245)
> Champollion deciphered the wrinkled granite hieroglyphics.
> But there is no Champollion to decipher the Egypt of every
> man's and every being's face. Physiognomy, like every other hu-
> man science, is but a passing fable. If then, Sir William Jones,
> who read in thirty languages, could not read the simplest peasant's
> face in its profounder and more subtle meanings, how may un-
> lettered Ishmael hope to read the awful Chaldee of the Sperm
> Whale's brow? (449)
> Who can show a pedigree like Leviathan? Ahab's harpoon had
> shed older blood than the Pharaoh's. Methuselah seems a school-
> boy. I look round to shake hands with Shem. I am horror-struck
> at this antemosaic, unsourced existence of the unspeakable
> terrors of the whale, which, having been before all time, must
> needs exist after all humane ages are over. (582)

Melville's purpose is to conjure the impression that the Whale is as
mysteriously silent as the Sphynx, as inscrutably unknowable as a
hieroglyph, as ominously formidable as a pyramid; and that, furthermore, he is more ancient than the Pharaohs and more durable than
humankind. And Melville well succeeds in making us realize that he
will inevitably and eternally block the quester's path.

Just as important as the pyramid as a symbol of Secular Reality in
Moby-Dick is another symbol derived from another ancient civilization, the complex of walls or labyrinth. Thus Queequeg's body is tattooed over with an "interminable Cretan labyrinth" (52), tattoo-

ings which comprise a "complete theory of the heavens and the earth, and a mystical treatise on the art of attaining truth" (612). But no one is competent to understand the inscribings, and this, of course, is just Melville's point: that no one may know Final Truth, neither Queequeg nor even Ishmael who is saved from death by the coffin onto which Queequeg had faithfully copied his markings. Queequeg, the passive one,[7] does not try to conquer the labyrinth and is not tempted. Not so Ahab, who inveighs at the sight of the coffin, "Oh, devilish tantalization of the gods!" (612); and who is found, one evening, "with the charts of all four oceans before him . . . threading a *maze* of currents and eddies, with a view to the more certain accomplishment of that monomaniac thought of his soul" (267). (Italics added.)

As for Ishmael, he is, as several commentators have noted, a compromise between Ahab and Queequeg.[8] On the one hand, his dispensation is the perpetual quester's, to traverse the labyrinth in endless pursuit. For he too seeks the White Whale, a phantom-correlate of that narcissistic image in the fountain, his own identity, what he calls "the ungraspable phantom of life." Both are equally elusive, and, in Ishmael's mind, inextricably connected. Nothing is more indicative of the Ahabian aspect of Ishmael's personality than the fact that even after the cataclysmic disaster of the *Pequod* and his survival on the open sea, he sails again (and presumably again and again) on a whaler (567).

But Ishmael's dispensation is also Queequeg's—to realize the impossibility of conquering the labyrinth. In fact, again utilizing the symbol of the maze, Ishmael admits the futility of questing:

> Were this world an endless plain, and by sailing eastward we
> could forever reach new distances, and discover sights more
> sweet and strange than any Cyclades or Islands of King Solomon,
> then there were promise in the voyage. But in pursuit of those
> far mysteries we dream of, or in tormented chase of that demon
> phantom that, sometime or other, swims before all human hearts;
> while chasing such over this round globe, they either lead us on
> in barren mazes or midway leave us whelmed. (316)

The reference to "that demon phantom that . . . swims before all human hearts" intimates, by its very ambiguity, the coalescence for Ishmael of the impossible quests for self-realization and Moby Dick.

Thus as the Queequeg in him qualifies the Ahab, his willingness to act—to permanently make Ahab's cause his own, to slay the White Whale and penetrate the heavenly realm—is reduced to a wish to act, to a skeptic's wish to discover if that realm really exists. As he himself says,

> With a frigate's anchors for my bridle-bitts and fasces of harpoons for spurs, would I could mount that whale and leap the topmost skies, to see whether the fabled heavens with all their countless tents really lie encamped beyond my mortal sight! (360)

But it is not Ishmael, but Ahab's successor, Pierre-Enceladus, who eventually throws himself at the ramparts of heaven in order to determine whether there is aught or "naught" beyond. Ishmael carries the counterbalancing Ahab and Queequeg and is not unlike the *Pequod*, weighted down with a Kantian's and a Lockean's whale's head on either bow: crippled but not decisively disabled. Like a rudderless boat, Ishmael yaws—his mood perpetually shifting from negation (the "damp, drizzly November in my soul" when we first meet him) to affirmation (sitting in the Spouter-Inn with Queequeg, "No more my splintered heart and maddened hand were turned against the wolfish world") back to negation ("Ahab's quenchless feud seemed mine"), back to affirmation (in the sperm squeezing scene, "I forgot all about our horrible oath"), world without end.

Nevertheless, at least twice in his career Ishmael explores what seems to be the realm of the Absolute. Once in the Bower of the Arsacides he wanders like Theseus, string in hand, through the ribs of a dead whale-god disguised by false priests as a live one, and for once, unsurprisingly, he does not lose his way in the labyrinthine maze. But neither, his tattooed statistics to the contrary, does he grasp the one grand hooded phantom: bleached bones but not Moby Dick. The second instance also indicates that whenever man thinks he has gained knowledge of the Absolute, he is guilty of solipsism. Daniel Hoffman reminds us that, at the Spouter-Inn, "Ishmael does see what lies behind the pasteboard mask," but again appearances are deceptive:

In his bedchamber . . . was 'a papered fireboard representing a man striking a whale.' Queequeg's first act on entering—before he even knows that Ishmael is in the room—is to remove this paper screen, and, there between the sooty fire-dogs, *he himself puts the image of his own god*. The pasteboard mask conceals nothing that man has not put there.[9]

Drawn simultaneously, then, in two directions, Ishmael is the qualified quester, the median between the insanely hyperactive Ahab and the passive Queequeg, at once committed to questing and retreating before its final extravagances. For failure to retreat means succumbing to the phantoms: death by Moby Dick; narcissistic absorption. It leads to the potentially fatal allegorism of Henry Thoreau who once wished he could live as a "subjective, heavily laden thought, in the midst of an unknown and infinite sea."[10] But Thoreau, like Ishmael, fortunately knew better: that in the sea of consciousness, as in the sea herself, drowning men do drown. Yet even if questing be futile, Ishmael must not give it up entirely. For he knows that only the sailing quest is sufficient to drive the dampness from his soul and regenerate his spirit; he *must* tempt himself with phantoms, for if grasping the White Whale, as Ahab does, is the fatal embrace, then only the sailing search for him is being truly alive.

Ishmael survives through compromise and through the dialectic of his vision:

And so, through all the thick mists of the dim doubts in my mind, divine intuitions now and then shoot, enkindling my fog with a heavenly ray. And for this I thank God; for all have doubts: many deny; but doubts or denials, few along with them, have intuitions. Doubts of all things earthly, and intuitions of some things heavenly; this combination makes neither believer nor infidel, but makes a man who regards them both with equal eye. (480)

In short, both Melville and his surrogate preserve themselves because both accept a wisdom that is woe, and both reject a woe that is madness.

But there can never be a permanently happy ending for Ishmael. There will be joy and sorrow, life and death, but there will never be, as Richard Chase observes, life *"through* death."[11] "Would that a man could do something and then say—It is finished," Melville wrote Evert Duyckinck, but, for Ishmael, the questing will never be done. Like Johah, he is spewed forth from the whale-like, ivory-laden *Pequod*, discharged, in effect, from the jaws of death: but only to quest again.[12] His fate reminds us in part of Father Mapple's, for that good man had once been trapped beneath the arched ribs of the whale:

> "In black distress, I called my God,
>   When I could scarce believe him mine,
> He bowed his ear to my complaints—
>   No more the whale did me confine.
>
> "With speed he flew to my relief,
>   As on a radiant dolphin borne;
> Awful, yet bright, as lightning shone
>   The face of my Deliverer God." (71)

To the unquestioning believer the whale is no obstacle to the God beyond, and Father Mapple emerges in the presence of the Lord. But Ishmael, "neither believer nor infidel," surfaces in the material world, a wandering orphan still. For him there can be no enduring transcendence; his—Melville's—is the barest of affirmations. And thus if Ishmael never achieves the stasis of a Golden Mean, he does, at least, attain a *modus vivendi*—one fraught with anxiety and disjunction, to be sure, but a *modus vivendi* nonetheless. In Melville the price is high for the privilege of diving.

If Ishmael, then, instinctively respecting whatever gods may be, quests through life with shortened sail, the Captain of the *Pequod* finds little necessity for caution. For if Ishmael's fate, in the modern jargon, is a perennial anxiety, Ahab's is a perennial alienation. He is what Starbuck calls him, a blasphemer, and there is nothing admirable in the vilifier of the gods—his ranting, name-calling, hatred and *hubris*. And yet, as a quester, he is indisputably distinguished. A seasoned veteran of the hunt, he has wandered, like the ancient Hebrews, for forty years; and is now, at fifty-eight, this master of magic, science, and whaling-lore, supremely equipped for his final battle (683). He may thrust down his "humanities," but his bravery and skill remain undiminished. He is a magnetic leader of men, surrounded by a superb crew and has assembled, under the tutelage of Fedallah, an élite corps. His harpoon, of nail-stubbs and steel razors, is the ultimate weapon of his craft, baptized in pagan blood and blessed in the devil's name. His boat, tried and trustworthy, is the best of its kind. In short, one knows that if Ahab, with his multitude of advantages, his preparation, determination, and skill, cannot penetrate the whale-wall, then no one can: that, once and for all, the White Whale will be captured or prove forever uncaptureable. And thus it happens that in the desperation of his quest, Ahab finally realizes the futility of his efforts and admits before he dies that "The dead, blind wall butts all inquiring heads at last" (658). Mad before, he is madness compounded now, for knowing that his cause is hopeless, still—while there is yet time to stop—like Macbeth, he drives and is driven to his fatal encounter.

Like Hawthorne, Melville argues an ultimate limitation of human knowledge and man's radical imperfectibility, and it is here, surely, that he exhibits tragic vision. Man may inch as close to ultimate answers as Ahab to Moby Dick, but he is doomed to final and inexorable rebuff. The disaster of the microcosmic *Pequod* and Ishmael orphaned once more—these images evoke in the reader nothing less than terror and pity. We are newly humbled and, in our humility, experience catharsis. Ahab, however, does not. Nor like Oedipus or Hester Prynne does he ever undergo a lasting transfiguration; and only in "The Symphony" chapter (when he weeps a solitary tear) is his redemption even momentarily conceivable. At the close—discounting his free will and magnifying his defiance—he wilfully plunges to his death. Yet Ahab is more than just melodramatic; perhaps not a tragic hero, certainly he is an epic one.[13] Of course he is not the sum of gentlemanly virtue. Achilles childishly sulks in his tent; Roland pridefully refuses to blow his horn until it is too late; Ahab is tyrannically incautious of the lives of others. But it is only the epic hero who does for society what society cannot do for itself, even if, as with Ahab, he does it unwittingly.

Ahab fronts the Whale for us, and we learn, through him, the final answer: that there is no final answer after all, and that the Whale, in his impenetrability, reflects and symbolizes our own ambiguous and fragmentary knowledge of the Cosmos, as much the questions we ask as the answers we seek. Ishmael may consign himself to doubt, but it is Ahab who establishes the Principle of Doubt beyond question. What then do we know of God? Only what we knew at the start: presumably that He is. The rest is Silence. Ahab, similarly, is ambiguous to the roots of his being, an ambiguity he inherits from his gothic progenitor, the Faustian hero-villain. He is, as William Ellery Sedgwick says,

> more than a whaling captain; he is man. He is man, sentient, speculative, purposive, religious, standing his full human stature against the immense mystery of creation.[14]

But Ahab is also, in Daniel Hoffman's words, "a false culture-hero, pursuing a private grievance (rather than a divine behest) at the expense of the mankind in his crew."[15] In truth, Ahab is both. At once culture hero and self-seeking culture bum, he engages the central metaphysical issue of his time and place, and his death is our victory.

Moby Dick is the supreme "*ur*-symbol"[16] of our literature, whose Meaning—as Ishmael well knows—no meanings may encompass, nor any Ahab comprehend; he must be sought in little, not in large, and he is inexhaustible. Consequently, in the first half of this essay we considered the Whale in a single context, as a symbol of the seeming duality of the Cosmos, and we emphasized Ahab's madly metaphysical quest for "evidence" of God, the doomed Romantic quest for a world behind the impenetrably Secular: the wall, labyrinth, maze, citadel, pyramid. Now we must consider the Primitive quest for a world within, the quest for sacrament and sexuality at the Sacred Center. But now it is Ishmael, not Ahab, who must chiefly guide us.

Almost from the very beginning of his career as an artist, Melville debated the paradox of bachelors, a paradox in that only bachelors live the two antithetical lives—one totally uncommitted to people or purpose and its converse, the life dedicated to the quest. On one hand, we have such uncommitted souls as Dr. Long Ghost in *Omoo*, King Abrazza in *Mardi*, the Captain of the *Bachelor* in *Moby-Dick* (who does not believe the White Whale exists), Plotinus Plinlimmon in *Pierre*, and the Narrator in "Bartleby." On the other, we have a continuing line of bachelor-questers: Tommo, Taji, Ishmael, Pierre, and Bartleby. If the putative quester is a married man, he must either reject marriage (as Ahab does) or reject questing (as Merrymusk in "Cock-A-Doodle-Doo!" does). For Marriage and Society preclude the quest just as the Quest and the Individual preclude marriage. In Melville no one can enjoy the benefits of both. Now whether this dilemma is a condition of the real world or a hurdle Melville himself erected in the path of his protagonists in order that they might avoid heterosexuality (or put the heavy price of guilt upon its attainment) does not principally concern us; what does is that the dilemma exists in the novels, that Melville recognized its presence, and that, in *Moby-Dick*, he rendered the solution he had but adumbrated previously in the relationships of Tommo and Toby, Typee and Dr. Long Ghost, Taji and Jarl, Redburn and Harry Bolton, and White Jacket and Jack Chase. To the paradox of bachelors Melville countered the marriage of males.

Ishmael embraces the pure, passive, unselfconscious Noble Savage, Queequeg; indeed, except in gender, Queequeg is not unlike Fayaway just as Ishmael, in the purity of his love, is not unlike Tommo. Thereafter they are "married" (84), go to bed again, and in "our hearts' honeymoon, lay I and Queequeg—a cosy, loving pair" (86). Pierre and Isabel also achieve high happiness in a darkened, lonely "hotel" room (the Apostles'), but, for all their mutual attraction, their "marriage" remains a fiction: they never sleep together and are never "a cosy loving pair."

Whether the intensity of the relationship between Ishmael and Queequeg subsides because, as is true in Melville, "marriage" kills love, or because, for novelistic reasons, Melville de-emphasized Queequeg's role in rewriting the book, one cannot finally say; but even if Queequeg does become a less important character in *Moby-Dick*, Ishmael still finds his greatest pleasure in male eroticism. In the

titillation of sperm-squeezing, Melville wryly reminds us, Ishmael
achieves a "corporateness" with his fellow men:

> Squeeze! squeeze! squeeze! all the morning long; I squeezed
> that sperm till I myself almost melted into it; I squeezed that
> sperm until a strange sort of insanity came over me; and I found
> myself unwittingly squeezing my colabourers' hands in it, mis-
> taking their hands for the gentle globules. Such an abounding,
> affectionate, friendly, loving feeling did this avocation beget; that
> at last I was continually squeezing their hands, and looking up
> into their eyes sentimentally; as much as to say,—Oh! my dear fel-
> low beings, why should we longer cherish any social acerbities,
> or know the slightest ill-humor or envy! Come; let us squeeze
> hands all round; nay, let us all squeeze ourselves into each other;
> let us squeeze ourselves universally into the very milk and sperm of
> kindness.
>
> Would that I could keep squeezing that sperm for ever! For
> now, since my many prolonged, repeated experiences, I have per-
> ceived that in all cases man must eventually lower, or at least
> shift, his conceit of attainable felicity; not placing it anywhere in
> the intellect or the fancy; but in the wife, the heart, the bed, the
> table, the saddle, the fire-side, the country. . . . (532-33)

As before, in his moment of solitary communion with Queequeg, Ishmael would again give up the quest (a product of intellect and fancy)
for the wife and the heart, a more realistic level of "attainable felicity." But as Ishmael—tied literally (and symbolically in marriage) to
the other end of Queequeg's "monkey-rope"—knows only too well:
marriage curtails freedom. If the savage slips on the whale's back, he
drags Ishmael under with him. Therefore, although there may be
greater latitude for action if the loved one is male, marriage and questing still prove fundamentally irreconcilable, and the paradox of bachelors remains unsolved.

The purity and innocence of Ishmael's homoerotic affections are
complemented by Melville's great scene of teeming, heterosexual energy, "The Grand Armada" chapter. The whales' spawning ground
is at "*the innermost heart* of the shoal." (496) (italics added)

> Yes, we were now in that enchanted calm which they say lurks

at the heart of every commotion. And still in the distracted distance we beheld the tumults of the outer concentric circles, and saw successive pods of whales, eight or ten in each, swiftly going round and round, like multiplied spans of horses in a ring.
. . . We must watch for a breach in the living *wall* that hemmed us in; the *wall* that had admitted us in order to shut us up (496).
(Italics added.)

Their boat is visited by "unsophisticated, and [in] every way innocent and inexperienced" whales while, beneath the water, mothers are seen nursing their young. Encapsulated within the sacred, womblike center, at the World Navel, Ishmael observes the sanctified rites of gestation and birth in a scene of pure fertility unparalleled in Melville. "We saw young Leviathan amours in the deep" (498), and one recalls how, in their walled-inland innocence, Tommo and the native girls frolicked in Typeean pools as if they were playful animals.

This is, in fact, the nourishing vision of love Ahab never experiences, and failing to attain the still point of a turning world, dies unredeemed. Ishmael concludes:

And thus, though surrounded by circle upon circle of consternations and affrights, did these inscrutable creatures at the centre freely and fearlessly indulge in all peaceful concernments; yea, serenely revelled in dalliance and delight. But even so, amid the tornadoed Atlantic of my being, do I myself still for ever centrally disport in mute calm; and while ponderous planets of unwaning woe revolve round me, deep down and deep inland there I still bathe me in eternal mildness of joy. (499)

In Melville's next book, Pierre, recognizing his incestuous desires, begs Isabel to "hark thee to thy furthest inland soul." But Isabel, who wishes finally to drown herself, has no inland soul, no sense of balance and stability upon which she can rely. She personifies the essential imbalance of *Pierre* as surely as Ishmael the balance of *Moby-Dick*.

As Ishmael penetrates the nucleus of his being, circumferential planets revolve about his vital center. Melville offers us here a perfect metaphor for the mandala-symbol, which "derives originally

from the 'enclosing circle,' the 'charmed circle,' the magic of which
has been preserved in countless folk-customs."[17] Dr. Jung continues:

> The 'circulation' is not merely motion in a circle, but means, on
> the one hand, the marking off of the sacred precinct, and, on the
> other, fixation and concentration.
>
> .   .   .   .
>
> The image has the obvious purpose of drawing a *sulcus primi-
> genius*, a magical furrow around the center, the *templum*, or
> temenos (sacred precinct), of the innermost personality, in order
> to prevent 'flowing out,' or to guard by apotropaeic means against
> deflections through external influences.

To be sure, mandala-symbols do "express the idea of a safe refuge,
of inner reconciliation and wholeness,"[18] but, as Jolande Jacobi asserts, they may as well represent "more or less approximate and tentative steps toward ultimate perfection and totality."[19] The latter remark more truly describes Ishmael's psychic condition; he is a much
nearer representative of the beginning of the individuation process
than of its consummation. Dr. Jacobi, as we have said, distinguishes
four "symbolic figures that are characteristic of the principal stages
of the process," and Ishmael as transpersonal Quester embodies only
the first stage—"the experience of the SHADOW" in the personal
unconscious. "The dark twin brother, between Ishmael and the unconscious sea, attached to him by an indissoluble bond—this Queequeg is Ishmael's shadow," John Halverson writes,[20] and adds that
"By his acceptance and assimilation of his shadow, Ishmael discovers
Eros, expressed as the sense of brotherhood and love."

By this assimilation the Quester is now prepared to delve beyond
the area of the personal unconscious—toward the collective unconscious—for "the integration of the shadow . . . marks the first stage in
the analytic process, and . . . without it a recognition of [the] anima
. . . is impossible."[21] For, as we know,

> The second stage of the individuation process is characterized
> by the meeting with the figure of the 'soul-image', named by
> Jung the ANIMA in the man, the ANIMUS in the woman.[22]

This stage is attained in *Pierre*.

In the Epilogue to *Moby-Dick* Ishmael again penetrates to the still center of a whirling mandala-symbol, the vortex. That in both instances the symbol of psychic harmony should follow severe natural (and, therefore, human) disorientation reminds us of Dr. Jung's remark[23] that mandalas "serve to produce an inner order—which is why when they appear in a series [as drawn by analysands], they often follow chaotic, disordered states marked by conflict and anxiety."

"Queequeg's coffin," according to John Halverson,

> is, as it were, the memory of the shadows, now assimilated. It appears at the 'vital centre' of the self. Having achieved the wholeness of self, Ishmael is safe alike from the savage sea-hawks of the ego which ravaged Promethean Ahab and from the voracious sharks of the unconscious.[24]

But perhaps we should say that Ishmael is only temporarily "safe," for, in fact, his individuation is hardly completed. Ishmael the Quester has just incorporated the Shadow, but Ishmael the quester must go down to the sea again after his rescue. As in the past, the Ahab and Queequeg of his being will struggle for dominance, each alternately gaining the upper hand.

In other words, the risk of the sea and the security of the land are the counter-tensions that, in perpetual antagonism, buoy Ishmael. And as they qualify his questing so that it is neither fatally passive nor fatally aggressive, they compromise his sexuality so that it mediates between heterosexual maturity and infantile regression. For Ishmael is torn in both directions. On one hand, as in the aftermath of the sperm-squeezing, he recognizes the importance of "the wife, the heart"; on the other, after Tashtego's "obstetrical" rescue, he speaks most favorably of the death which might have been, death in the womb of the whale's head:

> Now, had Tashtego perished in that head, it had been a very precious perishing; smothered in the very whitest and daintiest of fragrant spermaceti; coffined, hearsed, and tombed in the secret inner chamber and sanctorum of the whale. (445)

For such a death obviates the necessity of questing as well as the responsibility of living. In fact, continues Ishmael

Only one sweeter end can readily be recalled—the delicious
death of an Ohio honey-hunter [again deep inland!], who seeking honey in the crotch of a hollow tree [the pun is surely de-
liberate], found such exceeding store of it that leaning too far
over, it sucked him in, so that he died embalmed. (445)

As a child, Ishmael himself sought a return to the womb, for (as
Marie Bonaparte explicates a similar incident in "The Murders in the
Rue Morgue"), this desire, in symbol, is the obvious meaning of
Ishmael's mischief in trying to climb up his stepmother's chimney;
but she drags him out violently by the legs, forcing him into life—a
troublous and perhaps traumatizing method as that master obstetri-
cian Queequeg knows (see pp. 83-84). Then Ishmael is sent to bed
without supper, and his nightmare of "impotence" ensues.

Consciously aware of the desirability of marriage and a wife (perhaps for Ishmael, as for Taji, the greatest risk of all), but, at least
in part, unconsciously desirous of infantilism and death (the greatest
security of all), Ishmael is driven between these extremes to his homoerotic compromise. Therefore, although he is saved by Eros—as both
Freudian and Jungian critics agree[25]—and although his love for Queequeg is creative and enriching, his is, from the ontogenetic point of
view, a compromised sexuality nonetheless. It correlates exactly with
his qualified questing, but it does not imply a corresponding maturity.

As Ishmael is saved because he incorporates his Shadow, Ahab is
destined to die because he does not; because, unlike Ishmael, he refuses to commit himself to the only person aboard the *Pequod* whom
he loves and through whom he can be saved. Only Pip possesses
those "childish . . . or primitive qualities that would in a way vitalize
and even embellish [Ahab's] . . . existence," for only Pip is the "real
counterpart of [Ahab's] . . . conscious ego, the not or not sufficiently
lived side of [his] . . . psyche." Ahab is white, Pip is black. Ahab is
the Captain, Pip is the "most insignificant" of the crew (526). Ahab
is courageous, Pip is a coward. Ahab is *head*strong, Pip is "over ten-
der-hearted" (526). Ahab is usually solemn, Pip is usually laughing.
Ahab is an allegorist, Pip is a symbolist. Ahab craves death and risks
all on the sea, Pip "loved life, and all life's peaceable securities"

(526). Ahab makes a pact with the Devil and arraigns the gods for human suffering; Pip "saw God's foot upon the treadle of the loom" and comes to feel "indifferent" about human "weal or woe." (530).

Therefore, incorporating the Shadow would mean for Ahab what it means for Ishmael: reducing his vision of "attainable felicity," shifting his love from the quest to the family. And although Ahab *is* vulnerable where his wife and child are concerned—Pip elicits from him the tender feelings he would have reserved for them—Ahab finally, in his madness and desperation, turns not toward his good angel but toward his bad, toward Fedallah, in whom he recognizes his prophetic soul. But the tragedy of Ahab is that he is doomed regardless of what he does. By assimilating the Shadow in the personal unconscious, he must renounce the quest, for him a fate worse than death. By failing to assimilate the Shadow, he must confront Moby Dick inadequately armed in his transpersonal dimension, and that, as we know, is death itself.

If Ishmael is sexually immature, Ahab is sexually perverse, for, like Taji and Pierre, he too is parricidal and incestuous. And although it is true that Melville knew he had written a "wicked book," I very much doubt whether he was entirely aware of its deepest sexual import. Tommo effects his release by hurling a spear into Mow-Mow's throat; Taji divides the lacing of Yillah's tent with his cutlass; White Jacket rips open his water-logged jacket with his knife. These acts, symbolic of initiation, are instances of that typically American *rite de passage* in which sex is sublimated and replaced by violence—although, to a limited degree at least, they also imply that sexual energy is potentially creative. In *Pierre* and in such later works as "Benito Cereno" and *The Confidence-Man* possession and use of the phallic weapon suggests that sexual energy is unfailingly destructive (see, below p. 166). But in *Moby-Dick*, at the wavecrest of Melville's art, the connotations of the symbolic instrument, like the genital implications of the great Whale, are both creative *and* sinister.

On one hand, Queequeg rescues the drowning Tashtego from the womblike whale's head by plunging "his keen sword" again and again into it "so as to scuttle a large hole there." Then he hauls him forth, and Tashtego is reborn. But on the other hand, Ahab, in his

fanatically Oedipal compulsion, would penetrate the whale-wall,
which bears the characteristics of the Male (even as Taji stabbed
Aleema), and plunge his harpoon into Moby Dick's inner sanctum
where the Female Principle inheres (where Taji cutlassed Yillah).
But, as Newton Arvin, Dr. Murray, and several others agree,[26] in
Moby-Dick this Principle is Maternal, not Filial, and, therefore, Ahab's
hidden sexual desire is not to commit "secondary" incest with the Sister, like Taji, but the more grievous offense, "primal" incest with the
Mother. In this regard, W. H. Auden's comments seem to me decisive:

> In *Moby-Dick*, where Ahab's pride revolts against lack of ab-
> solute strength, against being finite and dependent, the sexual
> symbolism centres round incest and the Oedipus situation, because
> incest is the magic act of self-derivation, self-autonomy, with
> the annihilation of all rival power.
>
> .   .   .   .
>
> . . . the Oedipus fantasy is a representation in aesthetic terms of
> the fantasy of being a self-originating god, i.e. of the ego
> (Father) begetting itself on the self (Mother), and castration is
> the ultimate symbol of aesthetic weakness, of not being an
> aesthetic hero.[27]

At the end, in the act of hurling his harpoon, Ahab yields his sex
to the castrating Mother, for, as Harry Slochower asserts, Ahab

> . . . is [finally] . . . 'united' to the whale by his line. The umbilical
> cord is retied, and Ahab [strangled] sinks, like an infant 'voice-
> lessly' into the ocean by the side of the mystery he has been
> unable to fathom.[28]

Thus as Ahab seeks the zenith of metaphysical perversion in the quest
—to stab into the realm of Absolute Reality and slay God—so here
he seeks, presumably with unconscious intent, the correlative zenith
of sexual perversion. Like Oedipus who confronts the Sphinx, Ahab
confronts the "sphinx-like" whale, and, as, in final comprehension
of his act, Oedipus blinds himself, so Ahab, "as he beholds Moby
Dick about to pierce the hull of the *Pequod* . . . smites his forehead
and cries out: 'I grow blind; hands! stretch out before me that I may

yet grope my way. Is't night?' "[29] Ahab's monstrous desires, then, similarly proceed from a maddened brain and are similarly thwarted, but they inspire *Moby-Dick* to a hell-fire intensity far more hypnotic than the dream-like anxiety of *Mardi* or the manufactured fervor of *Pierre*.

As far as the Father is concerned, Ahab's mad purpose is not only to slay but to embrace him as well—and fatally embrace him he does. For Ahab is a kind of maimed Fisher King—even the baptism of his harpoon in blood suggests the sexual injury implicit in the Bleeding Spear motif—and he would restore his potency through conjunction with the phallus-shaped, divinely erotic Jove himself. But the Beast, like the weapons in *Moby-Dick*, is profoundly ambiguous: divine, yet malign—and so, as Ahab finally hooks Moby Dick, so the Whale finally ravages the *Pequod*, the oil-laden feminine vessel.[30]

Captain Ahab is Melville's first adult quester and the first who actively challenges the Great Mother—the White Whale; and, as with Taji, there are two ways, not just one, of evaluating his incestuous desires. In his ontogenetic character, Ahab exhibits an Oedipal neurosis in the classic Freudian sense; but, at the same time, by viewing him in his phylogenetic magnitude, we may locate his place in the history of the Quester whose development is in the direction of health, not sickness. By interpreting Ahab's Oedipal fate transpersonally, we recognize his heroic attempt to emancipate himself from the Mother through "regenerative" incest. Oedipus, writes Erich Neumann,

> . . . has no knowledge of what he has done and when he finds
> out, he is unable to look his own deed, the deed of the hero, in
> the face. Consequently he is overtaken by the fate that overtakes
> all those for whom the Eternal Feminine reverts to the great
> Mother; he regresses to the stage of the son, and suffers the fate
> of the son-lover. He performs the act of self-castration by putting
> out his own eyes.[31]

Ahab, similarly, has no conscious knowledge that he has sought the Mother; nor does he seem to realize it at the very end, although, interestingly enough, he does claim to suffer Oedipus' punishment.

> The blinding [of Oedipus] is no longer a puzzle for us. It sig-
> nifies the destruction of the higher masculinity, of the very thing

that characterizes the hero; and this form of spiritual self-castration cancels out all that was gained by his victory over the Sphynx. The masculine progression of the hero is thrown back by the old shock, the fear of the Great Mother which seizes him after the deed. He becomes a victim of the Sphynx he had conquered.[32]

Thus the phylogenetic progress of the Quester is partially undercut by Ahab's submission to the Great Mother, and this is perhaps why Melville's next protagonist, Pierre, is, like Taji, adolescent again.

Ahab's desperate battle with the Whale coincides with that stage of ego development Neumann calls the "dragon fight," a "fight [which] has three main components: the hero, the dragon, and the treasure,"[33] that is, the Quester, the Parents, and the Captive respectively. Melville himself identifies whales with dragons in *Moby-Dick*, and the adversaries in the dragon fight are very like those in the whale-hunt. According to Neumann,

The fight [of the Quester] with the dragon is thus the fight with the First Parents, a fight in which the murders of both father and mother, but not of one alone, have their ritually prescribed place.[34]

But, as I noted earlier, Ahab tries not merely to slay the Father; he means to embrace him as well, and their affiliation is essential if Ahab is to succeed in killing Moby Dick:

The slaying of the mother and identification with the father-god go together. If, through active incest, the hero penetrates into the dark, maternal, chthonic side, he can only do so by virtue of his kinship with 'heaven,' his filiation with God.[35]

Ahab, however, fails on all counts: to embrace and slay the Father, to mate with and slay the Mother. Thus he gives his life trying to achieve

The mythological goal of the dragon fight . . . the virgin, the captive, or, more generally, the 'treasure hard to attain.' It is to be noted that a purely material pile of gold, such as the hord of the Nibelungs, is a late and degenerate form of the original motif. In the earliest mythologies, in ritual, in religion, and in mystical literature as well as in fairy tales, legend, and poetry, gold and precious stones, but particularly diamonds and pearls, were originally symbolic carriers of immaterial values.[36]

In Melville gold and treasure—albeit "a late and degenerate form of the original motif"—are still symbolic carriers of immaterial values," of the reality of the Sacred and the Absolute.

I think, then, that of the ways in which Moby Dick may be regarded as symbol, two of the most appropriate are as the metaphysical duality of the Cosmos and as the life-energy, sacred and sexual, of the Center. Undoubtedly the two visceral demands of Ahab's being are metaphysical and sexual: to slay God if He exists or prove His absence if He does not; and to unite with the Mother and slay as well as embrace the Father. It is Melville's great triumph that as he made the symbolic elements of the Whale literally coextensive with one another —the realm of God and Sexual Energy one—so he made Ahab's quests seamlessly coincide and both depend on the hurling of one harpoon in an ultimately definitive act. But because the value of the Romantic Quest lies not in attainment but in the struggle therefor, Ishmael, not Ahab, is the book's only successful quester. For Ishmael engages a metaphysical problem he knows he cannot solve and discovers his deepest satisfactions in a sexual relationship he cannot consummate and in a perception of the Sacred he cannot maintain. Indeed, it may even be argued, as D. H. Lawrence first argued on behalf of another American hero, Natty Bumppo,[37] that Ishmael not only does not grow older (i.e., overripe with fulfillment) as the quest continues but that he grows younger and younger. His first sexual encounter in *Moby-Dick* is adult (sleeping with Queequeg); his second is adolescent (holding hands and squeezing sperm); but his third and last is natal. For in the book's final tableau, Ishmael emerges from the creamy pool as if reborn, and, like Nature herself ("The unharming sharks . . . with padlocks on their mouths"), he too experiences, in the cataclysm of death and rebirth, the real, if transient, peace of exhaustion. For Ishmael avoids the fate of the manic quester: crashing against or through the walls of dissatisfaction, a route that leads, inevitably, to further and further dissatisfaction. The very uncertainties of existence keep Ishmael young, and in the tensions of unfulfillment, he achieves a measure of real happiness.

B. PIERRE

Few would deny that as Melville strains the "limit of governable imagination"[38] in *Moby-Dick*, so in *Pierre* (1852) he plunges into an ungoverned reach beyond: his often intensely pure, annealed language becomes pockmarked and granulated; the moral center of *Moby-Dick* cannot hold in *Pierre* and disintegrates; the defects of plot and technique (never Melville's strongest points) are exacerbated; and just as the factual ballast of *Moby-Dick* unlooses itself in *Pierre*, so the legendary truth of the earlier novel becomes the fantasy fiction of the latter. From heroic triumph to heroic failure: *Pierre* is so badly flawed that one cannot but wonder how Melville could have plummeted so disastrously.

Several explanations, to one degree or another, participate in the truth: that Melville had not yet fully recuperated from the severe eyestrain and "psychoneurotic fatigue"[39] incurred in writing *Moby-Dick*; that he was depressed by a "moral conflict and an underlying will to wreck his self,"[40] and hence, not surprisingly, regarded his book with reckless disdain; that he chose a form (the novel)[41] and a theme (incest) that ran counter to his demonstrated talents as a romancer of sea-tales about men; that in fantasying his own familial relationships, he chose an area of experience he could not handle without fatally narrowing the gap between life and art;[42] and that he had begun to doubt the possibility (not to say validity) of language as a means of discovering or representing Final Truth (399).

All of these explanations, in some measure, help account for the outlandish lapses in taste, tact, and judgment, which disfigure *Pierre*, but all of them, it should be observed, are strictly local: none presupposes an overview of Melville's career, although from such a prospect a larger and more significant thesis about the specific achievements and failures in the canon emerges. In essence, it is this: that Melville was so obsessed with exhausting a theme that he never wrote a book just once and never wrote the same kind of good book twice. All of his novels, one might say, are either "companion-pieces" or "trilogies."[43] Thus, *Omoo*, bright and racy, should have completed the South Sea adventure cycle begun in *Typee*, but, no, Melville wrote the first (the narrative) part of *Mardi*, and it is dead weight. The novel of the metaphysical quest, begun in the second half of *Mardi*, reaches its esthetic culmination in *Moby-Dick*, but Melville, of course, added *Pierre*. The sparkling *Redburn* should have stood alone as the tale of a young man who traverses the path from Innocence to Experience, but Melville would write its sequel *White-Jacket*, in the main humorless and literary beside its predecessor. And, as for his satires on America and the Americans, *The Confidence-Man* is, quite frankly, a heavy-handed failure after *Israel Potter*, a light-fingered success. (*The Confidence-Man* is, to be sure, more ambitious and more significant for Melville's intellectual history, but *Israel Potter* is better literature.) What I am saying—and I shall have more to say on this subject after discussing *The Confidence-Man*—is that Melville was compelled not merely to explore, but to exhaust his themes and that this compulsion, more than the struggle for cash and the dimwittedness of his audience, is why half his books are "botches." That he thought otherwise merely affirms what we already suspected: that his creative faculty far outran his critical judgment. As an artist, he never learned to leave well enough alone.

In his personal relationships Melville also seems to have suffered from this same absolutist tendency. For instance, his estrangements from Nathaniel Hawthorne and Evert Duyckinck, his only heaven-born "chronometrical" and best earth-bound "horological" friend, respectively, seem to have resulted from a compulsion to drive these relationships to an *absurdum*. The manner in which Melville divinized his friendship with Hawthorne (". . . your heart beat in my ribs and mine in yours, and both in God's")[44] easily matches Pierre's noblest sentiments for Isabel, far exceeds Thoreau's idealization of friendship in *A Week* and could not but have embarrassed his correspondent who surely did not respond in kind. Melville's relationship with Duyckinck was much less intense, but again Melville seems to have demanded what he had no right to expect and what could not be fulfilled. Informal sponsor, advocate, employer, drinking companion, book lender, and loyal friend—Duyckinck had much to offer Melville, although armored as he was in a fastidiously Victorian sensibility, he could be neither wildly appreciative of *Moby-Dick* nor

share (or even condone) the unconventional sentiments of *Pierre*.
Nor could he conceive of literature as agonizing discovery. And, therefore, just as Melville cruelly satirized Hawthorne in the figure of the
unresponsive Plotinus Plinlimmon (who casually observes the mar-
tyr-like Pierre go to his doom), so too he satirizes Duyckinck as the
Editor of the *Captain Kidd Monthly*, who duns Pierre for a daguer-
reotype.[45]

The breach with Duyckinck was closed in September 1856, when
Melville came to New York from the Berkshires, and, as Leon Howard
has said, "sloughed off his four years of sensitive estrangement. . . ."[46]
But by then, of course, Melville had already begun to shorten sail,
and we are not surprised to learn that by 1878, the year of Duyckinck's
death, he "was spending almost as many evenings [at 20 Clinton
Place] as he had spent . . . [with Duyckinck] thirty years before. . . ."[47]
But the breach with Hawthorne was irreparable, and when the elder
man died in 1864, Melville was still not sure what had originally
driven them apart. The first stanza of "Monody" reflects his regret,
puzzlement, and sense of needless waste:

> To have known him, to have loved him
>   After loneness long;
> And then to be estranged in life,
>   And neither in the wrong;
> And now for death to set his seal—
>   Ease me, a little ease, my song![48]

The same compulsion that soured half his books soured his best friend-
ships as well.

Although Hawthorne once observed that Melville could "neither
believe nor be comfortable in his unbelief," in *Moby-Dick* Melville
does, for once, rest in the pondering repose of If. And, thus, for once,
he achieves no less in the balance of his sentences or the relation of
his characters than in the implications of his philosophy—a daringly
poised book, a Terror Stone which will not topple. But Melville
could not accept an anticipatory state, could not create again in the
spirit of negative capability, and, in consequence, programmatically
extended Pierre's transit from the transcendental mood which per-
vades *Mardi*, beyond the skepticism of *Moby-Dick* to an unregener-

ate atheism. Similarly, in these three books, Melville becomes more and more aware of the relationship between Secular Reality and the Absolute; in *Mardi* his expression of it is barely conscious (Aleema before and Yillah beyond); in *Moby-Dick* it is fully conscious (the Whale-wall before and the supposed "secret" within); in *Pierre*, as we shall see, it is overly self-conscious (the face of Plotinus Plinlimmon before and "Silence" beyond). This relationship, which Melville had half-knowingly advanced in *Mardi*, which he had intuitively controlled in *Moby-Dick*, he now intellectualizes in *Pierre*. In this context, Richard Chase's comment is particularly well-taken: "that *Pierre* is Melville's most contrived book, that here he is trying to make systematic and explicit use of his typical symbols. . . ." In other words, if one of the troubles with *Mardi* is that Melville wrote it knowing too little, one of the troubles with *Pierre* is that he wrote it knowing too much.

T he opening chapters of *Pierre* systematically recapitualate every Melvillean cliché of the earthly Eden: Saddle Meadows, the Glendinning feudal demesne, is on a plain surrounded by forests and mountains; that is, it is at the Sacred Center. Pierre, the nineteen-year-old descendant of heroes and sole heir of this ancestral kingdom, is in perfect health and near perfect spirits, robust, a devotee of polite literature, and in love with a maiden whose innocence parallels his own. He lives in sweet (albeit Oedipal) harmony with his mother and reveres the memory of his father, regards Nature as a "glorious benediction" (14) and God as transcendent and benign. "Would the god of sunlight decree gloom? It is a flawless, speckless, fleckless, beautiful world throughout; joy now, and joy forever!" (70). The prose of these chapters, sedulously aping that which it represents, is saturated in sentimentality and saffroned to a fare-thee-well, a blundering attempt to mimic the quality of life in the quality of language. Melville's purpose—at the willing sacrifice of his art—is to maximize the cloying, sickening sweetness, the hothouse disengagement, of Pierre's world in order to visit the largest lie with the largest truth.

Melville means to nurture this world to its finest flower before up-
rooting it ruthlessly and completely.

One beautiful spring morning Pierre and Lucy leave Saddle Meadows for "the wooded hills, whose distant blue, now changed into
a variously shaded green, stood before them like old Babylonian walls,
overgrown with verdure" (40). That is, they drive from the zone of
safety to the rim of danger, to the symbolic walls of Secular Reality.
And, therefore, it is not inappropriate—as if in response to vibrations
from without these walls—that Lucy intuits "some nameless sadness"
and dread; that she associates this dread with a certain face Pierre had
spoken of as haunting him, a face we later learn is Isabel's; and that
the discussion which ensues precipitates their first quarrel. What has
happened, of course, is that Isabel, or rather that sexual power which
is coincidental with her and of which she is the unnamed incarnation,
has already begun to drive a wedge between Pierre and Lucy. As the
scene ends, Pierre addresses the spirits of the air—like Ahab, he is a
master of invocation—and reaffirms his faith in Nature and Christ.
This ejaculation, however, serves but to frighten Lucy the more, and
she begs Pierre to "fly these hills, when, I fear, too wide a prospect
meets us. Fly we to the plain" (44). Pierre concurs, and a dozen lines
later Melville baldly remarks that "in the plain they find peace, and
love, and joy again" (44). But Melville's full intellectualization of
his symbol—to the extent of defining its values—robs it of its reso-
nance.

After escorting Lucy home, Pierre wanders behind his family's
mansion, and, as he falls to musing beneath a pine tree, sees, in an
hallucinatory moment, Isabel's face looking down at him. Like Ahab
contemplating the sphynxlike Whale, Pierre also realizes that the
face is the concealing mask of Secular Reality:

> '. . . what is that thou [Pierre asks the face] hast veiled in thee so
> imperfectly, that I seem to see its motion, but not its form? It
> visibly rustles behind the concealing screen. Now, never into the
> soul of Pierre, stole there before, a muffledness like this! If
> aught really lurks in it, ye sovereign powers, that claim all my leal
> worshippings, I conjure ye to lift the veil: I must see it face to
> face. Tread I on a mine, warn me; advance I on a precipice, hold

me back; but abandon me to an unknown misery, that it shall
suddenly seize me, and possess me, wholly—that ye will never do;
else Pierre's fond faith in ye-now clean, untouched—may clean
depart; and give me up to a railing atheist. Ah, now the face
departs. Pray heaven it hath not only stolen back, and hidden
again in thy high secrecies, oh tree! But 'tis gone—gone—
entirely gone; and I thank God, and I feel joy again; joy, which
I also feel to be my right as man; deprived of joy, I feel I should
find cause for deadly feuds with things invisible.' (47–48)

Despite the intimations of atheism, however, Pierre is still a Transcendentalist, unwilling, without further evidence, to attribute base
motives to Nature and God. But, at book's close, Pierre, like Ahab,
will be unable to discriminate between the "face" of Nature and the
"sovereign powers," will confuse the two, and, in the process, identify both as evil. For as Ahab regards the Whale as not just an inscrutable phantom but as a living allegory, the visible personification of
Evil, so Pierre finally concludes that Isabel is also not just an inscrutable phantom but his "Bad Angel" (425).

In Pierre's third encounter with Secular Reality, Melville makes
it quite clear that Pierre still regards Nature and God separately and
the former as gateway to the latter. But now impassioned by Isabel's
letter, which seems to indicate that they are brother and sister, Pierre
is no longer content to implore the "powers" to unveil themselves;
now he offers to smash through Nature directly. He addresses her as
if she were maliciously animate, and many critics have noticed his resemblance at this moment to Ahab, who would strike through the
pasteboard mask of the whale-wall:

'With myself I front thee! . . . Henceforth I will know nothing
but Truth; glad Truth, or sad Truth; I will know what is. . . . Thou
Black Knight, that with visor down, thus confrontest me, and
mockest at me; lo! I strike through thy helm, and will see thy face,
be it Gorgon! . . . From all idols, I tear all veils; henceforth I
will see the hidden things. . . .' (76)

It is Isabel, Pierre thinks, who finally kills him—by turning him to
stone; and Isabel herself has such a fatal premonition. "Tell me [she
asks him], do I blast where I look? Is my face Gorgon's?" (222).

But if Ahab and Pierre must both challenge symbolic barriers outside the self, only Pierre must challenge them within, for only he is
concerned with the legitimacy of motivation: if he is to establish a
holy relationship with Isabel, he must ascertain the purity of his
emotions. He must conquer "the infernal catacombs of thought" (58),
for at their heart "lurked the subtler secret"(59). His is, of course,
a futile task, and Melville, doubling the image, mocks him with rich
irony:

> Ah, thou rash boy! are there no couriers in the air to warn thee
> away from these imperillings, and point thee to those Cretan
> labyrinths, to which thy life's cord is leading thee? Where now are
> the high beneficences? Whither fled the sweet angels that are
> alleged guardians to man? (206)

Chapter VII, "Intermediate between Pierre's Two Interviews with
Isabel . . ." is perhaps the most crucial in the book, for in it Pierre decides that his feelings for her are pure, and he insists "that never,
never would he be able to embrace Isabel with the mere brotherly embrace, while the thought of any other caress, which took hold of any
domesticness, was entirely vacant from his uncontaminated soul, for
it had never *consciously* intruded there" (167). (Italics added.)
Melville's point, however, is that Pierre victimizes himself not just
because he unconsciously seeks an incestuous relationship but also because he would prove the spirituality of his feelings by an invalid
mode of ascertaining Truth; because, in his philosophical innocence,
he imagines that he has found a correspondence between *his* feelings
and the Spiritual itself. At the Terror Stone Pierre definitively tests
his faith in Transcendentalism and, in self-delusion, finds it not want-
ing.

The Terror Stone[50] is an enormous rock, "high as a barn," that
"hovered within an inch of the soil, all along to the point of teeter-
ing contact but yet touched not the soil" (154–55). At one end, "the
vacancy was considerably larger, so as to make it not only possible,
but convenient to admit a crawling man; yet no mortal being had ever
been known to have the intrepid heart to crawl there" (155). It
takes no little courage for Pierre to "slid[e] himself straight into the

horrible interspace" (157) and invoke the rock, because his original premise, the transcendental one from which all his difficulties follow, is that Nature is a conduit for divine sensation and that, if the "sovereign powers" so dispose, even insensate rocks will fall:

> 'If the miseries of the undisclosable things in me, shall ever unhorse me from my manhood's seat; if to vow myself all Virtue's and all Truth's, be but to make a trembling, distrusted slave of me; if Life is to prove a burden I cannot bear without ignominious cringings; if indeed our actions are all foreordained, and we are Russian serfs to Fate; if invisible devils do titter at us when we most nobly strive; if Life be a cheating dream, and virtue as unmeaning and unsequeled with any blessing as the midnight mirth of wine; if by sacrificing myself for Duty's sake, my own mother resacrifices me; if Duty's self be but a bugbear, and all things are allowable and unpunishable to man;—then do thou, Mute Massiveness, fall on me! Ages thou hast waited; and if these things be thus, then wait no more; for whom better canst thou crush than him who now lies here invoking thee?' (157–58)

In other words, Pierre is once again apostrophizing Secular Reality, but now he is exhorting it to crush him if Truth and the other heavenly qualities are not operable on earth. Therefore, when the rock holds, Pierre mistakenly concludes that not only does the Absolute exist, but that its virtues are potential in human conduct, and in his conduct in particular. Thus Pierre thoroughly convinces himself that he is a Christlike "chronometer."

On closer inspection, however, the Terror Stone seems not only mutely massive, but, most curiously, quasi-animate; indeed, very like a whale. It is "shaped something like a lengthened egg, but flattened more; and, at the ends, pointed more; and yet not pointed, but irregularly wedge-shaped" (154). Melville refers to the side of the Stone as a "flank," the summit as "fore-head like," one end as "haunched," and the other as the one Pierre crawls under. The fact remains, however, that despite Melville's allegorizing and despite Pierre's fearful response—as if he were entering the jaws of a great recumbent sphynx—the Stone is never anything more than a stone. In *Moby-Dick* Melville creates a totem figure of frighteningly suggestive power, but in *Pierre* he has himself become one of those false priests in the Bower of the Arsacides, who labors to imbue a dead whale, now an insensate rock, with artificial life.

Nevertheless, since Pierre, Servant of Truth and Enthusiast to Duty, is now convinced that he must acknowledge Isabel before the world, he forces himself into an untenable position: either destroy his mother (by calling Isabel his sister) or destroy his fiancée (by calling Isabel his wife). Melville symbolically expresses Pierre's existential frustration as a collision with Secular Reality: "he dashed himself in blind fury and swift madness against the wall, and fell dabbling in the vomit of his loathed identity" (201). Finally to protect his mother, Pierre resolves on the second course—but to little avail: Lucy swoons into a prolonged coma, and Mrs. Glendinning evicts him from their house and disinherits him. And, therefore, in the company of Isabel and Delly Ulver, a servant girl, who having been seduced, is also an outcast, Pierre leaves Saddle Meadows and comes to New York.

Ill-fortune, however, pursues him. His cousin, Glendinning Stanly, whom he had expected would receive him stylishly, disavows him, and it is only through the generosity of an old friend, Charlie Millthorpe, that Pierre and his entourage find lodging at the Apostles,' a reconverted church now tenanted by lawyers, philosophers, and other impoverished intellectuals. Pierre's apartment, in the building's new wing, is the second of his three homes, and the relationship among the three should not go unnoticed. At Saddle Meadows Pierre lived in the sacred glen, and as long as he was not a quester, did not feel the encapsulating effect of the "Babylonian walls." In New York City, however, the center at which Pierre resides—for he faces an inner courtyard—was formerly the church burial ground, but now that it has lost its holy purpose is, in effect, sacred ground desecrated. Furthermore, as Pierre's vistas were once spacious and beautiful, they are now restricted and unattractive:

> But except the donjon form of the old grey tower [Remember the imprisoned Donjalolo!], seemingly there is nothing to see but a wilderness of tiles, slate, shingles, and tin;—the desolate hanging wilderness of tiles, slate, shingles, and tin, wherewith we modern Babylonians replace the fair hanging-gardens of the fine

old Asiatic times when the excellent Nebuchadnezzar was king. (318)

In a quasi-autobiographical reflection, Pierre, now a struggling novelist dedicated to the promulgation of Truth, metaphorically describes his plight:

'Cast thy eye in there on Vivia; tell me why those four limbs should be clapped in a dismal jail—day out, day in—week out, week in—month out, month in—and himself the voluntary jailer!" (356)

But just as the symbolic walls become literal ones, so does the symbolic jail become Pierre's third and last "home." The pattern is fulfilled: the harder he struggles to overcome the walls, the nearer they impinge—until, finally, the "stone ceiling almost . . . [resting] on his brow," he dies in prison (424). The novel's final tableau reveals Lucy collapsed, Pierre and Isabel poisoned: at the stone center now is death unhallowed.

But long before Pierre reaches this final extremity, his survival—if not redemption—is still possible: for the god-drenched youth meets God and—irony of ironies!—fails to recognize Him:

As Pierre, now hurrying from his chamber, was rapidly passing through one of the higher brick colonnades connecting the ancient building with the modern, there advanced toward him from the direction of the latter, a very plain, composed, manly figure, with a countenance rather pale if anything, but quite clear and without wrinkle. Though the brow and the beard, and the steadiness of the head and settledness of the step indicated mature age, yet the blue, bright, but still quiescent eye offered a very striking contrast. In that eye, the gay immortal youth Apollo, seemed enshrined; while on the ivory-throned brow, old Saturn cross-legged sat. The whole countenance of this man, the whole air and look of this man, expressed a cheerful content. Cheerful is the adjective, for it was the contrary of gloom; content—perhaps acquiescence—is the substantive, for it was not Happiness or Delight. But while the personal look and air of this man were thus winning, there was still something latently visible in him which repelled. That something may best be characterized as non-

Benevolence. Non-Benevolence seems the best word, for it was
neither Malice nor Ill-will; but something passive. To crown all,
a certain floating atmosphere seemed to invest and go along
with this man. That atmosphere seems only renderable in words
by the term Inscrutableness. Though the clothes worn by this
man were strictly in accordance with the general style of any unobtrusive gentleman's dress, yet his clothes seemed to disguise
this man. One would almost have said, his very face, the apparently natural glance of his very eye, disguised this man.

·   ·   ·   ·   ·   ·   ·   ·   ·   ·   ·   ·   ·   ·   ·   ·

Now who was this man? This man was Plotinus Plinlimmon.
(341-342)

Although content, Plinlimmon also suggests a comcomitant Non-
Benevolence; there is an "inscrutableness" about him, and, strangest
of all, his "clothes" and "his very face . . . disguised this man," which
suggests that his outer surface is a mask. We have heard other things
about Plinlimmon too: from his study window Pierre has seen this
face looking at him, crying (silently) Vain! Vain! Vain! Fool! Fool!
Fool! Quit! Quit! Quit! but when Pierre "mentally interrogated the
face as to why it thrice said Vain! Fool! Quit! to him, there was no
response. For that face did not respond to anything" (345). In truth,
Plinlimmon does not speak; he is spoken for: his students, we remember, compiled his doctrinal lecture, "Chronometricals and Horologicals."

We may, then, identify the *face* of Plotinus, as we have already
identified Aleema, as another incarnation of Secular Reality, that inscrutable Reality which is a mask to the Beyond. And just as "Plinlimmon," as Dr. Murray reminds us,[51] is the name of a mountain in Wales,
so, as we noticed earlier, is Aleema described in mountain imagery.
But in *Mardi* the Absolute demonstrably—if but momentarily—exists, for Taji does penetrate Aleema and possess Yillah. In *Moby-Dick*
that Reality—now symbolized by that unknown realm within the
whale-God's body—presumably exists. But does anything exist beyond the face of Plinlimmon, this man-God Deist Nobodaddy?[52]
Only that ambiguous "silence [which] is the only Voice of our God."
And, therefore, just as the Whale tantalizes us by his godlike pres-

ence, so does Plotinus tantalize us by claiming the answer to Melville's final philosophic riddle:

'For he [the philosopher] will then see, or seem to see, that this world's seeming incompatibility with God, absolutely results from its meridian correspondence with Him.' (250)

But that part of the lecture which undoubtedly would have contained Plinlimmon's solution is—alas!—missing, just as Moby Dick is never penetrated. What really matters, however, is how one accommodates oneself to the knowledge that God is unknowable: Ishmael rests assured in the pondering repose of If; Plotinus whose book is entitled *EI* (that is, *IF* in Greek) is paralyzed by uncertainty. Nevertheless, his lecture ironically counterpoints Pierre's career, and a more careful reading of it might—but probably would not—have saved him, for like Ahab, "madness maddened" at the end of *Moby-Dick*, Pierre too is suicidally obsessed with revenge. Chronometrically-minded people, says Plotinus, usually work "*unique* follies and sins," for by failing to live chronometrically (as Pierre fails in the discovery of his incestuous desires), they fail to live horologically virtuous lives as well and run themselves into "moral abandonment, self-deceit and hypocrisy." Plinlimmon, therefore, advocates a strict adherence to the moral imperatives of Man, the Horologue, not God, the Chronometer—to the doctrine of "virtuous expediency." Plotinus, cynically well-versed in the ways of the world, knows that innocent boys with absolute passions always come to bad ends.

Melville himself regards Plinlimmon ambivalently. On one hand, he grudgingly admires the man who makes the sensible discovery that questing for absolutes is futile; in his maturity, Plotinus has kept his youth by retreating before the insurmountable obstacles of life. He is, in fact, for all his time-serving, one guide out of the quester's labyrinth, and he next appears, purified of Non-Benevolence as the "eminently safe" Narrator in "Bartleby." But, on the other hand, Melville bears an ill-concealed contempt for this disengaged philosopher. He is the latest instance of the Young Man's Aging Adversary whose genealogy includes such diverse worthies as Mow-Mow, Aleema, Satan in *Battle-Pieces*, and the blood-curdling surgeon of *White-Jacket*: for like Cadwallader Cuticle, one of his names is Welsh and both are polysyllabic and preposterous-sounding. Both men are of advanced age and both are—it is their major characteristic—Non-Benevolent, although only Plotinus elevates it to a philosophical principle. As Plinlimmon watches Pierre go to his doom without lifting a finger, so Cadwallader, after performing an unnecessary operation on a young sailor, inhumanly watches him bleed to death.

As Pierre struggles vainly with his book, his eyesight deteriorates: "the pupils of his eyes rolled away from him in their orbits," and, as they do, Pierre sinks into a "state of semi-consciousness, or rather trance. . . ." (402). It is then in this terribly overwrought condition that he experiences "a remarkable dream or vision" of the Mount of the Titans and the Cheopian pyramid.

> You saw Enceladus the Titan, the most potent of all the giants, writhing from out the imprisoning earth;—turbaned with upborne moss he writhed; still, though armless, resisting with his whole striving trunk, the Pelion and the Ossa hurled back at him; —turbaned with upborne moss he writhed; still turning his unconquerable front toward that majestic mount eternally in vain assailed by him, and which, when it had stormed him off, had heaved his undoffable incubus upon him, and deridingly left him there to bay out his ineffectual howl. (405–6)

Then, suddenly, the Titans, the "repulsed group of heaven-assaulters," arise and fling themselves once more at the Mount, and Pierre sees his own features on Enceladus' face, the primordial challenge re-enacted:

> Foremost among them all, he saw a moss-turbaned, armless giant, who, despairing of any other mode of wreaking his immitigable hate, turned his vast trunk into a battering-ram, and hurled his own arched-out ribs again and yet again against the invulnerable steep. (407)

In Pierre's overwhelming disillusion—his father's putative inconstancy and his mother's haughtiness; his betrayal of Lucy and his desire for Isabel; Glen's callousness and the incubus of authorship; financial and physical exhaustion—his faith in transcendentalism is extingushed. Pierre advances from "boyhood's thoughtless faith" to "disbelief" without "resting at last in manhood's pondering repose of

If" and becomes, in short, a railing "Atheist" (398). Melville, however, clearly disaffiliates himself from his hero believing that if Transcendentalism is untenable, Atheism is unnecessary. Melville may, in self-contradiction, characterize God as "Juggularius," the "Juggernaut-Juggler" in Dr. Murray's gloss,[53] whose Voice is Silence, but Pierre denies God completely and goes mad, for his career eventuates in homicide and suicide, "the stony walls all around [him] that he could not overleap. . . ." (396)

Pierre suffers in the extreme from what R. D. Laing calls "ontological insecurity," and there is a provocative relationship between the symptoms of this schizoid predicament and the sermons in stone by which Melville fashions his melodrama. Laing argues that the ontologically insecure person encounters three forms of anxiety—engulfment, petrifaction, and implosion—and I must direct the reader to *The Divided Self* for a close analysis of them. On receiving Isabel's letter, at the outset, Pierre is thrown into such turmoil that "he could not stay in his chamber; the house contracted to a nut-shell around him; the walls smote his forehead; bare-headed he rushed from the place. . . ." (77) At the end, in a "low dungeon of the city prison" he cannot escape, "the cumbersome stone ceiling almost rested on his brow. . . ." (424) In "The Pit and the Pendulum" this metaphor of engulfment, the challenge to one's autonomous identity, is represented in a surreal episode.

In *Pierre* the metaphor of petrifaction (i.e. depersonalization of oneself and of the other in one's eyes) is of course particularly apt. The Gorgon figures, Pierre's mother and of Isabel-as-his-mother, turn him to stone, reveal him in his lack of ontological autonomy, even as he himself reifies Isabel and Lucy. As he leaves the Apostles' for the last time, he passes Isabel who "sat petrified in her chair" and Lucy, "the marble girl [who] sat before her easel. . . ." (421) (When Millthorpe and Frederick Tartan come to visit Pierre and Lucy in jail, the turnkey wheezes his acknowledgement as he opens the cell door: "Kill 'em both with one stone, then." [426])

In the heart of young Pierre stands a marble shrine, a niched pillar which encloses "the perfect marble form of his departed father" and which supports "the entire one-pillared temple of his moral life. . . ."

(79) Implosion signifies the terrifying impingement of reality, the destruction, in this case, wrecked upon Pierre's shrined temple, and the emptiness, the nothingness, which ensues. Or as Melville says, "Better might one be pushed off into the material spaces beyond the uttermost orbit of our sun, than once feel himself fairly afloat in himself!" (335) This sense of being fairly afloat in herself is what induces Isabel, who prays for a vegetable motionlessness, to attempt suicide by drowning. Orphan and exile, her earliest memories center about an empty, boarded half-ruinous house whose fire-places are all in ruins—their bricks fallen into the hearth—and every hearth-stone with one long crack through it: Melville's version of the House of Usher.

From his first brush with the Babylonian walls to his ultimate collision with the Egyptian pyramid—a continuing confrontation with veil, catacomb, labyrinth, mountain, Terror Stone, wall, and face (of Isabel and Plotinus)—an increasing clarity defines Pierre's struggle and an increasing absurdity too, for nothing could be more absurd than Pierre flinging himself headlong at the ramparts of Heaven in search of a God he believes does not exist. The marvelous "Bartleby" indicates just how well Melville could exploit the Absurd, but in *Pierre* it is the Absurd that exploits Melville. Not for nothing, then, is the tone of *Pierre* viciously ironic and mocking, strident and hortatory. And little wonder that, as so much of the book indicates—the opening scenes at Saddle Meadows, the Testing at the Terror Stone, the figure of Plotinus Plinlimmon, and the perpetual interjections of the author—*Pierre* is as much a game, private joke, and tractate as it is serious fiction. More damaging still, as Marius Bewley puts it, is that the world of the novel is "a secondary act of [Pierre's] . . . own creation," not Melville's.[55] In truth, *Pierre* imitates the living novel as Enceladus imitates Ahab or the Terror Stone imitates Moby Dick.

A s I noted earlier, the love story of *Pierre* repeats in essence the love story of *Mardi*, although, in addition to making other changes, Melville transplanted his myth from the South Seas to Saddle Meadows.

Like Taji, whom he resembles, Pierre also finds himself attracted by two women, but we must not make the conventional assumption of Melville criticism that, from the outset, Lucy is opposed to Isabel. For, in point of fact, she is opposed to Mrs. Glendinning, and it is these two women who are drawn directly from their antecedents in *Mardi*, Yillah and Hautia respectively. Like Yillah, Lucy is asexual, innocent, passive, blonde, an angel from "Paradise" (46) who also has, on earth, a "secret inner shrine" (45)—not tent, but a bedroom. And just as Taji violates Yillah's holy sanctum, so Pierre violates Lucy's—although in that moment of violation Pierre is as much Aleema, who would sacrifice the maiden, as he is Taji, who would "rescue" her:

> Opening the door, he advanced slowly and deliberately toward her; and as Lucy caught his pale, determined figure, she gave a cry of groping misery, which knew not the pang that caused it, and lifted herself trembling in her bed; but without uttering one word.
>
> Pierre sat down on the bedside; and his set eyes met her terrified and virgin aspect.
>
> 'Decked in snow-white, and pale of cheek, thou indeed art fitted for the altar; but not that one of which thy fond heart didst dream:—so fair a victim!' (215)

Although the scene seems as appropriate for sexual seizure as for murder, it is "murder" Pierre commits, Aleema's crime, not Taji's. As Lucy swoons, her maid, Martha, cries, "Thou hast somehow murdered her. . . . See! she dies away at the sight of thee—begone! Wouldst thou murder her afresh? Begone!" (216). And, in any event, Pierre has already committed a kind of intercourse with Lucy (not, however, without her consent) in the book's opening pages. She is sitting at her opened window, "Upon the sill [of which] a snow-white glossy pillow reposes, and a trailing shrub has softly rested a rich, crimson flower against it" (1–2); Pierre stands beneath speaking of love with great extravagance:

> 'Fie, now, Pierre; why should ye youths always swear when ye love?'
>
> 'Because in us love is profane, since it mortally reaches toward the heaven in ye!'

'There thou fly'st again, Pierre; thou art always circumventing me so. Tell me, why should ye youths ever show so sweet an expertness in turning all trifles of ours into trophies of yours?'

'I know not how that is, but ever was it our fashion to do.' And shaking the casement shrub, he dislodged the flower, and conspicuously fastened it in his bosom. (2)

Like Inamorata and like Yillah, Lucy is not forcibly raped but rather willingly "deflowered." If the intercourse is more verbal than sexual, we should not be too surprised: all manner of sexual acts occur in *Pierre* in lexical or symbolic, but never literal, fashion.

As Lucy derives from Yillah, Mrs. Glendinning derives from Hautia. Both women are highly sexual and attractive (Mrs. Glendinning is not and Hautia does not seem to be a virgin); both are aggressive (212), domineering (22), demanding (112), and sophisticated in dress and taste; and, as if he were punning on "Hautia," Melville tells us that Mrs. Glendinning was "first fashioned" by "the Infinite Haughtiness' (105). Hautia, however, who derives in part from Spencer's Acrasia, is a sensualist, and Taji's first reactions to her are fear and disgust.Pierre, on the other hand, loves his mother, and she responds in kind. They play a little game calling one another "brother" and "sister," and on one occasion, they act out their incestuous fantasies as Pierre passes a "ribbon round her neck . . . crossing the ends in front" and tacking them there with a kiss (15). Mrs. Glendinning, who is not jealous of his asexual fiancée, approves the doubleness of her son's affections: "There," she says, kissing Pierre, "this is my cheek, and the other is Lucy's" (21).

In *Mardi*, Taji's choice is either/or, Yillah or Hautia; he cannot—even if he would—have them both. But in *Pierre* Melville introduces a third woman, one designed to reconcile within herself the opposing selves of the female character and, at the same time, fulfill Pierre's deepest desire. For Isabel promises to be both sexual Sister (hence the titillating possibility of incest) and asexual Wife (a woman Pierre can live, but not sleep, with). Like Mrs. Glendinning, she too is authoritarian (177), regal (179), and demanding (225), and both women, we are told, arch their breasts (69, 380). Isabel, however, is also like Lucy—saintly (139, 176), passive (226), and sweet (204), and, therefore, Pierre rejects his Mother-Sister and future wife for this new woman who purports to be both in one. Indeed, Isabel is Melville's one grand attempt to create the Whole Woman hinted at in the characterizations of Fayaway and Yillah. Unfortunately, she is not a successful integration of opposites, for her character remains hopelessly bifurcated. The trouble is not those strange fits of passion and heightened sexuality (178, 188, 205), which alternate with moments of repose and quietude—although, in context, they are improbable enough—but rather that she seems to be both too unselfconscious and overselfconscious to be credible. For instance, like Yillah, Isabel has "but very little" memory (369), is led by "dreamy promptings" (143), feels a certain affinity for another language she now no longer knows (French this time, not English), and cannot grasp or intellectualize the relationship between facts and ideas. "I comprehend nothing, Pierre; there is nothing these eyes have ever looked upon, Pierre, that this soul comprehended" (396). Pierre, in consequence, at times regards her as if she were a child or a primitive, remarking her "artless infantileness" and "changeless youthfulness" (164–65), and she, in turn, at times regards Pierre as if he were her parent:

> 'Thy hand is the caster's ladle, Pierre, which holds me entirely fluid. Into thy forms and slightest moods of thought, thou pourest me; and I there solidify to that form, and take it on, and thenceforth wear it, till once more thou moldest me anew. If what thou tellest me be thy thought, then how can I help its being mine, my Pierre?'

It is this unselfconsciousness and inability to rationalize that causes her to be unaware of her sexual appeal ("there is no sex in our immaculateness" 175); unaware that she is encouraging Pierre in his incestuous passion ("if thy sister can ever come too nigh to thee, Pierre, tell thy sister so beforehand" 391); and unaware of the presence of that passion when Pierre all but cries "incest" aloud and again invokes the encroachment of the walls:

> She blew out the light, and made Pierre sit down by her; and their hands were placed in each other's.
> 'Say, are not thy torments now gone, my brother?'
> 'But replaced by— by— by— Oh God, Isabel, unhand me!'

cried Pierre, starting up. 'Ye heavens, that have hidden yourselves in the black hood of the night, I call to ye! If to follow Virtue to her uttermost vista, where common souls never go; if by that I take hold on hell, and the uttermost virtue, after all, prove but a betraying pander to the monstrousest vice,—then, close in and crush me, ye stony walls, and into one gulf let all things tumble together!'

'My brother! this is some incomprehensible raving,' pealed Isabel, throwing both arms around him;—'my brother, my brother!' (320–21)

Yet although she is innocent, she is cunning (particularly after Mrs. Glendinning's death when she subsumes the role of the temptress and falls more nearly into opposition with Lucy). Indeed, only then does she really begin to understand the power of her sexuality and begin to use it deliberately: for instance, she opens a door while Pierre kisses her so that Lucy can see them (393). She becomes as jealous of Lucy as Mrs. Glendinning once was of her (368), calling Lucy "worthless" (368), as she had been called by Mrs. Glendinning, in deepest rage, "Some *slut*" (228). Isabel is at least four times described in snake imagery ("coiled," 226; "glided," 393; "slid," 411; "nestling," 425), and she bears in her "bosom a secret adder" (225). The path to her home in the woods is "serpentining" (131). And whereas, on one occasion (quoted above), she is unaware of the possibility of incestuous passion, on another, *earlier*, occasion, she seems quite well to intuit its presence:

> The girl moved not; was done with all her tremblings; leaned closer to him, with an inexpressible strangeness of an intense love, new and inexplicable. Over the face of Pierre there shot a terrible self-revelation; he imprinted repeated burning kisses upon her; pressed hard her hand; would not let go her sweet and awful passiveness.
>
> Then they changed; they coiled together, and entangledly stood mute. (226)

The fact is that Isabel is hopelessly double: "the object of the ardentest and deepest emotions of . . . [Pierre's] soul . . . transfigured in the highest heaven of uncorrupted Love" (167), Isabel finally becomes his Bad Angel and her sex the poison which finally kills him. " '[I]n thy breasts, life for infants lodgeth not, but death-milk for thee and me!—The drug!' and tearing her bosom lose, he seized the secret vial nestling there" (425).

Isabel is, in fact, a woman more suited to Poe than Melville; even her name is Poesque, and once—in the line "Yes, those envying angels did come down" (39)—Melville seemingly paraphrases "Annabel Lee." Isabel's face, we are constantly reminded, unites Beauty with Grief in a way that sublimates its sexuality, a conjunction Poe had previously made in "The Poetic Principle" of 1850; although the notion is common enough in romantic literature. *Pierre* also illustrates Poe's dictum that the Death of a Beautiful Woman is a supreme literary theme, and it borrows directly from "Ulalume": while the Poe-figure and Psyche, his soul, wander in the "ghoul-haunted woodland," they observe at the end of their vista "Astarte's bediamonded crescent"; similarly, when Pierre and Lucy ride to the forest region above Saddle Meadows, near the dangerous "Babylonian walls," Pierre suddenly exclaims in the astrological language reminiscent of "Ulalume": "Ha! I see Venus' transit now" (41). Both maidens respond identically: Psyche cries, ". . . oh, let us not linger!/Oh, fly! let us fly! for we must"; Lucy, "let us up, and fly these hills, whence, I fear, too wide a prospect meets us. Fly we to the plain" (44). Pierre and Lucy, of course, fly, but too late, for Isabel has already slid between them. The Poe-figure and Psyche proceed onward to the end of the vista where the tomb of Ulalume, his dead lover, intercepts them. That is, in each instance, the pure love of man for maiden is forestalled—psychologically by Isabel, literally and allegorically by Ulalume.[56]

In *Mardi*, Taji rejects marriage by pursuing Yillah and avoiding the marriageable Hautia; in *Pierre*, Pierre makes the same rejection by pursuing Isabel and avoiding the marriageable Lucy. It is irrelevant that in the earlier novel the rejected is the Dark Lady and in the latter the Light, for each quester realizes that his motive for "rescuing" the maiden is impure, and, in fact, in their first interview, Pierre finds Isabel sexually irresistible. What happens is that she plays the guitar for him, and, as Dr. Murray has pointed out,[57] the guitar "is

wittingly used by Melville as a womb symbol." (Pierre is entertained
on the first floor of the cottage; on the second, the seduced Delly
Ulver—Melville puns sexually on both names, "ulva" meaning womb
in Sanskrit—punctuates their conversation with her footsteps.) Isabel
plays "delicious sounds," music which, to the accompaniment of erotic
images, unquestionably arouses erotic impulses in Pierre. At first "the
sounds hung pendulous like glittering icicles from the corners of the
room; and fell upon . . . [Pierre] with a ringing silveryness; and
were drawn up again to the ceiling, and hung pendulous again, and
dropped down upon him again with the ringing silveryness" (148).

> . . . while with every syllable [of sound] the hair-shrouded form
> of Isabel swayed to and fro with a like abandonment, and sud-
> denness, and wantonness:—then it seemed not like any song;
> seemed not issuing from any mouth; but it came forth from
> beneath the same veil [Isabel's "long dark shower of curls"] con-
> cealing the guitar. (149)

At this moment Pierre reaches a reciprocal peak of sexual excitation.
"Now a strange wild heat burned upon his brow; he put his hand to
it," and when he does, the moment passes. "Instantly the music
changed; and drooped and changed; and changed and changed; and
lingeringly retreated as it changed; and at last was wholly gone"
(149)—the rhythm and repetition of the words apparently an attempt
to capture not only the spirit of the music but the declension of sex.

In one sense Isabel is rather curiously like Redburn: as an adult she
too does not quest, although in childhood, in temporary aberration,
she does. Like Redburn whose "insane desire" is to burst into the hull
of the glass ship, she has a "half-crazy" desire to find out what is at
the heart of her toy guitar. "Seized with this sudden whim, I un-
screwed the part [of the guitar] I showed thee [she is speaking to
Pierre] and peeped in, and saw 'Isabel' [her name inscribed]" (174);
that is, at the heart of her being, she finds her identity in her sex. She
is, one should add, at the time of her discovery in the first flowering of
adolescence (144–45). Her natural curiosity and the "wantonness"
of her playing; Pierre's plea, on recognizing his incestuous passion,
that she "unhand" him; the subsidence of his erotic impulses when
he touches his brow—these instances suggest that what Leslie Fiedler

remarked about *Moby-Dick* is also true of *Pierre*: that hand imagery "recurs in sensitive places" in the text: in *Moby-Dick*, notes Fiedler, in the sperm-squeezing scene and in Ishmael's nightmare, into which "it is tempting to read . . . a sense of guilt and powerlessness associated with the boy's special sin of masturbation."[58] In a comic vein, as we have already noted, masturbation is symbolized in the actions of Billy the tailor who "fiddles" when his wife won't have him; and, in a mood of resignation, in the Story of "The Fiddler" whose name is Master Betty (see below, p. 141). It is no accident that both are musicians, nor that a Carlo and Isabel play hand instruments too. (Melville's intuition came half a century before psychoanalysis suggested that playing a musical instrument in dreams is symbolic of onanism.) Finally we should note that the hollowed, often tapered enclosure is Melville's characteristic abstraction of the sexual organ, an image which ultimately merges with that of the Sacred Center to form a complex of life-energy symbols: the guitar (female); the fiddle (male); the organ (hermaphroditic); the whale (bisexual); the chimney (male or female); as well as such images of untapered enclosure as Inamorata's womb-room; Ishmael's coffin-buoy; the Typee and other fertile Valleys; the vortex which sweeps Ishmael to near death and ultimate rebirth and other mandala figures.

In their second interview, which not unnaturally begins for Pierre with feelings of guilt (168), Isabel again plays her guitar and again he responds to her sexual appeal—what Melville elliptically calls her "physical magnetism":

Now first this night was Pierre made aware of what, in the superstitiousness of his rapt enthusiasm, he could not help believing was an extraordinary physical magnetism in Isabel. And— as it were derived from this marvellous quality thus imputed to her—he now first became vaguely sensible of a certain still more marvellous power in the girl over himself and his most interior thoughts and motions;—a power so hovering upon the confines of the invisible world, that it seemed more inclined that way than this;—a power which not only seemed irresistably to draw him toward Isabel, but to draw him away from another quarter [Lucy of course]—wantonly as it were, and yet quite ignorantly and unintendingly; and, besides, without respect apparently to anything ulterior, and yet again, only under cover of drawing him to her. For over all these things, and interfusing itself with the sparkling electricity in which she seemed to swim, was an ever-creeping and condensing haze of ambiguities. Often, in after-times with her, did he recall this first magnetic night, and would seem to see that she then had bound him to her by an extraordinary atmospheric spell— both physical and spiritual —which henceforth it had become impossible for him to break, but whose full potency he never recognized till long after he had become habituated to its sway. (178)

But even as Pierre unknowingly falls beneath Isabel's unintending spell—thus Melville announces their original innocence—Pierre still expects to love her "with the pure and perfect love of angel to an angel" (181) and does not recognize his incestuous passion until he "coils" with her and experiences his "terrible self-revelation." He does not, however, at once reject this passion but, on the contrary, permits himself to be titillated by it. For although he attacks (166) and disavows (205–6) genuine marriage, he enters into a pseudo-marriage with Isabel (which is, after all, playing at incest because the "marriage" *is* pseudo—and is never consummated). The fact is that Pierre can no more commit incest with Isabel than Ahab can catch the White Whale. In *Pierre* it is done, like Lucy's defloration, lexically, not literally—again, only so to speak. Isabel, hearing that Lucy is to join them at the Apostles', becomes instantly jealous, falls into a faint, and, using the only weapon at her disposal, her sex, murmurs

'My bed; lay me; lay me!'
The verbal effect broke her stiffening enchantment of frost [cf. the "glittering icicles" of the guitar-playing sequence]; her thawed [cf "drooped"] form sloped sidelong into the air; but Pierre caught her, and bore her into her own chamber, and laid her there on the bed. (367)

That Melville knew sexual slang is, I think, undoubted: he was, after all, a sailor and serviceman before the mast; and what he did not learn from life, his favorite author, William Shakespeare, in whom he could find ample precedent, could supply. That he would use such slang in such puns as this one is also undeniable: the crude "archbish-oprick" joke in *Moby-Dick* is evidence enough. Whether "lay" (or, for that matter, "screw," upon which he could punningly neologize) was American slang in 1851 is, of course, hard to determine, but it seems to have been.[59]

It is only during their twilight encounter at the Apostles' that the titillations of incest become torturous, and it is then that Pierre makes the key decision of his later career, deciding—in accordance with his new insight—that he

'will gospelize the world anew, and show them deeper secrets than the Apocalypse!—I will write it, I will write it!' (321)

That is, he will become a religious artist-prophet, not remain just a literary dilettante. He does not, however, really try to reconstruct their lives—although on one occasion he does try to resist Isabel's "self-proffering form" (391)—because he feels that the task is im-possible:

For in tremendous extremities human souls are like drowning men; well enough they know they are in peril; well enough they know the causes of that peril;—nevertheless, the sea is the sea, and these drowning men do drown. (357)

Instead he compounds his sin and guilt by lying now to Isabel about his feelings for her just as he has previously lied to his mother, Lucy, Delly, and his schoolboy chum, Charlie Millthorpe. Like Hawthorne, he begins to feel the "heartless[ness]" of the observing artist (368) who has severed just and humane relationships in the pursuance of his art. For in the conviction that he is a "genius" (350), Pierre forces himself to slave eight and one-half hours a day on a book which, as Melville himself tells us, is immature (397).

Pierre's problems are compounded further when Lucy—now emer-gent from her swoon and convinced that she is his guardian angel—decides to join him and Isabel in New York. If she was asexual be-fore, she is positively angelic now. Nevertheless, her "terrible" (385) purity fascinates Pierre, and, before long, she displaces Isabel in his imagination, as she had, in fact, done twice previously:[60] ". . . more and more did she seem, hour by hour, to be somehow inexplicably sliding between them, without touching them" (397). But of course each time that Lucy dislodges Isabel, she is soon, in turn, herself dislodged, for, after Mrs. Glendinning's death, the girls do, more or less, become opposites, and Pierre cannot finally choose between them. Does he want "Lucy or God?" (213), or, as Melville puts it elsewhere, "The catnip [Lucy] and the amaranth [Isabel]!—man's earthly household peace, and the ever-encroaching appetite for God!" (405). (We are here provided with a good example of what Milton Stern calls "the richly reflexive character of Melville's use of words."[61] Isabel is metaphorically denoted "amaranth," while the woman whose personality she has in part subsumed, Mrs. Glendinning, is at the outset described in her "amaranthiness") (3). Lucy's emergence at the Apostles', then, may be taken as one last attempt on Melville's part to reconcile those opposing forces that had riven his protagonists for so long: Marriage (Lucy) and the Quest (Isabel).

Unlike Ishmael, who compromises his antagonistic desires, Pierre can find no mean between asexual marriage and incestuous sex. Nor is Ishmael's homoerotic solution available to Pierre, although, in his youth, he did cherish a reciprocated love for his cousin, Glendinning Stanly. Subsequent events, however, have driven them to the point of hatred: Glen is secretly jealous of Lucy's love for Pierre, and, in the wake of Mrs. Glendinning's disinheritance of her son, Glen disowns him as well. It has been remarked that in the reversal of the name "Glendinning" and in the fact that both "Pierre" and "Stanly" ultimately derive from words meaning "stone," that Glen is Pierre's alterego; and, in fact, Glen is precisely what Pierre is not—a scoundrel and a sophisticate; mannered, continentally educated, and at home in fashionable New York society. Glen is, in effect, Pierre's wickedly opposing self, the Pierre who not only would violate Lucy's "secret inner shrine" and commit "murder" there but who would, by marrying her, commit legalized rape as well. (Cf. her "secret inner shrine" with the "secret inner chamber and sanctum sanctorum" from which Queequeg rescues Tashtego obstetrically.) Melville is never explicit —here or elsewhere—about sex crime, but there is an unmistakable tone to his voice. For instance, it is Glen who, struggling with Lucy on the staircase at the Apostles', "defile[s her] by . . . his touches"

(382). And it is to Glen that Pierre screams, "By Heaven, had I a knife, Glen, I could prick thee on the spot" (281). But, perhaps, in cognizance of the sexual pun and in secret allusion to his fear that Glen would marry Lucy if he could, Pierre as much means that he would castrate Glen as stab him to death. And, in point of fact, Pierre does kill Glen by discharging both bullets from a brace of pistols (422)—a symbolic self-castration that is premonitory of his own suicide, for, as in Poe's "William Wilson," the protagonist kills himself soon after he kills his alter-ego.

Mutilation and death are, in fact, Pierre's final reward for being the Fool of Truth, for making the harrowing discovery that his passion for Isabel may very well have emerged "purely of an intense procreative enthusiasm" (416) and that—at the picture gallery where he sees *The Cenci* of Guido—the crimes for which he is responsible, psychologically if not literally, are incest and parricide. Melville's imagination, I think, boggled at establishing their actual occurrence, but actually portrayed or not, involvement in sexual passion, conjoined with his quest to overcome the wall, inevitably leads Pierre to maiming and suicide. Time and again his wound is suggested: when he identifies himself with the castrated Titan, Enceladus, "without one serviceable ball-and-socket above the thigh" (407); when he walks into his room at the Apostles' "and slowly shoot[s] . . . the bolt—which, for want of something better, happened to be an old blunted dagger—" (419)—no cutlass, no harpoon, no potent instrument, just "an old blunted dagger"; when he suffers deteriorating eyesight and fears the possibility of blindness; and, finally, when he cries, ". . . Pierre is neuter now!' (425). Not that "neuter" is not to be taken in more senses than one, but that one of those senses should be sexual.

In short, Pierre is a drowning man who, despite his discoveries, must drown, and fortunately Melville manages to recapture, in these final chapters, some of the cumulative intensity of the three days' chase in *Moby-Dick* and the sense of impending shipwreck that awaits the quester. "The dark vein's burst," mourns Charlie Millthorpe, kneeling at Pierre's side, "and here's the deluge-wreck-all stranded here!" (426). Nor does sexual vitality save those two other drowning men: Queequeg with "Sagittarius or the Archer" ". . . in the vicinity

of his thigh," and Felipe, the "new-wedded husband" of Hunilla in
"The Encantadas." Felipe's "body floated to the marge, with one arm
encirclingly outstretched. Lock-jawed in grim death, the lover-hus-
band softly clasped his bride, true to her even [Melville really means
"only"] in death's dream" (91). One recalls that Pierre and Isabel
lie together but once—again, only in death; in the book's last line:

> . . . her whole form sloped sideways, and she fell upon Pierre's
> heart, and her long hair ran over him and arboured him in ebon
> vines. (427)

For in Melville ideal heterosexuality is always the condition of death,
not life.

Pierre is split into two nearly perfect halves: the first thirteen chapters are set in Rural Saddle Meadows, the last thirteen in Urban New
York, and although Melville is obviously distinguishing between two
kinds of Society, his ultimate distinction is between two kinds of Culture.[62] For Saddle Meadows is, in several significant respects, a medieval world, and New York City a post-Renaissance one. Described in
terms of Ptolemaic astronomy, Saddle Meadows is a "closed" universe, encircled by a containing Babylonian "wall" as the "wall" of
the ninth sphere encircles the realm of the fixed stars; it is spatially
finite. Beyond the wall is the Empyrean; within, the sublunary organ-
ism Nature through which He reveals Himself by divine correspondence. Pierre believes he lives in direct communion with the transcendent God. The Divine Resident of Saddle Meadows is the
matriarchal Mary Glendinning, the "Queen" (13); her son is Pierre,
the Rock and would-be Christ, who, like the village folk, is a devout
Mariolotrist. In a secular sense, he reminds us, as he reminds William
Ellery Sedgwick, of Sir Galahad.[63] It is Pierre who wishes he had a
sister to champion (6) and who would confront in single combat the
"Black Knight . . . with visor down" (76). The economic structure
of Saddle Meadows is the feudal farmer-tenant system (11, 343);
the social order is hierarchical, and, at its center, is the Glendinning
family whose heritage is "richly aristocratic" (11). Pierre's grand-
father owned a "knight-making sword" (317).

But in Melville's vision the Medieval Universe is fatally tainted. Mary, not a true Queen of Heaven—in fact, a conspirer with Reverend Falsgrave—is without mercy or charity. And although she is still beautiful, she is "not very far from her grand climacteric" (17); by strict definition, "grand climacteric" refers to one's sixty-third year, but, loosely speaking, to a "critical year . . . of marked change, as in human life." And since she is "nearly fifty years old" (15), I should hazard that Melville means that she is nearing the end of her menstrual cycle. In other words, the sexual vitality that inspirits her and grants her her beauty is soon to die.

Like her, her son is also a simulacrum, a false Christ, as Dr. Murray alleges, not a true one (although I will cite only the bare bones of his argument here):[64]

> In the first place, Pierre is only nominally Christian. . . .
> In the second place, before meeting Isabel, Pierre is a natural unredeemed egoist. . . .
> Thirdly, since Pierre's Christ-like compassion is wholly bestowed upon Isabel, his feeling is markedly different from the evenly distributed loving-tenderness of Jesus. Jesus committed himself to a relationship with no other human being, notably with no woman. His only obligation was to God.

As a youth, Pierre used to spend

> long summer afternoons in the deep recesses of his father's fastidiously picked and decorous library; where the Spenserian nymphs had early led him into many a maze of all-bewildering beauty. Thus, with a graceful glow on his limbs, and soft, imaginative flames in his heart, did this Pierre glide toward maturity, thoughtless of that period of remorseless insight, when all these delicate warmths should seem frigid to him, and he should madly demand more ardent fires. (5)

The library: an apt emblem for Saddle Meadows herself—fastidious, decorous, beautiful, a society Spenserian, not Shakespearean, whose residents are unwilling to plunge to the axis of reality. In all, Saddle Meadows is an ambiguous world of green—of both youth and decay—an hermetically childish civilization, dominated by an aging Goddess and a false Savior.

Rejecting its insufficiency (if unable to recognize his own), Pierre moves into the post-Renaissance World of New York[65] but, in Melville's hands, the modern world fares no better than the medieval. Its Divine Inhabitant is no longer a Matriarch but the Male God of the Reformation. Except that, by 1851, God himself is post-Protestant, the uncaring Deist Nobodaddy who, never speaking, non-benevolently observes; a secular Deity living in an abandoned church: His Presence unfelt; His Voice Silence; His Universe "open," infinite without boundary; His Nature deanimate, no conduit to the Divine.

In such a universe, Transcendentalism (like the Dutch Reformed Creed of Melville's youth) is useless baggage, and Melville flails it with ridicule and scorn. Yet, at the same time, Pierre completely fails to achieve any rapport with Plinlimmon, a circumstance equally intolerable.

The politics of the modern world, embodied in the brainless Charlie Millthorpe, are not authoritarian but democratic, or better, mobocratic: "I have every confidence in the penetration and maganimousness of the people" (330), says Charlie, as he bids Pierre stump the state on the Kantian ticket.[66] Its society is not based in invidious feudal distinctions, but on the obliteration of all distinctions, for New York is a "vulgar caldron" (7), the last refuge of the dispossessed. And Pierre, allegorically the Earth in Richard Chase's exegesis,[67] who was once at the center of his universe is now, in New York, just another orbiting planet. New York is harsh and ugly, a stone city, ultimately ruinous to body, mind, and spirit. And yet it is the Real World, the only world, just as Saddle Meadows is the false Paradise from which Pierre has irrevocably disinherited himself. And this is the reason Melville intersperses so many vignettes in the second half of *Pierre*; why time and again, the characters whose original milieu is rural confront urbanites: stage-coach drivers, policemen, a prostitute, hotel-keeper, book-seller, porter, turnkey: all people of flesh and substance who explode into life. And whereas in *Moby-Dick* and *The Confidence-Man* a boatload (albeit, in the latter a Ship of Fools) is the symbol of collective humanity, the only instance of random humanity in *Pierre* is a disgorged brothelful. New York *is* the Modern World, Melville wants us never to forget, reality drained of appearance.

And so Melville's indictment is total, and *Pierre* is his supreme curse and malediction, his paradigm of disillusion: metaphysical failure, sexual failure, cultural failure; the failure of God, man, and civilization. And the failure too of the primitive ethos, the archetypal quest for the Sacred Center:

> Yet now, forsooth, because Pierre began to see through the first superficiality of the world, he fondly weens he has come to the unlayered substance. But, far as any geologist has yet gone down into the world, it is found to consist of nothing but surface stratified on surface. To its axis, the world being nothing but superinduced superficies. By vast pains we mine into the pyramid; by horrible gropings we come to the central room; with joy we espy the sarcophagus; but we lift the lid—and no body is there!
> —appallingly vacant as vast is the soul of man! (335)

The past is beautiful but false; the present is real but intolerable. How then shall Man recover the prodigiously eloquent synthesis of Beauty and Truth, Past and Present in the prairie city in the sea of *Moby-Dick*? Pierre's self-appointed task, in other words, is nothing less than the reunion of sundered halves, the association of sensibility; and he intends to offer the world nothing less than a new Revelation and a new Scriptures. "I will gospelize the world anew," he cries, "and show them deeper secrets than the Apocalypse" (321). And so, in quest of Final Truth, Pierre descends the "spiral stair in a shaft" and discovers only that the shaft is endless, that the vein in the marble, the crack in the hearth, has become a deepening abyss. Little Pip plunges to the unwarped, primal depths and returns with Heaven's Wisdom, but Pierre plummets endlessly through the bottom of the night.

A s never before in the Melville canon, the hero of *Pierre* confronts an unsymbolized representation of the Mother, the dominant and domineering Mrs. Glendinning; the conflict, in other words, is finally out in the open—although the language Melville uses to describe her coincides frequently with the language he uses to describe the Whale. Pierre is clearly her son-lover, one of those whom Neumann characterizes as "strugglers,"[68] and he far supersedes Ahab in the level of ego consciousness and degree of disengagment from the Mother he achieves. For, unlike Ahab who is unafraid, Pierre's

> fear of the Great Mother is the first sign of centroversion, self-formation, and ego stability. This fear expresses itself in various forms of flight and resistance [cf. Pierre's lying to his mother about Isabel and his flight to New York]. [But] the primary expression of flight, which is still completely under the dominance of the Great Mother is self-castration [Pierre's fate symbolically] and suicide [his fate literally].[69]

Nevertheless, Pierre does finally drive Mrs. Glendinning to her grave, although he does not struggle without assistance and, in fact, could not have succeeded alone. Isabel is his "femme inspiratrice," as Dr. Murray puts it[70]—an all-important relationship, to which we shall return.

In the books preceding *Moby-Dick* the Captive is never free of the symbol of the Mother-archetype. Inamorata is resident within the house; Fayaway, within the valley; and Yillah, as Mohi makes plain, is Hautia's prisoner:

> 'Listen; and in his own words will I recount the adventure of the youth Ozonna. It will show thee, Taji, that the maidens of Hautia are all Yillahs, held captive, unknown to themselves . . . .' [IV, 392]

But

> The transformation which the male [Ahab as transpersonal Quester] undergoes in the course of the dragon fight includes a change in his relation to the female, symbolically expressed in the liberation of the captive from the dragon's power.[71]

This captive, liberated from the Mother-archetype, appears in Melville's next book for the very first time; she is Isabel:

> In other words, the feminine image extricates itself from the grip of the Terrible Mother, a process known in analytical [that is, Jungian] psychology as the crystallization of the anima from the mother archetype.[72]

Indeed, Dr. Murray has long since identified Isabel as Pierre's anima, the feminine "soul-image" in the man.[73] Or, at least we should say that this is Isabel's role in the early stages of her relationship with Pierre. She is "anima-sister, both as the captive awaiting the deliverance and as the helper, is related to the higher masculinity of the hero, i.e., to the activity of his ego consciousness."[74]

> It is a tremendous step forward when a feminine, 'sisterly' element—intangible but very real—can be added to the masculine ego consciousness as 'my beloved' or 'my soul.' The word 'my' separates off from the anonymous, hostile territory of the unconscious a region which is felt to be peculiarly 'my' own, belonging to 'my' particular personality. And although it is experienced as feminine and therefore 'different,' it has an elective affinity with the masculine ego which would have been unthinkable in connection with the Great Mother.[75]

In the development of the transpersonal Quester, then, the separation of the Sister from the Mother cannot be underestimated, and, in fact, it is, as I have said, only through Isabel's inspiration—if not instigation—that Pierre is able to battle Mrs. Glendinning. "The freeing and winning of the captive form a further stage in the evolution of masculine consciousness,"[76] a stage, we recall, Ahab was not able to attain.

Unfortunately, however, Pierre is not able to *maintain* his psychological advance and soon begins to regress. That is, he soon finds himself under the control of another Mother-figure who dominates him much of the time; for, after Mrs. Glendinning's death—the point is crucial enough to repeat—Isabel, to some degree, assumes her character. On one occasion she asks Pierre if her face is Gorgon's (222), and although he answers "nay," it is quite clear that he will soon answer yes. And as befits a man whose name is Pierre, he does fall under her Medusan spell and is finally turned to stone. Freud's analysis of the Gorgon as the castrating mother is precisely what we should expect:

> We have not often attempted to interpret individual mythological themes, but an interpretation suggests itself easily in the case of the horrifying decapitated head of Medusa.
> To decapitate = to castrate. The terror of Medusa is thus a

terror of castration that is linked to the sight of something. Numerous analyses have made us familiar with the occasion for this:
It occurs when a boy, who has hitherto been unwilling to believe the threat of castration, catches sight of the female genitals, probably those of an adult, surrounded by hair, and essentially those of his mother.[77]

In the context of this remark we remember that Isabel asks her question of Pierre—". . . is my face Gorgon's?"—*after* he has watched her dance and sing with her hair-shrouded guitar; and, in fact, it is only after she asks her question—that is, after he becomes aware of the "threat of castration"—that he admits he is a symbolic castrate. Thus the personalistic interpretation meaningfully coincides with the transpersonalistic one, for, as Erich Neumann writes, the Gorgons are "uroboric symbols of what we might justly call 'the Infernal Feminine.' "[78]

Isabel, then, erstwhile holy sister, comes to resemble the Terrible Mother, but, as she does, so Lucy, prospective wife, becomes holy sister. And as it is through the agency of Isabel that Pierre is able to confront Mrs. Glendinning at the outset, it is through the influence of Lucy, his "Good Angel," that he is able to neutralize Isabel at the end. Thus Pierre overcomes the Mother not once but twice in a psychomachia of heroically purgative proportion, the profoundly sane act of a psyche discovering itself. But, as *Pierre* testifies, at what immense sacrifice! And therefore it is small wonder that women are generally absent from or consigned to minor roles in Melville's fiction throughout the rest of the fifties and that Melville does not represent (i.e., engage) the Terrible Mother again until *Battle-Pieces* (1866). For he needed time to recoup his powers and consolidate his gains before he could renew the struggle with her.

C. "BARTLEBY"

"Bartleby" (1853), Melville's first published fiction after *Pierre*, a deceptively simple tale told in a deceptively comic tone, is, nevertheless, the deadly-serious coda to Melville's metaphysical "trilogy," the gesture of an unreconstructed demonist. And, therefore, although "Bartleby" can be enjoyed without reference to the Melville canon— it is, after all, autonomous and self-illuminating—our appreciation of it deepens as we read it in context.

Bartleby is a wisp of a man who subsists on ginger-nuts, who glides quietly or is motionless, who lives hermit-like, who speaks almost nothing at all and who, eventually, does as little, preferring to stare from his window in a "dead-wall reverie." He is a solitary, in his way particularly American—consider the laconic Deerslayer or Thoreau at Walden; particularly Melvillean—consider Ahab on the quarterdeck or Taji in the open boat; particularly Modern—consider the non-communicative Gregor Samsa or Prufrock who thinks and thinks but talks and acts not at all. Bartleby is even particularly Urban, for it is in the city that the incidence of schizophrenia is highest. But if Bartleby is mentally ill, he is also spirtually ill, and there is a great difference between illnesses.

It has been pointed out by Richard Chase and others that Bartleby is a surreal representation of the artist—indeed Melville's own projection of the artist in a misunderstanding society—dislocated, unproductive, derided, and ridiculed.[79] But what has not been noted is the identity of Bartleby's employer, the "eminently *safe*" Narrator (4), who succeeds by being "unambitious." He is, I think, the very same "author" about whom Melville wrote these words in his review of Hawthorne's *Mosses*:

> It is true that but few of them [American writers] as yet have evinced that decided originality which merits great praise. But that graceful writer who perhaps of all Americans has received the most plaudits from his own country for his productions—that very popular and amiable writer, however good and self-reliant in many things, perhaps owes his chief reputation to the self-acknowledged imitation of a foreign model, and to the studied avoidance of all topics but smooth ones. But it is better to fail in

121

originality than to succeed in imitation. He who has never
failed somewhere, that man cannot be great.

In accordance with our tale the Narrator is an elderly gentleman, a
New Yorker, and a lawyer who would, if information were available, write Bartleby's biography. He once did legal work for John
Jacob Astor (4), and, on one occasion during the course of the story,
pays "fugitive visits to Manhattanville and Astoria" (42). As a literary figure, our Narrator is none other than Washington Irving, born
in New York, a lawyer in his youth, and now, in 1853, an elderly
gentleman whose principal concern is biography (*Life of Oliver
Goldsmith*, 1849; *Mahomet and His Successors*, 1850); who published *A History of New York* in 1809 and *Astoria*, a glorification
of John Jacob, in 1836, and revised it in 1849.

Following this track of reasoning, may we also determine the actual
identities of Turkey and Nippers, Bartleby's "co-authors"? I think not,
for Melville seems principally concerned with establishing them as
opposites. For one thing, as Richard Fogle remarks, "Turkey is an
Englishman, Nippers an American, and Melville makes them national
types according to the mythology of the nineteenth century in which
the beefy, stolid English John Bull stands over against the lean and
restless Yankee."[80] Turkey is about sixty years old, is insolent only in
the afternoon, and is described as "flighty." But he is associated with
earth as well as air—which may account for his nickname—because,
like a knight, he deploys his columns of writing, puts himself at
their head, and gallantly charges his foe; his lustrous face is called
his "augmented blazonry," that is his heraldic coat-of-arms. Yet,
though vaguely aristocratic, he dresses poorly, and drink is his recurring problem. His opposite, Nippers, is about twenty-five years old, is
irritable only in the morning and is described as "fiery." But he is associated with water as well as fire since he is called "piratical," and
thus Melville would seem to have divided the elements between them.
Nippers is a "ward-politician," a rather proletarian occupation for
one's spare time; he dresses well, but constantly suffers from indiges-
tion (5–11).

If Bartleby is a portrait of the artist, he is also a representative
man. In this variegated world of great heroes like Ahab and great

fools like Pierre, Melville focuses on this obscure individual, who appears suddenly out of nowhere, whom no one knows or cares to know, who knows no one; about whom nothing is known—neither parentage, birthplace, nor even family name: a mythically anonymous figure. At first he works "silently, palely, mechanically," a cog in the legal machine. And we who are neither heroic nor foolish enough to identify ourselves with Ahab or Pierre are, or can readily envision ourselves, small enough to become Bartlebys. In his regimented world there is no place for craft creativity, and Bartleby, the anonymous cipher, has the least creative job of all, copying. Of course he soon breaks down, but one wonders whether it is his eyes or his spirit which really gives way. The implicit alternative to Bartleby's drudgework is the high romantic art of Lord Byron (12), and, in this tale, there are no opportunities for expression between these extremes. Does Bartleby perhaps remind us of that other fittingly silent, forlorn man trapped in the workaday world he never made, the character portrayed by Charlie Chaplin? He well may, for Bartleby too is something of a comic figure. But his fate is not amusing, and it haunts us.

We are similarly affected by the Narrator. He is remarkably—to borrow Conrad's phrase—like "one of us." In fact, his conscience is our conscience, and we see ourselves reflected in his actions. Can we doubt then that he is really a very decent chap, understanding and generous to the limits of reasonable behavior, even if he does believe that the "easiest way of life is the best" (4)? For instance, when Turkey, the scrivener who rages after twelve o'clock, makes blots on official documents, the Narrator can be persuaded not to fire him: "fellow-feeling," he calls it and compromises by giving Turkey less important papers in the afternoon. Then the Narrator discovers Bartleby's unwillingness to proofread copy; however, since he is doing a quantity of other work, since he is honorable and never absent, since he is "perfectly harmless in his passivity," and since it is clear that the Narrator has a "not inhumane temper," Bartleby is permitted to stay. His "eccentricities are involuntary," is the Narrator's opinion. Furthermore, by humoring Bartleby, the Narrator can, as he says, "purchase a delicious self-approval . . . a sweet morsel for my conscience." (17)

Of course, at times the Narrator is infuriated by Bartleby's refusals to cooperate, but he is careful never to do anything rash. His tie with the scrivener closens substantially one Sunday morning when he discovers that Bartleby is living in his law office. He reflects on Bartleby's "miserable friendlessness and loneliness." "The bond of a common humanity now drew me irresistibly to gloom. A fraternal melancholy! For both I and Bartleby were sons of Adam" (22–23). On further reflection, however, pity yields to common sense. If Bartleby is suffering from an "incurable disorder," as he manifestly is, concludes the Narrator, there is only one thing to do: get rid of him. And in truth no one wants an inexplicably and incurably disordered man on his premises. Of course their settlement will be amicable: the Narrator will give Bartleby twenty dollars above his salary, pay his expenses home, and even give him a letter of recommendation if one is requested. But, on the next day, the Narrator perceives Bartleby's "dull and glazed" eyes; pity overwhelms him, and he suggests Bartleby abstain from copying.

But Bartleby abstains permanently, and, therefore, when the pressure of business forces his hand again, the lawyer gives him six days' notice. Bartleby, however, does not leave as bidden, and our respectable Narrator is thoroughly perplexed. "Turn the man out by an actual thrusting I could not do; to drive him away by calling him hard names would not do; calling in the police was an unpleasant idea" (32). Falling into a state of nervous tension, he feels the "old Adam of resentment" welling within him. He remembers the story of how Colt, an infuriated businessman, alone with Adams, killed him (34); that is, how Cain, alone with Abel, once slew his brother.[81] The Narrator fortunately saves himself, as he tells us, from Old Testament wrath by recalling the New Testament injunction: " 'A new commandment give I unto you, that ye love one another.' " Thus he saves himself, he insists, by charity and love.

And with his new attitude toward Bartleby he "penetrate[s] to the predestinated purpose of my life. I am content. Others may have loftier parts to enact; but my mission in this world, Bartleby, is to furnish you with office-room for such period as you may see fit to remain" (35). But again business considerations intrude, this time of a more serious nature; his professional reputation is beginning to suffer. Now he *must* free himself of his "intolerable incubus" (37). In desperation he changes his office: he will leave his scrivener, if his scrivener will not leave him. But, within a few days, the new occupant of his old Wall Street address insists he is responsible "for the man you left there." The Narrator responds, with "an inward tremor," that "he is no relation or apprentice of mine, that you should hold me responsible for him." For he does feel qualms of conscience, and although he recognizes a certain "charitable prompting" to call at his old quarters, "a certain squeamishness" prevents him from returning (39).

In a final attempt to free himself from the scrivener, he suggests all sorts of jobs that might interest Bartleby (including that of a conversationalist!); he even offers to take Bartleby home with him until a satisfactory arrangement is worked out. All to no avail. Bartleby prefers to stay where he is, and the Narrator flees the building and the city. He reasons that since he has tried his best to protect Bartleby, he should feel "carefree and quiescent," but in fact he feels neither, for his conscience does not quite justify him in the attempt. Upon his return to New York he learns that Bartleby has been jailed. Pathetically, he tries to convince the prisoner that life in the Tombs—with the sky overhead and the grass underfoot—is not so bad, but Bartleby rejects him unequivocally. He bribes the grubman to feed Bartleby well, but Bartleby dies unfed.

Thus the Narrator is not "Non-Benevolent," but one who is willing to assist his fellow-man only within "reasonable" limits; as long as that assistance does not demand that he commit himself wholly. Do we not here recognize something in ourselves? For example, does a dime (or even a dollar) in a blindman's tin ever really assuage a guilty conscience and leave us "carefree and quiescent"? We can argue, of course, that neither the Narrator nor we are saints and that we should not be expected to sell all we have and give it to the poor; but even if we did, it would still, like providing Bartleby with living space, be only a first step in the right direction. We shall have to go further, for we are bidden to "love one another," and none of us is completely able to disregard this injunction.

Therefore, the lawyer who once regarded Bartleby as another son of Adam, a brother, who retold and, in effect, rewrote the story of Cain and Abel, who finely mouths the words of charity and love, does not finally remain his brother's keeper, and it is, indeed, ironic to watch him high-mindedly preach, but not practice, his Christianity. Somehow he never seems to understand precisely what it is he has failed to do. Not graced with Plinlimmon's insight, the Narrator never understands Bartleby as Plotinus does Pierre. Plinlimmon will not help a man in trouble; the Narrator seemingly cannot. His is as much a failure of nerve and intellect as of love. In his one moment of illumination, he divines—too late—the spiritual chasm which separates him from the scrivener. "Ah, Bartleby!" he cries, "Ah, humanity!" And that cry haunts us too.

Let us dwell more carefully on this haunted and haunting quality, which is perhaps the major effect of the tale. In addition to the reason I have already adduced—our identification with both major characters in a tale of man's inhumanity to man—let us suggest another, the several strange disparities of plot and structure: the disparity between the thinness of the plot (an obscure man lives for a while and then dies—the coroner will undoubtedly say of malnutrition) and its profound significance as a redaction of one of man's most meaningful stories; and, second, the disparity between the Narrator's retelling of the plot (which he consistently undervalues) and that significance. For we sense throughout that we are in the presence of something more important than the Narrator's words and limited comprehension signify. In both instances, a gnawing semi-apprehension grips us. And, finally, there is the disparity between the rational Narrator and the tale itself, which seems to be taking place in a whimsical fairyland where one of the major characters seems to be crazed and two minor ones enchanted.

The central meaning of this tale, however, can be richly annotated by comparing Bartleby with Pierre, for Bartleby re-enacts, in strangely altered terms, Pierre's New York career. Pierre comes to the city and dies there in jail; Bartleby suddenly emerges in New York and also dies there in jail. Previously, Pierre had quarters in a lawyers' building; Bartleby had quarters in a lawyer's office. Solitary Pierre, we are told, might have been alone at the Pole; Bartleby, we are told, is a "bit of wreck in the mid-Atlantic." Both men, like Melville himself, are writers, and both suffer from eyestrain and overwork. Pierre ultimately declares himself "neuter"; Bartleby is apparently sexless. Other parallels will follow, but, having established the essential connection, let us describe the great difference between them. Pierre is garrulous and articulate; Bartleby is silent and enigmatic. Pierre is a man of deed and action; Bartleby is a man of thought and preference. Pierre is intemperate and harried; Bartleby is sober and spiritualized. In a word, Pierre is active, and Bartleby is passive. Pierre is also a man, and Bartleby is often referred to as a ghost. And it is significant that as Pierre dies in one book, Bartleby should emerge in the next, for Bartleby is the burnt-out and resurrected image of his former self, Pierre made passive. We are not—I should hastily add—entirely unprepared for this strange resurrection. Both Captain Ahab (after being dismasted by Moby Dick) and Lucy Tartan (who swoons into a lengthy coma) are both resurrected as people temperamentally other than their former selves.

In his last days (the time of our tale) Bartleby, like Ahab and Pierre, obsessively confronts Secular Reality. But whereas the aggressive questers ram against and apostrophize the whale-wall, Bartleby, a passive quester, just stares at it from a three-foot distance through his private window in the lawyer's office. In point of fact, though, he learns exactly as much (or, rather, exactly as little) from it as Ahab and Pierre learned before him: exactly nothing. Bartleby, however, to a culminatory degree, is trapped by and within external surfaces, by "the terror and implacability of existence," in Mordecai Marcus' phrase.[82] In front of the only other two windows in the office there are also stone walls, one black, the other white, and it is impossible for Bartleby to see around, beyond, or through them.[83] Furthermore, Bartleby deliberately confines himself, as much as possible, behind a green screen (12), itself ironically symbolic of his own "one insular Tahiti." He is walled in, in this ironic tale of Wall Street. And just as Melville refers to a whale's head as a "cistern" in *Moby-Dick*, so in "Bartleby" the lawyer's office is said to be surrounded by a "cistern" (5), however dry—an allusion to its enveloping sterility. For Bartleby who lives and works not only within confining walls but within a confining cistern too has, in effect, been swallowed by the whale, is imprisoned and cannot escape. Tashtego, we recall, was reborn from a whale's head in the "obstetrics" scene in *Moby-Dick*, but Bartleby dies in the Tombs (womb?) "huddled at the base of the wall, his knees drawn up, and lying on his side . . ." (45) in the fetal position, unreborn. For unlike Father Mapple who, in the whale's belly, calls upon his Deliverer God and is rescued, the Melvillean quester doubts His operativeness on earth and dies. In Melville God never answers those, like Ahab, who would force His secrets, nor those, like Pierre, who ask for signs, nor those, perhaps like Bartleby patiently before the wall, who expect those signs revealed. The final irony of Bartleby's situation is that we, as readers, know what is behind the wall, and we know it is not worth having, the Encantadan landscape of "grimy backyards and bricks." (11) Absolute Reality, as Pierre said of Virtue, is "trash."

The geography of the lawyer's office—in which Bartleby sets up light housekeeping—is reminiscent of only one other setting in all of Melville: Inamorata's womb-apartment, which the Youth invades. Both rooms are on the second story and seem to have no connection with the ground below. The Youth enters through a window; Bartleby stands, as if paralyzed, before one. The apartment is resplendently decorated with paintings of love, symbols of fertility and fruitfulness; the lawyer's office, on the other hand, has but one decorative object, an austere bust of Cicero, who himself once studied the law. The décor of the room, in other words, again bears some psychological relation to its occupant: in a barren "womb," in a barren season, a plaster-of-paris bust—fittingly lifeless and hollow in a tale which symbolizes the failure of love and the Quester's resubmission to the Great Mother.

Although I shall not deny that Bartleby is, at least to some degree, "deranged" (as the Narrator says), "luny" (as Ginger Nut says), and "schizophrenic" (as some critics say), I would maintain the spiritual as well as clinical etiology of his illness. For as a Melvillean quester, his behavior betrays a familiar pattern, and there is really no difference, save in matter of temperament, between Ahab, "madness maddened," throwing himself at a whale he finally knows he can never catch and Bartleby standing before a wall in the Tombs he knows he can never penetrate. Acting as if by reflex—for each knows all hope is gone—each dies in defiant confrontation: one, aggressively, wishing to die; the other, regressively, perhaps wishing he had never been born.

But as a counterpoise to man's insanity, Bartleby is not unblessed with heaven's sense. Like Pierre, he too is trying to establish significant contact with another human being, a quest even more important than his attempt to penetrate the wall. In his private way he is seeking (not a sister, but) a father, the Narrator himself. (This search for the father is, as Richard Chase has perceived, a common Melvillean motif.) And now we suddenly understand the crazy logic behind Bartleby's "I should prefer not to"; he is trying, through seemingly irrational conduct, to make the Narrator respond chronometrically, that is, in a saintly, not a human, way. Of course, Bartleby knows what being rational and reasonable is; on one occasion he even quite frankly admits that he "would prefer not to be a little reasonable." For Bartleby knows that being reasonable and explaining himself and his quest would give the Narrator, a kindly gentleman, the opportunity to act—reasonably. Out of an understanding and generous heart, the Narrator, intellectually aware of Bartleby's plight, might even offer to adopt him. What could be more generous? But such an adoption, born of the understanding intellect, would be a human or horological act of charity. And Bartleby seeks a chronometrical relationship, one which may not be verbalized, one which must emerge solely and with all possible purity from the heart not the head, one which passeth human understanding and reasonable human behavior. The Narrator cannot be asked to commit himself; he must do so of his own free will. He must make a supreme effort of conscience to accept Bartleby not on his own terms but on the scrivener's. But the Narrator, a bachelor, one uncommitted to life, cannot love, and Bartleby fails in his impossible quest.

There are several other ways in which Bartleby's career also parallels Pierre's. For instance, long before each man meets his death, each has, in effect, been warned to stop questing—in the form of a "hell-glimpse" into the human personality. For Pierre it is his recognition of incestuous desire for Isabel, whom he has tried to love spiritually. For Bartleby it is the knowledge, gained at the Washington Dead Letter Office, that love and charity, pardon and hope, the significant things men live by and need most, always come a little too late to do any good. Both questers, then, have learned something about man so important that it should be powerful enough to crack the false opinion each harbors about himself: that he can form a holy relationship with a fellow mortal. Pierre is immediately disillusioned by this "hell-glimpse," summarily concludes that spiritual values do not exist, but disregards the warning nonetheless, and plunges to final homicide and suicide. Whether Bartleby is similarly disillusioned at the Dead Letter Office we may only suppose, but he too continues trying to live the chronometric life. Our tale records his failure, and his fate parallels Pierre's. For both men agree to die in prison when life is no longer worth living, after it proves, once and for all, horological.

Just before his death, however, Pierre dreams that he is Enceladus flinging himself against the insurmountable walls of heaven. With the grass under his feet and the sky over his head, he has tried to scale the Cheopian pyramid to the Ultimate, but Secular Reality has defeated him. This same situation recurs in "Bartleby," when the passive quester stands forlornly in the Tombs:

> The surrounding walls, of amazing thickness, kept off all sounds behind them. The Egyptian character of the masonry weighed upon me [says the Narrator] with its gloom. But a soft imprisoned turf grew under foot. The heart of the eternal pyramids, it seemed, wherein, by some strange magic, through the clefts, grass-seed, dropped by birds, has sprung. (45)

Milton Stern, writing of *Pierre*, suggests that grass in the apparently sterile mountains of Pelion and Ossa symbolizes "the cyclic life-death continuum—the immortality of mortality. . . ." "The images of stone and green," he continues, "suggest that man's only immortality is his collective and historical mortality—the heritage of each generation handed down to the next in all the awful responsibilities of time."[84] Nor is it then accidental that when Bartleby dies, his head, like Pierre's is touching the cold stone. For Bartleby also fails to protect the human heritage, on behalf of the grass communicates with the stone.

Søren Kierkegaard, who died in 1855, wrote "the comical is present in every stage of life, for wherever there is life there is contradiction, and wherever there is contradiction the comical is present. . . . In truth, no age has so fallen victim to the comic as this." Wylie Sypher, interpreting Kierkegaard, adds, "and the most absurd contradiction of all is that man must risk everything without insurance against losing everything. This is precisely what ordinary 'Christians' refuse to do, Kierkegaard finds; they wish to find a 'safe' way to salvation, to find God without being tormented, and to base faith on what is probable, reasonable, assured."[85] The Narrator, we remember, is an "eminently *safe*" man and a reasonable one too, but Bartleby—and I have tried to suggest the same about his creator—risks all without insurance.

A tale like "Bartleby," as Sypher says of Dostoyevsky, embodies the "frightening ['comic'] clarity of the grotesque reducing life, as totally as tragedy, by means of a perspective that foreshortens everything, to absurdity."[86] Here, for instance, is an example of "frightening ['comic'] clarity," the kind of comedy Melville tried, but with little success, at the end of *Pierre*. While Bartleby is waiting patiently for death, the Narrator introduces the ungrammatical grubman to the scrivener. When they are alone again, the Narrator remarks that his friend is a "little deranged." "Deranged? Deranged is it?" repeats the grubman. "Well, now, upon my word, I thought that friend of yourn was a gentleman forger; they are always pale and genteel-like, them forgers. I can't help pity 'em—can't help it, sir" (45). Here then is Bartleby dying, with all its terrible present and primeval significance, and here is the grubman pitying genteel-like forgers (The ironies multiply, for the copyist *is*, after all, a kind of forger.) This scene causes a "laughter so raw that it brings grimaces hardly to be distinguished from tragic responses. The force of this comic 'shock' is like the 'qualm' stirred by tragedy; it can disorient us, 'disturb' us as confusedly as tragic calamity."[87] This force is the essence of "Bartleby."

In sum, then, in its redaction of man's archetypal predicament; in its compelling recreation of two representative men, two unforgettable images of ourselves; in its introduction of Biblical, mythic, and symbolic dimensions; in its spare, lean prose which moves swiftly, directly, and inexorably from climax to climax to conclusion; in the slow and horrifying growth of the reader's comprehension as he watches it unfold; in its surreal collocation of absurd grotesquerie (imagine Turkey sealing a document with a ginger-nut!) and moving pathos; in its narrative mastery and effortless delineation of character: in all these ways and by all these means, "Bartleby" is a superbly conceived and executed tale—extraordinarily affective, profounding disquieting—with the exception of *Moby-Dick*, Melville's most successfully realized fiction.

4. Quelled Enthusiast

"Cock-A-Doodle-Doo!" through
"Fruit of Travel Long Ago"

With *Moby-Dick, Pierre,* and "Bartleby," Melville plunged to his inmost leaf, and, afterwards, although there was much left to say, it must have seemed to him that there was little left to discover. He had posed some essential questions: Can Man know God? Can Man love Man? Can Man freely create?—and had supplied an omnibus "NO—in thunder." He had vicariously participated in the lives of his heroes: Ahab, who seeks God and dies; Pierre, who would love Isabel and fails; Bartleby, who would write but cannot. And, therefore, although Melville persevered in the '50s—seventeen more short stories, two novels, a travel journal, and a volume of poetry—the thrust and intensity that mark the prose of his major phase is no longer evident. And as his "NO" becomes more and more definitive, his work also announces a gradual discouragement with and disengagement from the quest. But the *problem* of the quester did not disappear simply because it was proved unsolvable: the splendid labyrinth, Melville now realized, was really a cul-de-sac, but his quester was trapped in it nonetheless.

In his first story after "Bartleby," Melville took immediate relief in gallows' humor: the certainty of despair (after the anxiety of hope) is its own compensation. The narrator of "Cock-A-Doodle-Doo!" is a farmer (that is, an inland resident) who has, in effect, retired from the quest. He is no longer young and is obviously drained of energy.

It was a cool and misty, damp, disagreeable air. The country looked underdone, its raw juices squirting out all round. I buttoned out this squitchy air as well as I could with my lean, double-breasted dress-coat—my overcoat being so long-skirted I only used it in my wagon—and spitefully thrusting my crab-stick into the oozy sod, bent my blue form to the steep ascent of the hill. This toiling posture brought my head pretty well earthward, as if I were in the act of butting it against the world. I marked the fact, but only grinned at it with a ghastly grin. (119)[1]

Bartleby never feels a "comic shock" in butting against the natural world, and, therefore, never realizes that the joke is on him, but the protagonist of "Cock-A-Doodle-Doo!" has learned the futility of questing and marks his symbolic act with a "ghastly grin." His general mood, however, is one of depression, and the weather is only one reason why. He remembers how a "good friend and thirty other good fellows were sloped into eternity" (120) in a railroad accident; he sees his "miserable-looking set" of calves, "six abominable old hair-trunks wandering about here in this pasture" (123). He thinks of his creditor, who duns him every Sunday in church; of sick babies; and, in the language of a minor Lear, of his own dyspeptic health:

> Yet what's the use of complaining? What justice of the peace will right this matter? Yea, what's the use of bothering the very heavens about it? Don't the heavens themselves ordain these things—else they could not happen? (121)

Then in his despair he hears a cock crow—

> *Glory be to God in the highest!*' It says those very words as plain as ever cock did in this world. . . . It plainly says—'*Never say die!*' (123)

and, like Whitman's child in "Out of the Cradle" who understands the song of the "he-bird," the narrator professes to understand the song of the rooster without the intermediation of symbols, as if he too were a kind of super-Transcendentalist. Immediately he feels better and soon feels "wild"; the weather clears; his fields blossom; the train, which he had formerly called an "iron fiend" and a "death monopolizer," now "chirps"; his creditor no longer disturbs him; even his kine dance happily. He soon discovers that whenever the cock crows, his mood shifts radically from deep depression to maniacal joy; and that his "philosophy of life" shifts from submission to the Absurd to espousal of the Ideal:

> I bowed my head, and felt forlorn—unjustly used—abused—unappreciated—in short, miserable.

Hark! like a clarion! yea, like a jolly bolt of thunder with
bells to it—came the all-glorious and defiant crow! Ye gods, how
it set me up again! Right on my pins! Yea, verily on stilts! (134)

For Chanticleer is, after all, a Transcendental fowl and was used by
Emerson and Thoreau as the symbol of regeneration and renewal,
the herald of the dawn, a bird of pride, self-reliance, and solitary
scorn (128). His golden color (139, 145) also indicates his Transcendental nature, another instance of Melville's use of gold to symbolize the Absolute. The narrator, his head turned completely, deter-
mines to buy the rooster even if it means clapping another mortgage
on his house, a mortgage he knows he cannot afford: like Ahab, he
seeks an animal whose name is a phallic pun and whose body supposedly incarnates the Ideal.

Melville also suggests the phallicism of the cock by associating him
with musical instruments: for instance, the cock crows like a "bugle"
(128), and one remembers how in "The Paradise of Bachelors" one
of the aging gentlemen handles but does not blow an obviously phallic "bugle" or "horn" (194)—which in turn reminds us of the phal-
lic-horn imagery of *Moby-Dick* (see above, p. ——). The cock's
nickname is "Trumpet" (141), and it is perhaps not without significance that the narrator of "Cock-A-Doodle-Doo!" himself an aging
bachelor, is called a "trump"—the cock's name apocopated! In any
event, the narrator traces Chanticleer through his crowing to the cottage of a poverty-stricken wood sawyer named Merrymusk, but the
sawyer knows the value of his bird and refuses to sell him at any price.

Born in Maryland (pronounced Merryland), Merrymusk's early
adventures parallel his creator's: like Melville, he too was once a
wandering sailor, who jumped ship (in Batavia, not Typee), caught
a fever (cf. Melville's wounded leg), and came near dying, but ral-
lied, reshipped, and finally landed in America. Then striking "for the
Northern interior" (137)—away from the sea of his youth—Merrymusk, like that other ex-sailor John Marr (see below, p. ——), retires
from the quest and becomes an inland man. That he is married and
has four children (Melville had already fathered three at the writing
of the tale) further indicates the seriousness of his renunciation. But
even more important to him than his family is his rooster, and man

and fowl are not only identified with one another in name and sexual energy (the word "musk" derives from the Sanskrit for testicle) but also in final fate (they both die happily) and centrality of vision.[2] Merrymusk is a man who has suffered and is suffering but whose spirit is indomitable:

> He was tall and spare, with a long saddish face, yet somehow a latently joyous eye, which offered the strangest contrast. His air seemed staid, but undepressed. He wore a long, gray, shabby coat, and a big battered hat. This man had sawed my wood at so much a cord. He would stand and saw all day long in a driving snow-storm, and never wink at it. He never spoke unless spoken to. He only sawed. Saw, saw, saw—snow, snow, snow. (135)

Like Merrymusk, the rooster also concentrates on what he does best and also manages to mitigate the hard knocks of the absurd world:

> Nor did it sound like the foolish, vain-glorious crow of some young sophomorean cock, who knew not the world, and was beginning life in audacious gay spirits, because in wretched ignorance of what might be to come. It was the crow of a cock who crowed not without advice; the crow of a cock who knew a thing or two; the crow of a cock who had fought the world and got the better of it, and was now resolved to crow, though the earth should heave and the heavens should fall. It was a wise crow; an invincible crow; a philosophic crow; a crow of all crows. (127)

But to the degree that each resigns himself to his fate and dies unresistingly, he denies the intelligence of his vision. Thus from his deathbed Merrymusk proclaims his health and the health of his dying wife:

> 'And the children?'
> 'Well, All well.'
> The last two words he shouted forth in a kind of wild ecstasy of triumph over ill. (145)

Needless to say, the children also die without suffering; and then the cock dies, the symbol of spiritual and sexual transcendence, although he lives on in the heart of the narrator, who, "under all circumstances crow[s] late and early with a continual crow," permanently manic at last (147).

If the story is not without ambiguity, it is because ambiguity inscribes itself upon its final meaning. We recognize in Merrymusk's stoicism a regulative principle the more impassioned narrator would do well to possess, but, at the same time, we cannot but observe that Merrymusk is doomed by his own best virtue. Similarly, as the golden cock dies, we mourn that Idealism cannot survive the world, but, at the same time, we rejoice in his death, for, alive, he tragically misguides the minds and hearts of men. For instance, the narrator is so overwhelmed by his crowing that

> I saw another mortgage piled on my plantation; but only bought
> another dozen of stout, and a dozen dozen of Philadelphia
> porter. Some of my relatives died; I wore no mourning, but for
> three days drank stout in preference to porter, stout being the
> darker color. (144) [cf. his anguished reaction to the death of
> his friend, noted above.]

But the saddest of all truths in "Cock-A-Doodle-Doo!" is that inland residents (like sea-farers), people who possess the Ideal (like people who seek it), people who are sexually vital (like those who are impotent) are *all* vulnerable: Melville perversely exhausts all possibilities of salvation, an old trick of his, taking an idea and driving it to an *absurdum*. And if the harmless and "normal" Merrymusk is doomed, then who is safe? "Cock-A-Doodle-Doo!" is Melville's apologia, his way of excusing himself for giving up the quest. But if he convinced his mind to withdraw, he hardly convinced his heart, and, as a section of his next work, "The Encantadas," indicates, he paid the price of regret for the necessity of denial.

"Sketch First" of "The Encantadas," "The Isles at Large," is a diabolically unmediated vision of the natural world:

> A group rather of extinct volcanoes than of isles; looking much
> as the world at large might, after a penal conflagration. . . .
> (49). Cut by the Equator, they know not autumn, and they know
> not spring; while already reduced to the lees of fire, ruin itself can
> work little more upon them. The showers refresh the deserts;
> but in these isles, rain never falls. Like split Syrian gourds left
> withering in the sun, they are cracked by an everlasting drought
> beneath a torrid sky. . . . (50) Little but reptile life is here

found: tortoises, lizards, immense spiders, snakes, and that
strangest anomaly of outlandish nature, the *iguana*. No voice, no
low, no howl is heard; the chief sound of life here is a hiss. . . .
(50–51) In no world but a fallen one could such lands exist. . . .
(51) Apples of Sodom, after touching, seem these isles. (53)

In Melville's allegory, the "peculiar reptile inhabitant" of this hell
on earth is the giant tortoise, the implacable quester:

> . . . there is something strangely self-condemned in the appearance
> of these creatures. Lasting sorrow and penal hopelessness are in
> no animal form so suppliantly expressed as in theirs. . . . (53)

(One thinks first of Bartleby, self-condemned, entombed, hopeless.)

> As I lay in my hammock that night, overhead I heard the slow
> weary draggings of the three ponderous strangers along the
> encumbered deck. Their stupidity or their resolution was so great,
> that they never went aside for any impediment. One ceased his
> movements altogether just before the mid-watch. At sunrise I
> found him butted like a battering-ram [as if he were Pierre]
> against the immovable foot of the foremast, and still striving,
> tooth and nail, to force the impossible passage. That these tor-
> toises are the victims of a penal, or malignant, or perhaps, a
> downright diabolical enchanter, seems in nothing more likely than
> in that strange infatuation of hopeless toil which so often pos-
> sesses them. I have known them in their journeyings ram them-
> selves heroically against rocks, and long abide there, nudging,
> wriggling, wedging, in order to displace them, and so hold on
> their inflexible path. [Like Pierre's] their crowning curse is
> their drudging impulse to straightforwardness in a belittered
> world. (57–58)

The "penal, or malignant, or perhaps . . . downright diabolical enchanter," who abuses the quester is God, once an "equivocal conjuror,"
soon to be a Confidence Man.

The tortoise, however, is not only the quester but also the object
of the quest, just as Moby Dick is finally lure *and* assailant, and like
the Whale, he is of "dateless, indefinite endurance" (57). "What
other bodily being possesses such a citadel [except, of course, the
Whale] wherein to resist the assaults of Time?" (57). The exterior

of both creatures is "impregnable" and covered with "ciphers," and just as the Whale is presumably Secular and Sacred, so the tortoise has two sides, one dark and melancholy, the other bright and yellowish. Simply because one "cannot turn the tortoise from its natural position . . . and expose his livelier aspect," one should not "declare the creature to be one total inky blot" (56)—the mistake, we remember, is Ahab's not Ishmael's. Like the Whale and Golden Cock, the Tortoise is also the putative sanctum of the Absolute. "Ye oldest inhabitants of this, or any other isle, said I [to the tortoises], pray, give me the freedom of your three *walled* towns" (57). (Italics added.) And Melville, the youthful adventurer of 1841, seems to have taken that liberty, for

> . . . next evening, strange to say, I sat down with my shipmates, and made a merry repast from tortoise steaks and tortoise stews; and supper over, out knife and helped convert the three mighty concave shells into three fanciful soup-tureens, and polished the three flat yellowish calipees into three gorgeous salvers. (59)

But now, in 1853, Melville himself is a retired quester, although "leaving the crowded city to wander out July and August among the Adirondack Mountains," he still recalls, "as in a dream . . . other and far distant rovings in the baked heart of the charmed isles. . . ." (54). He remembers "the sudden glimpses of dusky shells, and long languid necks . . . [protruding] from the leafless thickets. . . ." (54) "I can hardly resist the feeling that in my time [for he knows his time of questing is done] I have indeed slept upon evilly enchanted ground." (54) And he is haunted by his experiences:

> Nay, such is the vividness of my memory, or the magic of my fancy, that I know not whether I am not the occasional victim of optical delusion concerning the Galapagos. For, often in scenes of social merriment, and especially at revels held by candlelight in old-fashioned mansions, so that shadows are thrown into the further recesses of an angular and spacious room, making them put on a look of haunted undergrowth of lonely woods, I have drawn the attention of my comrades by my fixed gaze and sudden change of air, as I have seemed to see, slowly emerging from those imagined solitudes, and heavily crawling along the floor, the

ghost of a gigantic tortoise, with "Memento*****" burning in
live letters upon his back. (54)

. . . scarlet letters burnt into the tortoise's back, memorializing the
death of the quest. "Did you ever lay eye on the real Equator?" Melville challenges the armchair admiral. And then, more pertinently,
"Have you ever, in the largest sense, toed the line?" (69).

One of the most fascinating of the Encantadas is the "least unproductive," Barrington Isle.

> 'I once landed on its western side,' says a sentimental voyager
> long ago [Melville himself in a moment of reminiscence], 'where
> it faces the black buttress of Albermarle. I walked beneath
> groves of trees—not very lofty, and not palm trees, or orange
> trees, or peach trees, to be sure—but, for all that, after a long sea-
> faring, very beautiful to walk under, even though they supplied
> no fruit.' (77)

This island is a "secure retreat, an undiscoverable hiding place . . .
in the centre of a vast and silent sea" (76), "a harbor of safety, and
a bower of ease" (77)—Melville's Great Good Place. It is populated
by buccaneers who make occasional forays into the outer world, but
who are, in the main, content to sit and philosophize on the stone
benches they have built for themselves. Many of them, Melville admits, "perpetrated the greatest outrages," but there were others "whose
worst reproach was their desperate fortunes—whom persecution, or
adversity, or secret or unavengeable wrongs, had driven from Christian society to seek the melancholy solitude or the guilty adventure
of the sea"—one thinks, for instance, of Taji ("persecution" by the
Captain of the *Arcturion*), Ishmael and Melville himself ("adversity"), and Ahab ("unavengeable wrongs"). Tommo's experience is
recaptured in "Sketch Ten":

> A sullen hatred of the tyrannic ship will seize the sailor, and he
> gladly exchanges it for isles which, though blighted as by a
> continuous sirocco and burning breeze, still offer him, in their
> labyrinthine interior, a retreat beyond the possibility of capture.
> (113)

Barrington Isle (if not all The Isles at Large) is not very unlike Melville's own Adirondack refuge, a quasi-paradise for bachelors.

As the sailor no longer toes the line, so another projection of self, the artist, no longer seeks Truth. Ahab and Ishmael are now retired buccaneers; Pierre and Bartleby give way to Helmstone, a poet in "The Fiddler" who ultimately renounces his art. Although he is at first desolated by adverse criticism, Helmstone's spirits revive under the influence of Hautboy, a man of forty who looks like a boy of twelve and who, as a twelve-year-old prodigy named Master Betty (another sexual pun on a name),[3] once dazzled British audiences with his fiddling. Now living in obscurity, Hautboy amuses himself and his companions by playing folk airs: in other words, he has compromised his high art, disavowed his great fame, and embraced a regressive sexuality.

Nevertheless, Hautboy is extraordinarily happy. At a circus performance, Helmstone watches him and is astonished by what he sees:

> Such genuine enjoyment as his struck me to the soul with a sense
> of the reality of the thing called happiness. The jokes of the
> clown he seemed to roll under his tongue as ripe magnum bonums.
> Now the foot, now the hand, was employed to attest his grateful
> applause. At any hit more than ordinary, he turned upon Standard
> [a mutual friend] and me to see if his rare pleasure was shared.
> (234)

Although Hautboy's behavior seems childish, Helmstone does not lose his respect

> Because all was so honest and natural, every expression and atti-
> tude so graceful with genuine good-nature, that the marvelous
> juvenility of Hautboy assumed a sort of divine and immortal air,
> like that of some forever youthful god of Greece. (234)

For Hautboy possesses what all the manic questers lack, the "low, enjoying power" and "a certain serene expression of leisurely, deep good sense." He is a parody of Plinlimmon.

> Good sense and good humor in him joined hands. As the conver-
> sation proceeded between the brisk Standard and him—for I
> said little or nothing—I was more and more struck with the ex-
> cellent judgment he evinced. In most of his remarks upon a variety
> of topics Hautboy seemed intuitively to hit the exact line between

enthusiasm and apathy. It was plain that while Hautboy saw
the world pretty much as it was, yet he did not theoretically
espouse its bright side nor its dark side [as the questing tortoise
apparently does]. Rejecting all solutions, he but acknowledged
facts. What was sad in the world he did not superficially gainsay;
what was glad in it he did not cynically slur; and all which was
to him personally enjoyable, he gratefully took to his heart. It was
plain, then—so it seemed at that moment, at least—that his
extraordinary cheerfulness did not arise either from deficiency
of feeling [cf. Pierre's estimate of himself] or thought [cf.
his estimate of Charlie Millthorpe]. (235–36)

Nevertheless, Helmstone remains unconvinced of Hautboy's genius:
if he is happy, reasons the poet, it is because he is not, like me, an
ambitious dreamer," because "Nothing tempts him beyond common
limit. . . ." "For a genius to get rid of his genius [as Hautboy has
seemingly done] is as impossible as for a man in the galloping con-
sumption to get rid of that" (237). But then he hears Hautboy play
"Yankee Doodle" (Melville once wrote for a newspaper of that
name), and he is "transfixed by something miraculously superior in
the style" (239). No doubt about it: "*With* genius and *without* fame,
[Hautboy] . . . is happier than a king" (240). "Next day I tore all my
manuscripts, bought me a fiddle, and went to take regular lessons of
Hautboy" (240), thereby embracing, in a stroke, the denial of serious art and its analogue, mature sexuality.

Hautboy is a truly preposterous character (even more than Merrymusk) because he is created on the arbitrary assumption that a quester
can become a non-quester through an effort of will. In point of fact,
however, such a conversion is impossible. Only the non-questers, Jack
Chase and Rolfe (of *Clarel*), are abundantly endowed with serenity,
good sense, and intelligence, and are still believable persons. But Melville was trying desperately to draw the analogy between the Fiddler
and himself as two neglected geniuses who could thrive without public recognition.

Melville's generic name for the individual who glories in defeat is
"The Happy Failure," and this is, in fact, the title of another of his
stories. In this tale, a man who has worked for ten years on a swamp-

draining invention gleefully acknowledges the failure of his experiment. His contraption is a

> multiplicity of convoluted metal pipes and syringes of all sorts and varieties, all sizes and calibres, inextricably interwreathed together in one gigantic coil. It looked like a huge nest of anacondas and adders. (228)

It is housed in

> a huge, shabby, oblong box, hermetically sealed. The sphynx-like blankness of the box quadrupled the mystery in my mind.
> (223)

James Baird has interpreted the image of the anaconda in Melville's work as symbolic of the Urwelt, the pre-rational *"original world,"*[4] and in "The Happy Failure" this universe is concealed by a now familiar symbol of Secular Reality, a covering, sphynxlike and blank. In other words, the quester has sought to control the natural forces of the unseen world, and—as symbolized by the machine he cannot operate and the swamp he cannot drain—he fails. As ever, the quester suffers from the madness of over-reason, but as soon as he relinquishes the idea of questing, his head no longer denies his heart. His decision to give the mechanism to his faithful black, who "can sell the old iron for tobacco-money," (231) elicits this rejoinder:

> 'Dear massa! dear old massa! dat be very fust time in de ten long 'ear yoo hab mention kindly old Yorpy. I tank yoo, dear old massa; I tank yoo so kindly. Yoo is yourself again in de ten long 'ear.' (231)

The story is of course susceptible of other interpretations as well: for instance, the anaconda-machine may well symbolize the hidden and tangled realm of undifferentiated (not specifically sexual) drives —the Unconscious; here it is split apart from the Conscious mind (by being buried in the hermetically sealed box) and consequently unable to make itself felt—a circumstance tragic indeed for the author who spoke with such instinctive authority in *Moby-Dick*. From another point of view, we may regard "The Happy Failure" as symbolic of Melville's career as creative artist. With *Typee*, nine years previous (if not ten), he had begun writing novels and with *Mardi* had acquired his characteristically aggressive stance: now he would drain the swamp of the popular mind, drain it of its misconceptions and show it Truth. But the swamp of course refused to cooperate, and the machine broke down and was almost broken up by its inventor; similarly, Melville soon stopped writing (his fiction constantly prophesies his estate), and there is some evidence that in his failure and frustration he directed some of his anger against himself.

"The Happy Failure," then, like "The Fiddler," is another pathetically unfortunate tale in which Melville, certain now of the sterility of questing, tries to accept defeat gracefully. But his tone rings false, and his argument lacks conviction. "Boy, I'm glad I've failed," says The Happy Failure. "I say, boy, failure has made a good old man of me. It was horrible at first, but I'm glad I've failed" (231). And, at his deathbed, his nephew remarks:

> . . . as I took my last look at his venerable face, the pale resigned lips seemed to move. I seemed to hear again his deep, fervent cry—'Praise be to God for the failure!' (232)

And it is a cry that echoes hollowly for nearly forty years until that other "happy failure," the first and only convincingly drawn one in the Melville canon, Billy Budd, finally redeems it with his "God bless Captain Vere!" and redeems too the Fiddlers and Jimmy Roses, abortive attempts at final reconciliations.

Jimmy Rose, protagonist of a tale which bears his name, is a once-wealthy businessman who ultimately swallows his pride and accepts a genteel poverty. For it is "pride" (253), as symbolized by the peacock wallpaper in his home that inevitably leads to his downfall:

> In short, the original resplendence of the peacocks had been sadly dimmed on that north-side of the room. . . . [M]any of the once glowing birds seemed as if they had their princely plumage bedraggled in a dusty shower. (243)

The bedraggled peacock should also be taken as a sexual pun, and, in fact, it establishes the analogy between the failure of Jimmy's mercantile career and the impotence of his solitude and bachelordom. And, as is frequent in Melville, there is a sexual pun on a character's name: when he was successful, Jimmy rose. But his triumph is in the past, for now he is fallen.

Like "The Happy Failure," "The Lightning-Rod Man" and "The Bell-Tower" also concern themselves with Man's short-sighted attempt to impose his will on Nature. In the former, a door-to-door lightning-rod salesman, who plies his trade during electric storms, is rebuffed by a householder—but again the tale has underground levels, and means, finally, much more than it says. The salesman claims that only his product offers complete protection from Nature's fury and that, by its judicious use, Man can, in effect, influence the ways of God on earth. Although he is a Confidence Man in his techniques of persuasion—he brandishes his rod as if it were a magic "wand" (216) —he very probably does believe in his product: "*Mine*," he asserts proudly, "is the only true rod [read 'God']" (216).[5] In allegorical terms, the salesman is a conventional religionist, a believer in a wrathful, but mollifiable, Deity.

Without his talisman, however, he offers no guarantee, although he is not without provisional advice: when the thunder crashes, seek the center of a room and stay there, he suggests, and, in fact, on entering the mountaineer's home, he takes a place "in the *exact middle* [the '*safest part*' (218)] of the cottage" (213). (Italics added.) His prospective client, on the other hand, perversely lingers in what seems to be the most dangerous place of all—near the outer wall:

'The current [explains the salesman] will sometimes run down a wall, and—a man being a better conductor than a wall—it would leave the wall and run into him.' (218)

The Lightning-Rod Man, that is, retreats to the place of primal innocence, according to the original version of Melville's myth, whereas the householder, believing that God's ways are good if finally inscrutable, stands exactly where he pleases and does not try to anticipate the workings of Diety. He is, we soon discover, a Transcendentalist:

'Who has empowered you, you Tetzel, to peddle round your indulgences from divine ordinations? The hairs of our heads are numbered, and the days of our lives. In thunder as in sunshine, I stand at ease in the hands of my God. False negotiator, away! See, the scroll of the storm is rolled back; the house is unharmed;

and in the blue heavens I read in the rainbow, that the Deity
will not, of purpose, make war on man's earth.' (221) (Italics
added.)

But the Lightning-Rod Man does not leave without a struggle and,
in fact, becomes violent:

> The scowl grew blacker on his face; the indigo-circles enlarged
> round his eyes as the storm-rings round the midnight moon. He
> sprang upon me [with] his tri-forked thing ... (221), a polished
> copper rod, four feet long, lengthwise attached to a neat wooden
> staff, by insertion into two balls of greenish glass, ringed with
> copper bands. (214)
>
> . . . .
>
> I seized it; I snapped it; I dashed it; I trod it; and dragging the
> dark lightning-king [who is rather Ahabian in complexion] out
> of my door, flung his elbowed, copper sceptre after him. (221)

It is, as Richard Chase has intimated,[6] a castration scene, and the
point of it is essentially this: unlike the Transcendentalist who, so to
speak, "accepts the universe," the man who persists in trying to control the forces of Nature and God must fail—be he Ahab, Pierre, or a
contemptible seller of lightning-rods—and his failure is not infre-
quently symbolized by a sexual injury.

The moral of "The Lightning-Rod Man" is even more forcibly ap-
plied in "The Bell-Tower," the tale of a Renaissance artist-mechanic
who would build "the noblest bell-tower in Italy," but whose pride
finally outruns his skill. In the cause of his craft, Bannadonna ruthlessly kills a workman with a caster's ladle, and when a splinter of
the dead man's scalp contaminates the molten mass, suppresses knowledge of the bell's fatal imperfection. In other words, Bannadonna
challenges both the Law of God and the Law of Nature and, in his
pride, expects to escape retribution. But his most arrogant act of all
is the construction of a mechanical carillionist, for, through the
agency of this soulless being, he seeks, like Ahab,

> to solve nature, to steal into her, to intrigue behind her, to procure
> some one else to bind her to his hand;—these, one and all, had
> not been his objects; but, asking no favors from any element
> or any being, of himself, to rival her, outstrip her, and rule her.

He stooped to conquer. With him, common sense was theurgy; machinery, miracle; Prometheus, the heroic name for machinist; man, the true God. (369–70)

(*To solve* Secular Reality, as if she were a puzzle or a maze; *to steal into* her, as if she contained the Absolute; *to intrigue beyond* her, as if she shielded the Absolute from sight.)

It is, therefore, a matter of elementary poetic justice that, as Bannadonna has slain, he should in turn be slain; that as he has inhumanly treated a fellow man, he should in turn be treated inhumanly by the monster he had created. And, one afternoon, while intently sculpting the figure of Una on the clock's face, Bannadonna forgets the time of day in the eternity of Art and is clubbed to death from behind by his automaton. In his role as artist, his death cannot but elicit our sympathy: for, like Pierre, he becomes the Fool of Truth, staring at Una, as Ishmael warns us not to stare at the fire, until it inverts him. But, as mechanic, in this Hawthornesque tale, Bannadonna seeks to uncover, *regardless of cost*, the secrets of the created universe and, in this role, deserves no pity whatever.

His inventions, metaphors of himself, are also short-lived: the mechanical man is immediately destroyed by the Luddite-like magistrates of the town; the bell in the "groined belfry" reveals its fatal blemish by cracking the first time it is rung; and the shaft collapses a year later. We may interpret the Fall of the Bell-Tower as symbolic of "cultural failure" as well as of "castration"[7]—neither the Jungian nor the Freudian reading invalidates the other—although only the latter is presently relevant: Bannadonna pays the quester's price for pride, maiming and death.

Those who survive unscathed are the non-questing Bachelors of the Inner Temple, an enclave of silence and slow time off bustling Fleet Street, a "cool deep glen, shady among harboring hills . . . in the stony heart of stunning London" (185); the Sacred Center, a Paradise where time is told "not by a water-clock" but a "wine-chronometer" (that is, by Heaven's "chronometric" time) (193). At the fertile heart of this Typeean landscape live the "Brethren of the Order of Celibacy" (189), bachelor-lawyers, like the encapsulated Narrator in "Bartleby," who also believed that the "easiest way of life is the best." Their mode of life enchants the Melvillean protagonist:

> Ah! when I bethink me of the sweet hours there passed, enjoying such genial hospitalities beneath those time-honored roofs, my heart only finds due utterance through poetry; and, with a sigh, I softly sing, 'Carry me back to old Virginny!' (189)

The song and its title are absurdly inappropriate, but Melville cannot resist a rueful pun: "Carry me back to old Virginity" is what he really sings, to an innocent day without care and worry and sex, when life was a Paradise for Bachelors:

> The thing called pain, the bugbear styled trouble—those two legends seemed preposterous to their bachelor imaginations. How could men of liberal sense, ripe scholarship in the world, and capacious philosophical and convivial understandings—how could they suffer themselves to be imposed upon by such monkish fables? Pain! Trouble! As well talk of Catholic miracles. No such thing. (193)

Perhaps the key word in the story is "snug": bachelor cells are "snug" (189), and so is bachelor furniture (190), and, at the end of a dinner party (". . . household comfort . . . was the grand trait of the affair" [193]), some of the guests are "driven snugly" home (195). In their insularity as non-questers, they reject knowledge of evil for childhood's pleasure, fulfillment for anticipation. For instance, after the bachelors dine, the narrator watches his host lift "an immense, convolved *horn*," (194), and

> Not having heard that our host was a performer on the *bugle*, I was surprised to see him lift this horn from the table, as if he were about to blow an inspiring blast. But I was relieved from this, and set quite right as touching the purposes of the horn, by his now inserting his thumb and forefinger into its mouth; where-upon a slight aroma was stirred up, and my nostrils were greeted with the smell of some choice Rappee. It was a mull of snuff. It went the rounds. Capital idea this, thought I, of taking snuff about this juncture. This goodly fashion must be introduced among my countrymen at home, further ruminated I.
> [*cf.* sperm-squeezing as a more vigorous example of human corporateness.]

The remarkable decorum of the nine bachelors—a decorum
not to be affected by any quantity of wine—a decorum unassailable
by any degree of mirthfulness—this was again set in a forcible
light to me, by now observing that, though they took snuff very
freely, yet not a man so far violated the properties, or so far
molested the invalid bachelor in the adjoining room as to indulge
himself in a sneeze. The snuff was snuffed silently, as if it had
been some fine inoxious powder brushed off the wings of butter-
flies. (194) (Italics added.)

The host holds his phallic horn or bugle but does not blow it; then
the bachelors take snuff but restrain themselves from sneezing; before retiring, some of the guests read the aphrodisiacal *Decameron*
—like holding the horn and inhaling the snuff—another mode of
stimulation without consummation. For the bachelors willingly experience life at second hand, just as they are content to substitute
(unknowingly, we may assume) one physiological pleasure for another, eating for sex. For that is how, I think, one may interpret their
elaborate seven-course feast—ox-tail soup, turbot, roast beef, mutton
and turkey and chicken-pie, game fowl, tarts and pudding, cheese
and crackers—bountifully consumed with claret, sherry, ale, and port.
One thinks of the native feasts in the bachelor grove of Typee and of
the lusty appetites of the harpooners aboard the *Pequod*. In Melville,
the orgy is always at table, never in bed.

"The Paradise of Bachelors" and "The Tartarus of Maids" comprise a "diptych," and, as the word suggests, their juxtaposition is not
casual. Melville, in fact, is playing at paradox: in Paradise, there is
fertility and age but no sex; in Hell, there is sterility and youth and
sex. "The Tartarus of Maids" is an anatomical allegory, set in the
womb (a "hollow . . . called the Devil's Dungeon," through which
runs Blood River [196]); a heavy-handed, grim, and embarrassingly
unfunny tale. The process of reproduction is allegorized as a paper-
making factory run by maids (the product is generally "foolscap"
—that is to say, fools) and, to the Dungeon, in search of a cheap and
dependable source of envelopes, comes a "seedsman," (196), that is,
a dealer in sperm:

Flaked all over with frozen sweat, white as a milky ram, his

nostrils at each breath sending forth two horn-shaped shoots of
heated respiration, Black, my good horse, but six years old,
started at a sudden turn, where, right across the track—not ten
minutes fallen—an old distorted hemlock lay, darkly undulatory
as an anaconda. (197–98)

(As for the operations of the paper-making machine and the equivalently mechanical process of gestation and childbirth, let every reader
decipher the obvious allegory for himself.) The maids' overseer is a
bachelor whose nickname is "Old Bach" (204)[8]—the name of a cele-
brated composer and organist—and his assistant is a youth called
"Cupid." Nevertheless, despite their presence and the orgastic intrusion of the seedsman, the girls are, and always will be, virgins (210);
for even at the place and moment of birth Melville discovers an in-
alterable sterility.[9]

Melville composed two other diptychs—"The Two Temples" and
"Poor Man's Pudding and Rich Man's Crumbs"—and, in these stories,
his strategy is also one of paradox, of inverting common notions and
setting conventional beliefs on end. For instance, in "The Two Temples" Melville juxtaposes a Church and a Theatre and ironically suggests that it is the former that is enveloped in an atmosphere of religion and solemnity. Temple First, a New York City Church, is
repeatedly called a "magic lantern" and the ceremony performed
therein a "theatric wonder," and "some sly enchanter's show" (150,
153). And, like an enchanter, the priest "vanished from the scene,"
before reappearing "through the same side door, his white apparel
wholly changed for black" (153–54). The audience seems "one of
buried, not of living men; when, suddenly, miraculously, like the
general rising at the Resurrection, the whole host came to their feet,
. . ." (154); it is like a magical trick, Melville means, the same kind
that God the Conjuror performed at the Resurrection.

Temple Second is a London theatre located in a comparatively quiet
street. "It was like emerging upon the green enclosure surrounding
some Cathedral church, where sanctity makes all things still"—yet
another image of the still point at the fertile center. "Thinking it
might prove some moral or religious meeting, [the protagonist hur-
ries] . . . towards the spot" (159) but gains entrance only when a by-

stander charitably offers him a ticket. (In "Temple First," a beadle denies him entrance because of his shabby clothes.) Inside the theatre, the ticket-taker is "like some saint in a shrine" (162), and, from his seat, he observes an urchin "hovering like a painted cherub over the vast human firmament below" (163) and the rest of the audience, a "devout congregation" (160). They are, one is led to believe, the salt of the earth, although it is the *other*, the American, congregation who hear themselves so addressed. The narrator, however, is so over-whelmed that he involuntarily bows his head, forgetting, in a moment of "lunacy," that he is not in a "house of prayer" (163). As for the play, with Macready playing Cardinal Richelieu, it proves a complete success and affords Melville a final irony: the actor mimicks the re-ligious and delivers a more convincing performance that the priest had done before him.[10]

In "Poor Man's Pudding"—the title itself bespeaks paradox—a poet of comfortable means insists that a poor farmer is not really poor at all. The poet, suggestively named Blandmour, simply does not un-derstand the reality of life in the woods, and his Transcendental in-nocence is staggering: he believes that Nature is a "blessed almoner . . . in all things beneficent" (167), and, in consequence, he euphe-mizes the plight of the poor. Snow is "Poor Man's Manure"; melted snow, "Poor Man's Eye-Water"; rainwater (used as a leaven in bak-ing), "Poor Man's Egg"; rice, milk, and salt, "Poor Man's Pudding," etc. Blandmour's ideas, however, are less Transcendental than Thor-eauvian, and one of the evident purposes of this tale is to refute some of the arguments of *Walden*. (Unfortunately, Melville missed or—more likely—rejected the wit of Thoreau's exaggerations and answered the thrusts of irony with an unbecoming seriousness.) Thoreauvian economy becomes Melvillean poverty; philanthropy, uncalculated cruelty; homegrown beans, Poor Man's Pudding; a pleas-ant saunter, a forced march; architectural purity, damp necessity: in all, the reality of subsistence living for the ideality of woodland life: poor food and insufficient clothing, inadequate furniture and ill-burning fires, dampness of body and dampness of soul, disease and death. "You find rare wisdom in the woods," muses one character with devastating irony, for it is not the wisdom of *Walden* he finds but the wisdom of Solomon.[11]

 T he resignation of Merrymusk, the "deep, good sense" of the Fiddler, the acquiescence of the Happy Failure, the silence of Jimmy
Rose; the eviction of the Lightning-Rod Man, the fall of Bannadonna; the duality of the tortoise: all are instances of acceptance and
reconciliation, futile attempts to overrule the dictates of the heart.
But in "Benito Cereno" Melville reverts to his earlier pattern of disjunction: the dark (Babo) and the light (Cereno) do not conjoin but
collide, and, in one of his most effective pieces of fiction, we are once
more thrust into the ambience of "Bartleby," the penumbra of despair.

Benito Cereno, Captain of the San Dominick, is captured during a
slaves' rebellion, forced to cooperate with his captors, and kept in a
state of perpetual fear and trembling. For each day, at the insistence
of Babo, the black terrorizes him anew by shaving his throat but not
cutting it (save for one monitory nick) and shaving his face but not
cutting his beard (308). In other words, Babo not only toys with
Benito's life but, no less cruelly, with his sex—for, as I have indicated
earlier, Melville often uses the shorn beard as symbolic of loss of manhood (see above, pp. ———). We should also note that Benito's bedroom, the place of his daily humiliation, is littered with "four or
five old muskets," "a dented cutlass," and "a hacked harpoon" (305)
and that, at his waist, he wears a "scabbard, artificially stiffened"
(352)—obsolete, battered, or inconsequential weapons that symbolize dissipation of power, hollowness of being, and the absence of sexual energy. (Italics added.) (And, in point of fact, Benito is a "pale
invalid" with a hollow, racking cough.) Although no quester in the
usual Melvillean sense, Benito does have a mission to perform and
that mission is perverted by the scheming Babo, a kind of Confidence Man who carries two daggers (327); and surely it is not beside the point that one of The Confidence Man's disguises is as a seemingly meek Negro.

Benito, of course, has no choice but to submit: refusal means that
he must follow his leader, Don Alexandro, whose flesh was removed
from its frame and whose skeleton now is the ship's figurehead. The
Don was first set upon in his cabin by two muscular, hatchet-wielding

Ashantees, brought to the deck "half alive and mangled" (338) and there finally dispatched. Although it would be arbitrary to gloss "castrated" for "mangled," it is not without interest that the hatchet-wielders are elsewhere, with rich irony, called "organ-grinders" (273) —a pun we have previously encountered in the Melville lexicon, although never in so grim a context. In short, Benito has every reason to live in constant terror.

For that matter, so has the American, Amasa Delano, Captain of the *Bachelor's Delight*—except that he is too innocent to plumb the real meaning of his intuitions. So "singularly undistrustful" that he finds it difficult "to indulge in personal alarms, any way involving the imputation of malign evil in man" (256), Delano suspects, but cannot fully comprehend, that his life and sex are also jeopardized:

> Gingerly enough stepped good Captain Delano between . . . [the 'ominous file(s)' of 'hatchet-polishers'], and in the instant of leaving them behind, like one running the gauntlet, he felt an apprehensive twitch in the calves of his legs.
> But when, facing about, he saw the whole file, like so many organ-grinders, still stupidly intent on their work, unmindful of everything beside, he could not but smile at his late fidgety panic. (272–73)

Nevertheless, Delano collects these moments of dubiety—Cereno's strange "reserve," the "incompetence" of the seamanship on the *San Dominick*, the "twitch in [his] calves," an attack on a white sailor by a black, a young Spaniard skulking on deck, and "the strange questions put to him concerning his ship' ' (284). And

> By a curious coincidence, as each point was recalled, the black wizards of Ashantee would strike up with their hatchets, as in ominous comment on the white stranger's thoughts. (284)

Delano's recollections, in other words, are counterpointed by the castrating murderers honing their blades.

Throughout "Benito Cereno" Melville opposes the sexual and animal energy of the Negro (who bears hatchets, daggers, and razors) to the impotence of the White (who is associated with old, broken, or non-existent weapons). Babo, for instance, is once described as

"snakishly writhing" (327), and a Negro mother and her robust son
are depicted as doe and fawn:

> [Delano's] . . . attention had been drawn to a slumbering
> negress, partly disclosed through the lacework of some rigging,
> lying, with youthful limbs carelessly disposed, under the lee of the
> bulwarks, like a *doe* in the shade of a woodland rock. Sprawling
> at her lapped breasts, was her wide-awake *fawn*, stark naked,
> its black little body half lifted from the deck, crosswise with its
> *dam's*; its hands, like two *paws*, clambering upon her, its mouth
> and nose ineffectually rooting to get at the mark; and meantime
> giving a vexatious half-grunt, blending with the composed snore
> of the negress.
>
> The uncommon vigor of the child at length roused the mother.
> She started up, at a distance facing Captain Delano. But as if
> not at all concerned at the attitude in which she had been caught,
> delightedly she caught the child up, with maternal transports,
> covering it with kisses.
>
> There's naked nature, now; pure tenderness and love, thought
> Captain Delano, well pleased. (292) (Italics added.)

The only other suckling scene in Melville is of whales, the Grand
Armada Chapter of *Moby-Dick*: for good (the fawn and doe) or for
evil (the snake), the Negroes aboard the *San Dominick* are intensely
animalic and intensely sexual. So that when Cereno says that it is "the
Negro" who "cast[s] such a shadow upon" him, we must realize that,
consciously or not, Babo represents more to Cereno than just the principle of Evil incarnate. In Melville's complexly double vision, Benito
expresses a White Man's racial and sexual fantasy of the Negro
mythicized in hatred, just as Delano expresses its inverse, a White
Man's fantasy, as scurrilous and unreal, but one *mythicized in love*.
For instance, Delano is convinced of the Negro's docility, unfailing
good humor, and intellectual inferiority:

> There is something in the negro which, in a peculiar way, fits
> him for avocations about one's person. Most negroes are *natural*
> valets and hair-dressers; taking to the comb and brush congenially
> as to the castanets, and flourishing them apparently with almost
> equal satisfaction. . . . And above all is the great gift of good-
> humor. Not the mere grin or laugh is here meant. Those were

unsuitable. But a certain easy cheerfulness, harmonious in every glance and gesture; as though God had set the whole negro to some pleasant tune.

When to this is added the docility arising from the unaspiring contentment of a limited mind, and that susceptibility of blind attachment sometimes inhering in indisputable inferiors. . . . (306–7) (Italics added.)

And, therefore, Captain Delano patronizes the Negro—

In fact, like most men of a good, blithe heart, Captain Delano took to negroes, not philanthropically, but genially, just as other men to Newfoundland *dogs*— (307)

and believes in the spontaneous goodness of his "naked nature" just as he believes in the goodness of Nature herself. (Italics added.)

Benito, on the other hand, believes that the Negro is not only not good-humored but hates the White for making him a slave; that he is not really docile but feigns submission while waiting for his opportunity to revolt; that the Negro will revenge himself by flaunting his sexual dominance ("polishing his hatchet") and by terrorizing the White at his weakest point, his sense of sexual inferiority, before castrating him and, depending on what happened to the flesh deliberately removed from Don Alexandro's bones, possibly cannibalizing him as well. Fear and humiliation (if not sin and guilt), in other words a broken spirit as well as broken body slowly kills Benito Cereno; he has, all along, followed his leader, for without his sword, the symbol of his command, he has been, like Don Alexandro, a mere figurehead. And there is no use trying, at the penultimate moment, to remake history. Like Hester and Dimmesdale, he knows that a man cannot escape his past and that a new life in another country is impossible.

Captain Delano, however, is the eternally optimistic American:

'But the past is passed; why moralize upon it? Forget it. See, yon bright sun has forgotten it all, and the blue sea, and the blue sky; these have turned over new leaves.'

'Because they have no memory,' [Benito] . . . dejectedly replied; 'because they are not human.'

'But these mild trades that now fan your cheek, do they not

come with a human-like healing to you? Warm friends, steadfast friends are the trades.'

'With their steadfastness they but waft me to my tomb, Senor,' was the foreboding response. (351–52).

We are, then, once more in the ambit of the man who dies in the Tombs:

> 'Nothing reproachful attaches to you by being here,' [the Narrator tells Bartleby in prison]. 'And see, it is not so sad a place as one might think. Look, there is the sky, and here is the grass.'
>
> 'I know where I am,' he replied, but would say nothing more. . . . (43)[12]

But much more than the Narrator of "Bartleby," who also argues from Nature, Delano is transcendentally inclined, and his comprehension of good and evil, belief in God and disbelief, is keyed to the condition of the natural world:

> The next moment, with clenched jaw and hand, he passed Atufal, and stood unharmed in the light. As he saw his trim ship lying peacefully at anchor, and almost within ordinary call; as he saw his household boat, with familiar faces in it, patiently rising and falling on the short waves by the *San Dominick's* side; and then, glancing about the decks where he stood, saw the oakum-pickers still gravely plying their fingers; and heard the low, buzzing whistle and industrious hum of the hatchet-polishers, still bestirring themselves over their endless occupation; and *more than all, as he saw the benign aspect of nature, taking her innocent repose in the evening*; the screened sun in the quiet camp of the west shining out like the mild light from Abraham's tent; as charmed eye and ear took in all these, with the chained figure of the black, clenched jaw and hand relaxed. Once again he smiled at the phantoms which had mocked him, and felt something like a tinge of remorse, that, by harboring them even for a moment, he should, by implication, have betrayed *an atheist doubt of the ever-watchful Providence above*. (324) (Italics added.)

And, therefore, although Delano is, in part, "undeceived" (351) by the final turn of events, he never really understands why Cereno claims he must die and never understands that, for Cereno, the "bright sun . . . and . . . blue sky" have neither transfiguring power as fact nor—as they have for those who watch Billy ascend—redemptive value as symbol. Of the two visions of the Negro—Delano's dream and Cereno's nightmare—it is Cereno's that comes true. Although Babo no longer threatens him physically, Benito knows at the end— to Delano's astonishment and pain—that he can no longer be "saved" (352). The tragic penumbra that overshadows Bartleby, who is similarly misunderstood, overshadows Benito too. He is a victim; he is doomed; and he knows it.

In the main, Melville's Negroes are stereotyped as gentle or savage animals: for example, as fawns (Yorpy, in "The Happy Failure," Sambo in the "Old Zack" anecdotes, 1847) and does (Pip and his tambourine-playing ancestor, Billy Loon, in *Omoo*, a "jolly little Negro"); or as bulls (the Handsome Sailor in *Billy Budd*) and lions (Daggoo in *Moby-Dick*). But nowhere in an important role does Melville combine the lion with the doe and create a Negro who is more man than myth, more fact than fantasy, and, therefore, it is difficult to agree with Sidney Kaplan that Pip, Daggoo, and Fleece are "three greatly conceived characters."[13] Ironically, the most important dialect-speaking "Negro" in the canon is the fawning Black Guinea, the white Con Man disguised as a "negro cripple," and he poses us a special problem. Just what does Melville mean by describing him with his "black face rubbing against the upper part of people's thighs as he made shift to shuffle about . . .?" Is Melville suggesting the black is obscenely concerned with sex or that he is hypersexual? Or, since the Guinea is really white, is Melville's shaft really aimed at the white man who believes these allegations? Or is Melville, as in "Benito Cereno," simultaneously speaking from both sides of his mouth? None of these explanations is too subtle to be true.

A variant of Melville's most abject persona, the Happy Failure, is Israel Potter, the Unacclaimed Success (1855). Melville and Potter (the real Potter and the fictionalized) perform heroic deeds in art and war, and both go unrewarded; it is, in other words, not insignificant that although Melville knew the pamphlet recounting Israel's life *before* he wrote *Moby-Dick*, he chose not to use it until after "Bartleby," that is not until Israel's history bore some imaginative correlation to his own. And just as Melville lived almost his last forty years in virtual anonymity in New York, so Potter—as if Melville gloomily foresaw and were prefiguring his own fate—lives his last forty-five years, anonymously, in another stone city, London. Neither *Moby-Dick* nor wartime derring-do could guarantee them fame in their lifetimes, and posterity had to rescue them both. Melville surely felt an affinity for this unremembered patriot who had given himself so unsparingly.

But if Israel is finally buffeted by a neglectful world, his Revolutionary escapades are not without satisfaction, and he is, in fact, a success in ways that other Melvillean protagonists would wish to be but are not: for instance, Israel gains the affection of Captain John Paul Jones, who treats him as a son and whom Israel regards as a kind of father (128, 132), whereas Tommo sails under a tyrant, Redburn under a hypocrite, and White Jacket under a sottish brute. But the shipboard adventures of these three are quasi-autobiographical—as Israel's are not—and it is quite possible that the captains under whom Melville really sailed were not nearly as derelict as they appear in the novels. Perhaps Melville made them so in order to explain their utter disregard for his protagonists, who by his reckoning, were of superior mettle and, therefore, deserving the company of officers. (It is true, however, that most other men of authority in Melville—Ahab, for instance, or Plinlimmon, or even, as some would say, Vere—are not benevolent either.)

Israel also wins the trust of the renowned Dr. Franklin and the respect of King George III—wish-fulfillments of a commoner who, despite his genius, never hobnobbed with society or court. Through his ability to feign madness and through his "submissive quietude" Israel ingratiates himself with a group of English naval officers and does not, in the spirit of this diverting tale, live to regret it; that is, unlike Pip or Bartleby, two truly maddened Divine Inerts, Israel's willingness to place himself in the hands of others does not lead to his destruction; nor, in fact, does it lead to the flogging that White Jacket fears, for the British Captain is enlightened and his Master-at-Arms (think of Bland and Claggart!) is neither sadistic nor insidious.

If Israel is a quester at all (and during the Revolution, despite his avowed desire to return to America, he flits from one adventure to the next like the hero of *Omoo*), if he is a quester, it is only during the last two chapters, in which Melville rather absurdly telescopes his last forty-five years. His wish to return home is thwarted until after he begins to suffer the quester's malady, and although he never becomes monomaniac like Ahab nor "schizophrenic" like Bartleby—his questing impulse is, after all, not very strong—he does become pathetically, quixotically daft (233).[14] In short, Melville did not truly burrow into the terror-haunted regions of his mind in order to describe Israel's enforced vagabondage. One is reminded of *Omoo*, for it too is witty and picaresque, emphasizes plot and action, eschews religious and sexual symbolism, and almost completely rejects abstract analysis.

There is no better evidence of its concentration on surface than the scene in which Israel is hidden in the secret passageway of a chimney and remains concealed there for three days before escaping on the fourth (94ff). The episode fairly begs for symbolic treatment but Melville refrained. It is incorrect, therefore, to suggest that Israel seeks Absolute Reality within the wall or, once within, that he seeks it without. Nor is it wise to regard his emergence as a resurrection or, assuming the chimney a womb symbol (as one may in *Moby-Dick*), a rebirth. And although it is true that Israel is incarcerated by Squire *Woodcock*, the chimney is obviously not a phallus symbol either (as it is in "I and My Chimney") and the pun nothing more than a gentle jape. I do not mean, however, that *Israel Potter* is just a *divertissement*, and it is, in fact, a fairly serious (if not closely reasoned) Progress Report on the American Experiment. But it is, finally, an exquisite book, not a passionate one, for Melville, although interested in, was never viscerally concerned—except in *Battle-Pieces*—with the problems of politics and polity.

John T. Frederick notes that the three sections in *Israel Potter* "which are wholly Melville's . . . are strategically placed at the beginning, near the middle, and at the ending of the novel" and that the imagery in all three sections is related: the first chapter contains images of "solitude, immurement and confinement and of darkness and danger, expressed or latent in the details of the gorge, the scowling glen, and the walls. . . ."; chapter twelve contains the "account of Israel's incarceration"; and chapter twenty-six, his life in London, and is "shot through with the symbolic imagery of immurement and confinement, of stone and mud and death, of fog and mist and darkness."[15] Similarly, one may find many images of immurement and confinement in Melville's *Journal to the Near East and the Levant* (1856–57) and, in fact, Harrison Hayford has reminded us of the city walls and labyrinthine, mazelike streets of Jerusalem and Constantinople.[16] The point of relation between these images and those in *Israel Potter* is that, by and large, they *remain* images—however, as Melville himself would have said, "instinct with significance" they may be—and do not become realized symbols. As in *Omoo* and *Redburn*, so in *Israel Potter*: in Melville's lightest novels narrative action outweighs symbolic action.

Israel Potter falls into three distinct sections: Chapters 1–2 recount Israel's adventures before the Revolution; Chapters 3-25, his adventures during the Revolution; and Chapters 26–27, those after the Revolution; and during the central section of the book, Israel encounters three American heroes, Ben Franklin, John Paul Jones, and Ethan Allen, each an epitome of the national spirit. Franklin, whom he meets first, is, although "pastoral," keenly observant of "the main chance" (64):

> Having carefully weighed the world, Franklin could act any part in it. By nature turned to knowledge, his mind was often grave, but never serious. At times, he had seriousness—extreme seriousness —for others, but never for himself. Tranquillity, was to him [as it was to Plinlimmon] instead of it. This philosophical levity of tranquillity, so to speak, is shown in his easy variety of pursuits. Printer, postmaster, almanac maker, essayist, chemist, orator, tinker, statesman, humorist, philosopher, parlor man, political economist, professor of housewifery, ambassador, projector, maxim-monger, herb-doctor, wit. . . . (66)

But there is also in Franklin an undeniable touch of The Confidence Man (one of whose aliases, incidentally, is of a herb-doctor):

> 'Every time he comes in he robs me,' soliloquized Israel, dole-

fully; 'with an air all the time, too, as if he were making me presents.' (74)

And only The Con Man, in all of Melville, can shift masks as often as Franklin.

Through Franklin, Israel is introduced to Jones, the tattooed barbarian in gentleman's dress, the Ahab-like hero whose love of self exceeds love of country. Jones' victory over the *Serapis* offers Melville "a type, a parallel, and a prophecy":

Sharing the same blood with England, and yet her proved foe in two wars—not wholly inclined at bottom to forget an old grudge—intrepid, unprincipled, reckless, predatory, with boundless ambition, civilized in externals but a savage at heart, America is, or may yet be, the Paul Jones of nations. (170)

Con Man and predator: are they, then, the final fruits of democracy? Melville first seems to say yes: he links Franklin to Jones, and Israel to them both through extensive dialogue and dramatic sequence. Their affairs account for twelve of the middle chapters before Melville, seeming to experience a change of heart, introduces Ethan Allen as a corrective. But there is too little of America's mythic rejuvenator (less than a chapter and a half) to counterbalance the effort of Franklin and Jones, and what little there is comes, virtually, as an afterword (Chapter 21ff). Furthermore, Allen is neither as fully-fleshed nor as dimensional as his compatriots and never engages Israel in speech or action. Finally the introduction of Allen forces Melville into a direct contradiction. "America," he had said, "is, or may yet be, the Paul Jones of nations." But in describing Allen, Melville concludes:

His spirit was essentially Western; and herein is his peculiar Americanism; for the Western spirit is, or will yet be (for no other is, or can be) the true American one. (212)

Melville's final opinion in *Israel Potter*, then, is that Franklin and Jones may well, collectively, represent America's Past and Present, but only Allen represents her Future. And her Future lies in the West, the land—as Allen never stops reminding us—of Christian Gentlemen: four times he declares that he is a "Christian"; four times that

he is a "gentleman"; and twice that he is a "Christian gentleman."
We can hardly help getting the point, particularly when we learn that
Israel lives forty-five years in London, "this cindery City of Dis" (227)
a Hell on earth, yearning all the while to reach the New World.
Finally, on Bunker Hill Day, 1826, the unsung hero returns to Boston
and, thence, to the ruins of his family's homestead in the Berkshires,
where he discovers that the last remaining member of his family went
west "more than thirty years previous. . . ." (239). But Israel can go
no further and dies in the East, still short of the Promised Land, a
displaced person in a kind of purgatorial limbo.

Of the loose triads in *Israel Potter*—Franklin, Jones, Allen; Past,
Present, Future; Hell, Purgatory, Heaven; London, the American
East, and West—only the last members closely relate to one another:
Allen, the Future, the West beyond the mountains, the quester's
heaven of Christian Gentlemen. For *Israel Potter* is, after all, a novel
of anticipation, the left panel of the diptych, like *Omoo*, like *Redburn*,
like *Moby-Dick*. But the apples of Sodom inevitably turn to ashes:
Mardi, *White-Jacket*, *Pierre*; and after *Israel Potter*, *The Confidence-
Man*, Melville's novel of "fulfillment" in the Territory Ahead.

If *Pierre*, reflecting Melville's own sexual crises and metaphysical
doubts, is an anguished book, *The Confidence-Man* (1857)—written
by one who had "pretty much made up his mind to be annihilated"—
is beyond bitterness and, therefore, curiously serene. The state of mind
that brought it forth is, perhaps, no better described than by Ishmael
in what is an uncannily premonitory gloss:

> There are certain queer times and occasions in this strange
> mixed affair we call life when a man takes this whole universe for
> a vast practical joke, though the wit thereof he but dimly discerns,
> and more than suspects that the joke is at nobody's expense but
> his own. However, nothing dispirits, and nothing seems worth
> while disputing. He bolts down all events, all creeds, and beliefs,
> and persuasions, all hard things visible and invisible, never
> mind how knobby; as an ostrich of potent digestion gobbles down
> bullets and gun flints. And as for small difficulties and worryings,

prospects of sudden disaster, peril of life and limb; all these,
and death itself, seem to him only sly, good-natured hits, and jolly
punches in the side bestowed by the unseen and unaccountable
old joker. That sort of wayward mood I am speaking of, comes
over a man only in some time of extreme tribulation; it comes in
the very midst of his earnestness, so that what just before might
have seemed to him a thing most momentous, now seems but a
part of the general joke. (Chap. xlix.)

In *The Confidence-Man* Melville accepts three barren contingencies:
that Chronometrical Virtues do not exist; that Man's life is a giant
joke, his "day" on earth April Fool's; and that the absurd and dying
universe is sailing straight to extinction. Although nihilist, *The Confidence-Man* is ironically like much else that Melville wrote in the
mid-fifties, a document of acceptance.

In its final tableau—the most dramatic in the book—Melville al-
legorizes his final meaning. As the lights of the universe dim, dim-
eyed Everyman, equipped with a money-belt, an insurance policy, and
a counterfeit detector, asks the Con Man what else he needs to be
saved. "Let me give a little guess, sir" is the polite reply. "Life-preserver?" Yes, of course, a life-preserver, and the Master of the Universe graciously gives him the three-legged stool he (Everyman) had
been sitting on, a stool with a hollow seat and a tin chamber pot fastened beneath. And, then, complaining of a foul odor—perhaps the
candle burns ill; but neither discount the pun on "stool"—the Con
Man extinguishes the last lamp of the Universe and "kindly" and
"with sympathy" leads the tottering old man away.

Melville maintains his ambiguity to the last line: "Something further"—presumably the Last Judgment—"may follow of this Mas-
querade." That is, as there may be a Last Judgment, there may very
well not be; there may be nothing at all. The only other alternative,
that the Final Rites will be conducted by the Con Man himself, is
equally forbidding, for, from one point of view, he is most obviously
the Devil: we watch him cheat and swindle as many passengers
aboard the *Fidèle* as he can; no question that he is a thorough-going
scoundrel. At the same time, however, he is God (albeit the Trickster)
a figure who appears recurrently in the Melville canon: in *Mardi*, He

is the "equivocal conjuror"; in *Moby-Dick,* "an unaccountable old
joker"; in *Pierre,* "Juggularius" the juggler; in "The Encantadas," an
"enchanter"; in "Temple First," a magician; in *The Confidence-Man,*
a quick-change artist. The Con Man is Devil *and* God: but that is not
all.

He first appears as Christ—his "aspect [is] . . . singularly innocent,"
his hat is "fleecy," his figure "lamblike," and he writes on a slate such
aphorisms as *"Charity thinketh no evil," "Charity believeth all things,"*
and *"Charity never faileth."* Nor does he try to swindle anyone, and
perhaps only a critic who lacks confidence will assume that his function is to subvert the passengers with Christian propaganda, for The
Confidence Man's *public* declarations avow precisely the same thing.
(Melville is always more sympathetic to sons and the Son than he is
to fathers and the Father.) Nevertheless, it would be an error to suppose that Christ and the Con Man are different people or even that
the Con Man is impersonating Christ; the truth is more devastating:
the Con Man *is* Christ, a deaf mute unable to speak to a world unwilling to listen. Except that he is not only Christ but Anti-Christ as
well, and Melville was surely aware that he parodied the Second
Coming preparatory to the Last Judgment; for, according to Christian legend, Anti-Christ is supposed to precede Christ, not follow him,
and Christ, who is supposed to be accepted by Mankind is scorned,
whereas Anti-Christ (who is supposed, finally, to be scorned) is, re-
versely, accepted by Everyman. Ishmael's warning comes true: that
in our despair we fail to discriminate among events, creeds, beliefs,
and persuasions; and conclude that God, the Devil, Christ, and Anti-
Christ are all one and all the same.[17]

In *Pierre,* the dissolution of the hero's metaphysic begins: in a
three-cornered struggle with himself, Pierre denies His existence,
seeks His presence, and blasphemes His absence, at once atheist, ag-
nostic, and believer. Pierre dies searching for and failing to find Truth,
and it was a struggle that Melville must well have understood he
could not afford to repeat, that the expenditure of emotional capital
was too great. In this light we realize that *Israel Potter* and almost all
the short stories (with the exception of "Bartleby," "Benito Cereno,"
and one or two others) form a kind of holding operation, a con-

cession to a "reasonable" view of the Universe. For in most of the stories Melville tries very hard to make us (and himself) believe that metaphysical distinctions can and should be made, that life does have two sides, a dark *and* a light.

But *The Confidence-Man* re-establishes the suicidal negation of *Pierre*, and Melville ends by finding Final Truth neither splintered unrecognizably nor distinguishably dual but—and how monstrous the irony!—incarnated in The Confidence Man, as it had once been unitized in the Whale. At the same time, Melville levels most human distinctions, creating just three kinds of people: knaves, fools, and misanthropes. The knaves constantly argue for absolute faith in Man, Nature, and Providence; the fools constantly succumb to their arguments; and the misanthropes forever preach absolute distrust. Melville's reduction, in other words, excludes all the truly humane positions and quite frankly discounts the promise of Western Man *Israel Potter* adumbrates: there is no frank, bluff, hearty Ethan Allen in *The Confidence-Man*; the wounded "Titan" is his nearest caricature. In the same way the hero of *Pierre* emerges, reduced to a one-legged cynic, frustrated by life, if not by death. Like Pierre at the end of his life, the cynic is also a "godless" and "pitiless man [who] . . . has lost his piety," (24) and is a "raver" (26). (He also seems to be a "discharged custom-house officer"—as if Melville were once more predicting his own future.)

Although we are never told just how the peg-legged cynic is reduced to his desperate circumstance, we *are* told the history of another defeated man, China Aster. China is a candle-maker who, at the instigation of his "friend," Orchis, agrees to manufacture his candles from sperm, not tallow. Orchis lends China the money necessary for his new venture but ultimately forecloses the account, driving China into bankruptcy; attempts to recoup his losses destroy his health and lead directly to his death. Orchis incarnates the well of sexual energy, now polluted and poisoned, for he perverts the creativity implicit in sex. His name derives from "testicle" in Greek, and like the Lightning-Rod Man he carries a tipped cane; but he is a betrayer of sperm. And China can no more castrate Orchis than anyone aboard the *Fidèle* can overthrow the Con Man (who, significantly, is often described in snake imagery).[18] The point is that from *Moby-Dick* to *The Confidence-Man*, the period in which the decline and defeat of the young quester is decisively recounted, the weapon that once symbolized his aggressive sexuality has now passed into the hands of his adversary—from Ishmael to Ahab, from the householder to the Lightning-Rod Man, from China Aster to Orchis. And, perhaps most fitting of all, the hatchets belong now to the Ashantees, not Benito Cereno. Tommo once slew Mow-Mow with a Polynesian spear, but in "Benito Cereno" that spear is finally reclaimed by its rightful, dark-skinned owner. The transfer of temporal power and sexual vitality is complete.

The villain of *Pierre* also reappears in *The Confidence-Man* in strangely altered terms: Plinlimmon, the non-benevolent philosopher, becomes Mark Winsome, the misanthropic idealist. (It surely reveals more of Melville than of his intended victims that he should ridicule two such unalike people as Hawthorne and Emerson as Plinlimmon-types.) The Confidence Man himself has no antecedent in Melville unless he be the atheist anti-quester Jackson, and after the Con Man only Claggart is so deliberately intent upon perverting the good impulses of a fellow traveler. The Con Man, in other words—as far as the Melville canon goes—is precisely what Melville calls him, "an original" (277)—not Quixote, Hamlet, or Milton's Satan, but an original nonetheless. And, according to Melville's logic, since there is no room in one book for two "originals," the Con Man has no antagonist who can overturn him. For neither Charlie Noble (another swindler), nor Mark Winsome, nor Egbert his disciple routs him, and if they, in turn, do not succumb, it is only because they are as soulless as he. Only a Bulkington, one imagines, could have challenged the Con Man and not yet lost his humanity (Bulkington is forever the "second" original!) but by 1857 Melville no longer believed in the existence of Bulkingtons.

The Confidence-Man is Melville's tale of life beyond the Alleghenies, the "inevitable sequel," as Lewis Leary has justly said, to *Israel Potter*;[19] but whereas the earlier novel, however well realized, is irretrievably minor, *The Confidence-Man* could well have been major. It fails because it suffers, in an extreme way, from the same difficulty that checked Melville in those other novels that are also the last of a sequence, *Mardi*, *White-Jacket*, and *Pierre*: the compulsion to exhaust a theme and/or drive its action beyond the limits of the natural world. Think of Melville's groups of novels in their relation to Secular and Absolute Reality and this notion will come clearer. *Typee* and *Omoo* are preoccupied with life in the South Seas; but the narrative half of *Mardi* is an overwrought fantasy of that life, and the symbolist half is perpetually concerned with the Ideal beyond those seas. *Redburn* captures the salt of ocean and the stench of Liverpool; but *White-Jacket*, a tired book by an overworked author, first submerges us in endless shipboard detail, then focuses on the *Neversink* moving allegorically to her final destination. *Moby-Dick*, brilliantly anagogic, never forgets the ribs and terrors of the Whale; but *Pierre*, offering the myths of Saddle Meadows and New York, forever occupies an unreal realm. *Israel Potter* leaves its hero *before* the mountains; but *The Confidence-Man* starts and finishes beyond those mountains. In other words, some of Melville's novels—*Typee, Omoo, Redburn*, most of *White-Jacket*, and *Israel Potter*—for better or worse, concentrate on the natural world and invoke the Spirit of Place before the Wall; other novels—most of *Mardi, Moby-Dick,* and *Pierre*—for better or worse, concentrate simultaneously on this world and the next and invoke not only the Spirit of Place before but also the Tension of Passage through the Wall. That leaves *The Confidence-Man*, which, since it takes place exclusively beyond the Wall, profits from neither Place nor Tension, and this is why it lacks "plastic . . . fictive and dramatic power. . . ."[20]

As in the cindery landscape of "The Encantadas," the world of *The Confidence-Man* is virtually devoid of human or spiritual value. The few good men aboard the *Fidèle* (like the Methodist minister who will not believe that the "crippled negro" is really The Con Man) are very like the do-gooding tortoises, blindly going forth, they know not whither. But, as literature, the Encantadan Hell is as plastic, fictive, and dramatic as one could wish because Melville was, in effect, describing a hellish natural world—and the latter is a perfect symbol for the former; but if Melville were to have described the Mississippi landscape in *The Confidence-Man*, he would perforce have had to describe much of it as beautiful country, and such description would hardly be apt symbols for Tartarus. This is the reason, I am quite sure, why Melville suppressed at least one passage of intense visual beauty that he had composed for *The Confidence-Man*, and why this nihilistic novel is deliberately underwritten.[21] Choosing to concentrate on the "real" world beyond, eschewing the world of sense, Melville drove the craft of fiction through the fabric of appearance and emerged not with a novel but with a dialogue. Rushing precipitously into the realm of Essence, he indulged himself to a degree that no romancer can afford; he had lost not only all confidence in the world beyond but, more important for his art, denied that it could or should be revealed by the world before. As a symbolist of prose fiction, Melville collapsed on the edge of paradox—a collapse as instrumental as the so-called "nervous breakdown" he almost suffered in drawing him to Europe and the Near East for a rest cure.

One is reminded that a newspaper critic of Melville's lecture, "Statues in Rome" (1857–1858), complained that "excepting for [his reported] conversation with the lady about the head of Tiberius, one would hardly have guessed that he had ever been in Italy at all."[22] This charge is interesting not merely because it is true but because it is the one often brought against *The Confidence-Man*: that there is little indication, as the novel proceeds, that the action is taking place aboard a vessel moving down a great river. This may well be the novel's fatal flaw, but it does not indicate a diminution of talent as much as an imbalance in its application. For as *The Confidence-Man* shuns the sensuously descriptive passage—renouncing "Beauty" for "Truth"—so "The Piazza," its exact contemporary and counterpart, is fraught with loving emblems of creation and is dedicated not to "Truth" but "Beauty," to Illusion and to the necessity of Illusion. ("Statues in Rome," on the other hand, incontinently rejects Life for Art.) The point is that Melville's mistrust of the natural world here reaches its epitome: *The Confidence-Man* disregards it, and "The Piazza" insists that it is a "fairyland."

From his piazza one day, the narrator sees "some uncertain object . . . mysteriously snugged away, to all appearance, in a sort of purpled breast-pocket high up in a hopperlike hollow, or sunken angle, among the northwestern mountains"—but "so situated as to be only visible, and then but vaguely, under certain witching conditions of light and shadow" (440–41):

> Indeed, for a year or more, I knew not there was such a spot, and might, perhaps, have never known, had it not been for a wizard afternoon in autumn—late in autumn—a mad poet's afternoon; when the turned maple woods in the broad basin below me, having lost their first vermilion tint, dully smoked, like smouldering towns, when flames expire upon their prey; and rumor had it, that this smokiness in the general air was not all Indian summer—which was not used to be so sick a thing, however mild—but, in great part, was blown from far-off forests, for weeks on fire, in Vermont; so that no wonder the sky was ominous as Hecate's cauldron—and two sportsmen, crossing a red stubble buck-wheat field, seemed guilty Macbeth and forboding Banquo; and the hermit-sun, hutted in an Adullam cave, well towards the south, according to his season, did little else but, by indirect reflection of narrow rays shot down a Simplon pass among the clouds, just steadily paint one small, round, strawberry mole upon the wan check of Northwestern hills. Signal as a candle. One spot of radiance, where all else was a shade.
>
> Fairies there, thought I; some haunted ring where fairies dance. [Thus truly a "purple" passage.] (441–42)[23]

The following May he sees a rainbow "resting its further end just where" (442) he had marked the spot and remembers that "if one can but get to the rainbow's end, his future is made in a bag of gold" (442)—again Melville introduces the image of hidden gold as symbolic of the Absolute.

A few days later the narrator sees a "golden sparkle" (442) in the same place, the glass of a cottage window reflected; another day it appears to be a "silver buckler" (443); then a "golden mountain-window" (444). Unable to restrain his romantic imagination any longer, and using "golden-rods" and the "golden flights of yellow-birds" (444) to guide him, he sets forth for "fairy-land."

> . . . I wore a light hat, of yellow sinnet, with white buck trowsers—both relics of my tropic sea-going. (447)

. . . .

"I'll launch my yawl—ho, cheerly, heart! and push away. . . ."
(444) For although he travels on horseback and afoot, Melville's
metaphor for travel (like the narrator's clothing) is nautical. Indeed,
to reach his goal, he must cross an "ocean":

> For not only do long ground-swells roll the slanting grain, and
> little wavelets of the grass ripple over upon the low piazza, as
> their beach, and the blown down of dandelions is wafted like the
> spray, and the purple of the mountains is just the purple of the
> billows, and a still August noon broods upon the deep meadows,
> as a calm upon the Line; but the vastness and the lonesomeness
> are so oceanic, and the silence and the sameness, too, that the first
> peep of a strange house, rising beyond the trees, is for all the
> world like spying, on the Barbary coast, an unknown sail. (440)

In a way, the narrator is Taji reincarnate (although now his metaphor-
ical companion is his yawl, not Jarl), and the maiden he finds at the
cottage is Yillah resurrected:

> Pausing at the threshold, or rather where threshold once had
> been, I saw, through the open door-way, a lonely girl, sewing at
> a lonely window. A pale-cheeked girl, and fly-specked window,
> with wasps about the mended upper panes. I spoke. She shyly
> started, *like some Tahiti girl, secreted for a sacrifice*, first catching
> sight, through palms, of Captain Cook. (447) (Italics added.)

Together they enact the disillusioning scene that never takes place in
Mardi, the scene in which the youth who consciously seeks the Ideal
finally finds it.

Like her cottage, which on near inspection proves to be battered,
leaky, gray and unpainted, Marianna is weary, wakeful, lonely, and
alone. Neither gold nor the ideal maiden is anywhere to be found.
The narrator is surprised that Marianna is vastly unhappy and remarks—as if he were Taji remembering Yillah's joy as the acolyte of
the priest Aleema and, later, as his lover—

> 'I have heard that, for this wakeful weariness, to say one's
> prayers, and then lay one's head upon a fresh hop pillow—'
> (452)

But she interrupts him:

'Look!'
Through the fairy window, she pointed down the steep to a
small garden path near by—mere pot of rifled loam, half rounded
in by sheltering rocks—where side by side, some feet apart,
nipped and puny, two hop-vines climbed two poles, and, gaining
their tip-ends, would have then joined over in an upward clasp,
but the baffled shoots, groping awhile in empty air, trailed
back whence they sprung [symbolizing the failure of love].
'You have tried the pillow, then?' [asks the narrator].
'Yes.'
'And prayer?'
'Prayer and pillow.'

Marianna says what Yillah was never permitted to say: that neither
religion ("prayer") nor sexual love ("pillow") brings transfiguring
happiness. But, in her disillusion, Marianna harbors one illusion
still: that her weariness would be cured

'. . . If I could but once get to yonder house [the narrator's own,
which, in the sunlight, seems "marble"], and but look upon
whoever the happy being is that lives there! (452)

Though thoroughly disabused himself, the narrator conceals his
knowledge and replies humanely:

'. . . For your sake, Marianna, well could [I]wish that I were that
happy one of the happy house you dream you see; for then you
would behold him now, and, as you say, this weariness might
leave you.' (452–53)

But how pathetic that the erstwhile Truth-Seeker should deny his vision, that the deep-diver should accept his immolation! And how
pathetic too that the organic vision of Beauty and Truth which carries
Moby-Dick to such exalted heights, should first dichotomize into the
halves of *Pierre* and, finally, disintegrate into "The Piazza," on one
hand, and *The Confidence-Man* on the other! Indeed, Melville would
not write significant prose again until he could reconceive the relation
between this world and the next, between the spheres of love (as
exemplified by Billy) and the spheres of fright (as exemplified by
Claggart)—that is, not until *Billy Budd*.

A n analogue to, if not source of, Melville's treasure hunt in "I and
My Chimney" is a trope in *Moby-Dick*. Tashtego, searching diligently
for the proper place to break into the captured Sperm Whale's great
Heidelburgh tun—into his head where Essence supposedly inheres—

> proceeds heedfully, like a treasure-hunter in some old house,
> sounding the wall to find where the gold is masoned in. (340)

In "I and My Chimney" Melville reverses the simile and compares
the chimney with a whale and a pyramid, two other familiar symbols:

> The architect of the chimney must have had the pyramid of
> Cheops before him; for, after that famous structure, it seems
> modeled, only its rate of decrease towards the summit is consid-
> erably less, and it is truncated. From the exact middle of the
> mansion it soars from the cellar, right up through each successive
> floor, till, four feet square, it breaks water from the ridge-pole
> of the roof, like an anvil-headed whale, through the crest of
> a billow. (377–78)

William Ellery Sedgwick has perceptively identified the chimney,
"excavated on each floor for certain curious out-of-the-way cupboards
and closets, of all sorts and sizes," with the White Jacket, "with [its]
. . . great variety of pockets, pantries, clothes-presses, and cupboards."[24]
Both may well be, as Sedgwick asserts, symbols of "Melville's crotch-
ety ego," but, primarily, I think, they are symbols, like the whale and
pyramid, of the complex barrier world of Secular Reality. So too, for
that matter, is the house that surrounds the chimney, except that it is
not merely complex but veritably "labyrinthine." It is, says Melville,
"like a philosophical system" (389), for, however closely one explores
it, one finds neither final answers nor final exits:

> Going through the house, you seem to be forever going some-
> where, and getting nowhere. It is like losing one's self in the
> woods; round and round the chimney you go, and if you arrive at
> all, it is just where you started, and so you begin again, and
> again get nowhere. Indeed—though I say it not in the way of
> fault-finding at all—never was there so labyrinthine an abode.
> (389)

Henry Pommer reminds us of Melville's reminiscence of *Paradise*

Lost in his *Journal of a Visit to London and the Continent* (1849–1850)—

> Last evening was very pleasant. Walked the deck with the German, Mr. Adler till a late hour, talking of 'Fixed Fate, Free-Will, fore-knowledge absolute' etc.

—and of the succeeding line which Melville surely knew but did not quote, "And found no end, in wand'ring mazes lost."[25] The house was built by the narrator's late kinsman, Captain Julian Dacres, and "dacres," as Merton Sealts has pointed out, is an anagram for "sacred"[26] (although it should also be remembered that Blake's chimney sweep is Tom Dacre). Richard Chase's comment is also pertinent here: "As usual the hidden mystery is to be connected with the father [that is, the spiritual father, Captain Dacres], for "the impenetrable secret of the chimney is the God whom it is vanity to try to understand."[27] But how many questers Melville sent into the labyrinth before he finally admitted they were "getting nowhere!"

The chimney is twelve feet square at the base and "Very often," the narrator tells us, "I go down into my cellar, and attentively survey that vast square of masonry. I stand long, and ponder over, and wonder at it" (380). In short, the narrator is as fascinated by his chimney (and its truly "sacred" center) as Redburn is by his glass ship, and as Redburn, in a moment of temporary madness, would break his way within and uncover gold guineas supposedly secreted there, so the narrator, similarly beguiled, would try to undermine the chimney's foundation, that mysterious artifact ancient as the Urwelt:

> It has a druidical look, away down in the unbrageous cellar there, whose numerous vaulted passages [the labyrinthine avenues of Secular Reality], and far glens of gloom, resemble the dark, damp depths of primeval woods. So strongly did this conceit steal over me, so deeply was I penetrated with wonder at the chimney, that one day—*when I was a little out of my mind*, I now think—getting a spade from the garden, I set to work, digging round the foundation, especially at the corners thereof, obscurely prompted by dreams of striking upon some old, earthen-worn memorial of that by-gone day when, into all this gloom, the light of heaven entered, as the masons laid the foundation-stones, peradventure

sweltering under an August sun, or pelted by a March storm. Plying
my blunted spade, how vexed was I by that ungracious interrup-
tion of a neighbor who, calling to see me upon some business,
and being informed that I was below, said I need not be troubled
to come up, but he would go down to me; and so, without ceremony, and without my having been forewarned, suddenly discovered me, digging in my cellar.

'Gold digging, sir?'

'Nay, sir,' answered I, starting, 'I was merely—ahem!—merely
—I say I was merely digging—round my chimney.'

'Ah, loosening the soil, to make it grow. Your chimney, sir,
you regard as too small, I suppose; needing further development,
especially at the top?'

'Sir!' said I, throwing down the spade, 'do not be personal. I
and my chimney—'

'Personal?' (380–81) (Italics added.)

He is, as he admits, momentarily insane, and, consciously or not, he
is "digging for gold"; his friend's captious irony is not without
point. But in a more personal sense, his purpose may well be, as Richard Fogle suggests, "self-mutilation," and, in fact, one would be
hard pressed to explain the intimacy he enjoys with his chimney ("Personal?") unless one accepted its covert phallicism.[28] But "self-mutilation" is, I think, too strong a term: he seems rather to suffer the
embarrassment of one caught at private sexual play—with his trun-
cated chimney and blunted spade.

The chimney has been razed at the top in a "surgical operation"
(379)—its owner, that is, is metaphorically wounded although not
fully impaired:

Often I think how grapes might ripen against my chimney. How
my wife's geraniums bud there! Bud in December. Her eggs,
too—can't keep them near the chimney, on account of hatching.
(384)

(The pun on eggs is a joke, and no one, I trust, sees Melville's private
life reflected therein.)[29] The narrator's wife,

advanced in years, as she know she must be . . . seems to
think that she is to teem on, and be inexhaustible forever. She

doesn't believe in old age. At that strange promise in the plain of
Mamre . . . [his] old wife, unlike old Abraham's, would not
have jeeringly laughed within herself. (385)

Moreover, the woman is as cancerously energetic as she is rampantly
fertile and, with her two daughters, campaigns to have the chimney
torn down completely. In short, she embodies Melville's current notion that sexual energy operates for destructive, not constructive,
ends, and although she carries no weapon, one psychologizing critic
has noted that she wields her finger as if it were one.[30] The women
wish not merely to renovate the old house—which they foolishly
think they can accomplish by destroying its backbone—but also to
unearth the secret treasure they have heard is hidden somewhere in
the chimney. That is, they are not questing for the Ideal, but for
buried gold, and their interests—like those of the gold-hunters in
Mardi, Harry Bolton and Stubb—are purely materialistic. Thus, if
the narrator's madness is temporary—rather like Ishmael's alternative resolve to link his spirit to Ahab's—his wife's (albeit to a lesser
degree) *is* Ahab's, a monomania against which the narrator must constantly guard himself:

> But worst of all was, that time I unexpectedly returned at early
> morning from a visit to the city, and upon approaching the house,
> narrowly escaped three brickbats which fell, from high aloft,
> at my feet. Glancing up, what was my horror to see three savages,
> in blue jean overalls, in the very act of commencing the long-
> threatened attack. Aye, indeed, thinking of those three brickbats,
> I and my chimney have had narrow escapes. (407)

A comically shrewish termagant—yet who would deny that she and
her two daughters, three "savages," seriously try to molest the narrator?—she is a parody and perversion of the heroic quester, a kind
of Dame Van Winkle; and he, "a dozy old dreamer" (385), a retired
quester who has long since embraced his uselessness, is a kind of Rip.
But only a kind: he is alert enough to realize that total destruction of
the chimney implies not only symbolic castration but also the loss of
his remaining household influence, a social as well as sexual dimin-
ishment. And he is wise enough to resist.

In their search for gold the women ally themselves with a certain

engineer-surveyor of the district, a "Mr. Scribe," who measures the
chimney, makes several calculations and grandly announces that there
is surely a secret chamber within. Mr. Scribe, however, is not to be
trusted; for a fee he is apt to "misdescribe," and, in fact, the narrator
rids himself of this troublemaker with a fifty dollar bribe. Scribe is the
arch-Materialist—peen hammers and measuring tapes bloom in his
wake—whose final incarnation is the geologist Margoth in *Clarel*.

But is there a secret closet within the chimney, and, if there is, does
it contain gold? Melville mocks not only the questions, which he
leaves unanswered, but their proponents, the antic wife and the absurd surveyor. Knowledge of the Absolute, as in *Moby-Dick*, is left
deliberately ambiguous—although now Melville leaves no doubt of
his opinion of the quest for it:

> ... even if there were a secret closet, secret it should remain, and
> secret it shall. Yes, wife [says the narrator], here for once I must say
> my say. Infinite sad mischief has resulted from the profane bursting
> open of secret recesses. Though standing in the heart of this
> house, though hitherto we have all nestled about it, unsuspicious
> of aught hidden within, this chimney may or may not have a
> secret closet. But if it have, it is my kinsman's. To break into that
> wall would be to break into his breast. (406)

To quest, he now knows, is to desecrate, not to preserve; to destroy,
not to create. The narrator keeps faith with History, Appearance, and
Order and finds final happiness in pipe and chimney.

A companion piece of this story is "The Apple Tree Table," and,
as before, the characters are a "matter-of-fact wife" (414), a "Democ-
ritus" in linsey-woolsey; two highly impressionable daughters whose
names again are Anna and Julia; and a husband whose distant forebear is once more from *The Sketch Book*. One midnight, while reading his Cotton Mather—the same author who undoes poor Ichabod
Crane—the husband suddenly hears a mysterious ticking and suspects ghosts. "Could Cotton Mather speak true?" (421) he wonders
fearfully. His daughters, of course, have no doubt: the ticking does
seem to come from the table, and the table does have devil's-claw
feet; ergo. . . . But his wife chooses rather to confront the Unknown,
in the tone of a mock Ahab addressing the elements:

When breakfast was cleared away she took my watch and, placing it on the table, addressed the supposed spirit in it [the table], with a jocosely defiant air: 'There, tick away, let us see who can tick loudest.' (421)

As it happens, the table does not answer.

That night her husband discovers the source of the ticking: a bug which had been embedded in the wood finally wormed his way free. Small consolation for his daughters, however, who panic again: bugs frighten them even more than ghosts! But his wife, thoroughly devoid of wonderment at the marvels of Nature, vigorously rubs the table top with roach powder in order, as she says, to "whip [the ticking] . . . out of it" (428). Nevertheless, on the third night, a second bug materializes, and, like the first, he too is "a fiery opal" (432), with the "sparkle of a glorious sunset" (432)—like the golden cock, emblematic of Essence. And, like the cock, both bugs die soon after they reach the light of common day—such is man's tenuous grasp of the Eternal.

Both bug and table are shown to a certain Professor Johnson, and the lucid, if somewhat prosy, professor explains the mystery in strictly naturalistic terms (434). Perhaps he is, as Frank Davidson surmises, another caricature of Oliver Wendell Holmes (the first, according to Merton Sealts in his cited article on "I and My Chimney," being Mr. Scribe).[31] Whether these assumptions are true or not, we may be certain that in both stories Melville is respectfully amusing himself at the expense of those who would rationalize "metaphysical" phenomena. But in his blacker moods, wrath would replace respect, and he could well cry of the historian and euhemerizer "Heartily wish Niebuhr & Strauss to the dogs" and mean it.[32]

Melville left America 11 October 1856 and visited the British Isles, the Near East, and the Continent before returning home 19 May 1857. Although his experiences, fragmentarily recorded in his *Journal*, were to be most useful in writing *Clarel* (published 1876), he made immediate use of his journey: the lecture on "Statues in Rome" and, in 1860, a volume of poetry, which Scribner's rejected. Of these poems presumably written in the late '50's but not published until 1891, in the section of *Timoleon* called "Fruit of Travel Long Ago," three particularly interest us—"Pausilippo," "The Great Pyramid," and the "L'Envoi"—for they embody certain recrudescent images and fantasies that suggest the continuity of Melville's art. For instance, the theme of "Pausilippo" is the martyrdom of the artist, a theme first enunciated in *Pierre* soon after Melville realized that "though I wrote the Gospels in this century, I should die in the gutter."[33] In fact, before we examine the quasi-Melvillean harpist of "Pausilippo" who has, so to speak, "played himself out," it would be wise to examine first his distant ancestor, young Pierre, as he becomes aware of his gifts, at the outset of his career.

Melville's most violent tale of initiation recounts how the nineteen-year-old poetaster of "The Tropical Summer: A Sonnet" is swiftly transformed into the would-be author of The Great American Novel; how, disavowing his youthful pretensions and renouncing his home and parents, he ambitiously attempts that novel in the Bohemian quarter of New York; and how, in consequence of his own immaturity, he overreaches himself and fails. Indeed, his eventual suicide in part results from (and in part is symbolic of) this failure, for it is the incubus of an unfinished book that drains his energy, strains his eyesight until he is almost blind, and distracts his mind to a nightmare of castration and death. Although it is absurd to identify the features of Melville's portrait or the events of his career with such chiaroscuro, both portrait and career do reflect the truth, imaginatively distorted. For the moment, then, let us not deal in exact correspondence.

As his surviving juvenilia indicate, Herman Melville was also a teenage author, who, perhaps like Pierre, "had frequently done that which many other boys have done—published" fugitive magazine pieces (and, perhaps, been as unaccountably puffed for them). Surely the overwritten "Fragments" are as trivial as any of those "first-fruits of genius" (304) Pierre takes from his own "writing-desk" (219) and burns. Or, perhaps, by the "first-fruits of ['published'] genius" Melville is alluding to his own first two novels, *Typee* and *Omoo*, novels which received high praise at publication but which he scorned as "Peedee" and "Hullabaloo" in 1849, as " *'Typee' 'Piddledee' etc*"[34] in 1860, and in *Pierre* (1852) as much admitted were the products of an unoriginal mind:

> And in the inferior instances of an immediate literary success, in very young writers, it will be almost invariably observable, that for that instant success they were chiefly indebted to some rich and peculiar experience in life [like adventuring in the South Seas], embodied in a book, which because, for that cause, containing original matter, the author himself, forsooth, is to be considered original; in this way, many very original books, being the product of very unoriginal minds. (304)

Like Pierre, Melville did not realize that he had an original mind —that is, that he had "genius" (*Mardi*, Ch. clxxx; *Pierre*, 360)— until the wiring of his first book of serious proportion, *Mardi*. It is, of course, his third novel, but, in the foreshortening of his career, is very much like Pierre's abortive first. Both books, for instance, were written not only for esthetic and idealistic reasons but also to provide ready cash. Lombardo (read Melville) bestirred himself to write his *Koztanza* (read *Mardi*) in order "to procure his yams" (Ch. clxxx); Pierre, similarly, is confronted with the "prospective menace of being absolutely penniless, unless by the sale of his book, he could realize money" (333). For, like Pierre, who has undertaken the support of a family, Melville married during the composition of *Mardi*; but just as Pierre's novel is "least calculated to pecuniary profit in the end" (397), so *Mardi* was a financial disaster. In both instances, the profit is purely intellectual: Pierre knowingly grows "wiser" and "profounder" (359), and Melville regarded his experience in similar terms: "Had I not written & published '*Mardi*' [sic], in all likelihood, I would not be as wise as I am now, or may be," he confided to Duyckinck.[35] Pierre's book, however, is destined to fail as literature because its author is "goaded, in the hour of mental immaturity, to the attempt at a mature work . . ." (470), a circumstance, as *Mardi* reveals on almost every page, which similarly befell Melville, but with this difference: that whereas the author of *Mardi* is partially aware, Pierre is completely unaware of his immaturity. Thus even as Melville defends *Mardi*, he reluctantly scores some of its faults—self-criticism and correction Pierre never entertains.

There is, however, one major flaw in *Mardi* which Melville either failed to recognize or chose not to admit, but which he specifies, as if to repair his shortsightedness, as one destructive element in Pierre's novel—the unassimilated quality of "book-knowledge":

> A varied scope of reading, little suspected by his friends, and randomly acquired by a random but lynx-eyed mind, in the course of multifarious, incidental, bibliographic, encounterings of almost any civilized young inquirer after Truth; this poured one considerable contributory stream into that bottomless spring of original thought which the occasion and time had caused to burst out in himself. Now he congratulated himself upon all his cursory acquisitions of this sort; ignorant that in reality to a mind bent on producing some thoughtful thing of absolute Truth, all mere reading is apt to prove but an obstacle hard to overcome; and not an accelerator helpingly pushing him along.
>
> . . . .
>
> He did not see,—or if he did, he could not yet name the true cause for it,—that already, in the incipiency of his work, the heavy unmalleable element of mere book-knowledge would not congenially weld with the wide fluidness and ethereal airiness of spontaneous creative thought. He would climb Parnassus with a pile of folios on his back. (333–34)

As *Mardi* alienated more readers than it pleased, so Pierre's novel-in-progress-"a blasphemous rhapsody," (420) according to Steel, Flint & Asbestos, as they refuse to publish it—would surely have met the same reception; both authors, however, did receive the dividends of Fame for their earlier, less serious work. Not, to be sure, that anyone offered to publish Melville's Collected Works in an Illustrated Edition (as the firm of Wonder and Wen, Peter Pence illustrating, solicits Pierre), but Melville too was the passion of autograph-hunters (297); was dunned for a dagguerotype he did not give (298); did, according to legend, eventually write an autobiographical essay (300); was asked to lecture if not on Universal Knowledge then on the South Seas—as in fact he did in 1859 after his reputation had considerably declined (296); and who knows but that, in the flush of youthful lionizing, ladies did not also flatter him with their albums? (295).

Finally, we should note that, like Pierre, Melville also bid farewell to home and family at nineteen (to go to Liverpool) and, if he did not make his leave permanent or die young, he did from his twenty-first year, bury himself in the South Seas, not to emerge until four years later. Then he wrote *Typee*, prelude to *Mardi-Moby-Dick-Pierre*, what Melville calls, in allusion to these two phases of his career, this "shallowly expansive embayed Tappan Zee [the bay of Typee] of my otherwise deep-heady Hudson. . . ." (304). As he had done with *Mardi* and as Pierre fails to do with his novel, Melville slaved to finish *Moby-Dick* in New York, and it is, as a thousand have concurred, The Great American Novel, the novel Pierre futilely tries to write.

Nevertheless, despite the magnitude of his achievement, Melville regarded himself as a writer who had failed, and, in part of course, he was right: everything, including his masterpiece, is flawed to lesser or greater degree. But Melville always measured himself by the highest standards—would have been, in fact, the American Shakespeare —and saw himself less in terms of what he had done than in what he might do. "Leviathan is not the biggest fish," he wrote after finishing *The Whale*; "I have heard of Krakens."[36] *Pierre* is that very beast, a monstrous octopus that strangles the artist in its tentacles, and, in *Pierre*, Melville, for the first time, melodramatizes his martyrdom; but not for the last. Therein follows those later projections of self, the writers, Bartleby and Helmstone; and the musicians, Master Betty and Silvio. The latter is the aging harpist of "Pausilippo," and through him Melville mythicizes the "failure" of his life's work:[37]

> Clandestine arrest abrupt by night;
> The sole conjecturable cause
> The yearning in a patriot ode
> Construed as treason; trial none;
> Prolonged captivity profound;
> Vain liberation late. (243)

It is a strange kind of fantasy for a nineteenth century American —the totalitarian nightmare. Authority in *Pierre* (as represented by Plinlimmon) may rebuff the artist with contempt and indifference, but in the European context of "Pausilippo" it plots against him with a conspiratorial facelessness and duplicity. Silvio emerges from prison too late; too late for Melville too, for if he finally achieves the inner freedom to disregard his countrymen, he has had, in the exchange, to watch his art wither and to swallow the bitter gall of unsuccess. Melville too is "released" from the demands of his art, but only after his will to create has been permanently diminished:

> A man it was less hoar with time
> Than bleached through strange immurement long,
> Retaining still, by doom depressed,
> Dim traces of some aspiring prime.
> Seated he tuned a homely harp
> Watched by a girl, whose filial mien
> Toward one almost a child again,
> Took on a staid maternal tone.
>
> .   .   .   .
>
> Hillward the quelled enthusiast turned
> Unmanned, made meek through strenuous wrong,
> Preluding, faltering; then began,
> But only thrilled the wire—no more,
> The constant maid supplying voice,
> Hinting by no ineloquent sign
> That she was but his mouth-piece mere,
> Himself too spiritless and spent. (243–44)

"Immurement long"—how Melvillean the penalty!—walled-in, and, in consequence, deprived of Accomplishment and Fame. Forced now, like the Fiddler, to renounce High Art for Folk, for the "homely harp." "But only thrilled the wire—no more," a harpist unable to sing: an artist *manqué*, a victim "Unmanned," a quester "quelled." And then the harping "ceased."

> In low and languid tone
> The tideless ripple lapped the passive shore;
> As listlessly the bland untroubled heaven
> Looked down as silver doled was silent given
> In pity—futile as the ore! (245)

Heaven "bland untroubled" is where the Con Man is Master, Heaven which does not promise the possibility of transcendence. In Jerusalem,

Melville noted in his *Journal* for 26 January 1857, "The mind can not but be sadly & suggestively affected with the indifference of Nature & Man to all that makes the spot ['Zion'] sacred to the Christian. . . . [O]n Olivet every morning the sun indifferently ascends [think of Billy Budd who also ascends!] over the Chapel of the Ascension."[38] To the harpist silver is "silent given/In pity," but Melville never really succeeds in transmuting the dross of self-pity into the ore of poetry.

If the artist is victimized, rendered impotent, and finally silenced, the seeker for Truth suffers a worse, if less humiliating, fate, as Melville reaffirms in "The Great Pyramid":

> Slant from your inmost lead the caves
> And labyrinths rumored. These who braves
> And penetrates (old palmers said)
> Comes out afar on deserts dead
>   And, dying, raves. (255)

Madness and death: Melville has, as if obsessively, retreated beyond the nihilism of *The Confidence-Man* to the agony of *Pierre* and reimagined (if not reparticipated in) the fatal quest; and, then, with an "Envoi" concludes the "Fruit of Travel Long Ago." The hero, now gratefully returning to home and wife, exhibits the same ambivalence Melville attributed to him (and to himself) in *Pierre*:

> My towers at last! These rovings end,
> Their thirst is slaked in larger dearth:
> The yearning infinite recoils,
>   For terrible is earth.

> Kaf thrusts his snouted crags through fog:
> Araxes swells beyond his span,
> And knowledge poured by pilgrimage
>   Overflows the banks of man.

> But thou, my stay, thy lasting love
> One lonely good, let this but be!
> Weary to view the wide world's swarm,
>   But blest to fold but thee. (256)

Dorothee Metlitsky Finkelstein tells us that "in Islamic tradition Kaf, a mythical mountain range surrounding the earth, forms the boundary between the visible and invisible worlds":[39] in other words, Kaf is another name for Secular Reality, and the quondam quester is now only too happy to find refuge therein.

In *White-Jacket* Melville describes a fall from the mast, but we now know that Melville borrowed the incident from another man's book. For, like Redburn, the young Melville was sure-handed and footed, never suffered a fear of heights (and some masts were as high as six-story buildings), and, as far as we know, never got dizzy aloft. In 1849, at thirty, Melville traveled to London and "renew[ed] his youth by climbing to the masthead" of the *Southampton*.[40] Then in 1850, the same August day he met Hawthorne, Melville "found a projecting rock [atop Monument Mountain] which resembled the bowsprit of a ship, scrambled out to the dizzy end, and began to pull on imaginary rigging."[41] In 1860, aged forty-one, Melville sailed with his brother, Tom, to San Francisco and, en route, amused himself by climbing out onto "the flying jib boom," that is, out over the ocean, "for a magnificent sight of the full-rigged clipper riding the swells behind him."[42] I have documented Melville's affinity for high and dangerous places because of his most remarkable *Journal* entry for 3 January 1857:

[A pyramid] looks larger midway than from top or bottom. Precipice on precipice, cliff on cliff. Nothing in Nature gives such an idea of vastness. A balloon to ascend them. View of persons ascending, Arab guides in flowing white mantles. Conducted as by angels up to heaven. Guides so tender. Resting. Pain in the chest. Exhaustion. Must hurry. None but the phlegmatic go deliberately. Old man with the spirits of youth—long looked for this chance—tried the ascent, half way—failed—brought out—pale as death. Nothing so pathetic. Too much for him; oppressed by the massiveness & mystery of the pyramids. I myself too. A feel ing of awe & terror came over me. Dread of the Arabs. Offering to lead me into a side-hole. The Dust. Long arched way,—then down as in a coal shaft. Then as in mines, under the sea. The stooping & doubling. I shudder at the idea of ancient Egyptians. It was in these pyramids that was conceived the idea of Jehovah.

Terrible mixture of the cunning and awful. Moses learned in
all the lore of the Egyptians. The idea of Jehovah born here.—
When I was at top, thought it not so high—sat down on edge.
Looked below—gradual nervousness & final giddiness &
terror![43]

Melville goes within and does not, it is true, go mad, but in mounting
the outer wall of the pyramid, suffers "a pain in the chest," then "a
feeling of awe & terror," and, finally, at the top, though he himself
did not think it very high, "gradual nervousness & final giddiness &
terror." His attack, of course, could have been organic, but I think
what really happened was that Melville had finally confronted his
great symbolic obstacle and seen beyond. And the Beyond was Nothing.

5. The Art of Attaining Truth

Battle-Pieces through Billy Budd

W ith one exception, the writing of every serious book Melville published from 1851 through 1876—*Moby-Dick*, *Pierre*, *The Confidence-Man*, and *Clarel* (*Israel Potter* is not serious and the *Piazza Tales* is not a book)—caused him deep emotional distress; the exception is *Battle-Pieces and Aspects of the War* (1866). With one exception, Melville's family unfailingly preferred his light to his serious fiction; again the exception is *Battle-Pieces*, which they vigorously applauded. Melville sought government preferment on several occasions from the time of *Mardi*; and although *Battle-Pieces* was not specifically instrumental in advancing his cause or gaining him his Customs' Post, had his wartime sentiments been less conventionally patriotic, we may assume the book would have counted against him. In short, by striving less hard, Melville maintained his health, won the admiration of his family, and did not jeopardize his position, as the unconventional *Leaves of Grass* probably cost Whitman his job with the Department of the Interior. But of course Melville paid the price for easy success: only a handful of the seventy-two Battle-Pieces are successful poems, and some of the rest, in the word of Melville's sympathetic biographer, are clearly "hack."[1] At the least we should not want to part with "The Portent," "Misgivings," "The Conflict of Convictions," "The March into Virginia" (with its marvelously definitive line "All wars are boyish, and are fought by boys"), "Shiloh," and the last stanza of "Chattanooga," but for too much of the rest Melville's own words, apropos his own earlier abortive volume, are not unwarranted: "Of all human events, perhaps, the publication of a first volume of verses is the most insignificant. . . ."[2]

According to Melville, the Civil War was not merely between North and South, but, in its moral dimension, between "Right" and "Wrong," and he compares it to the battle between the loyal and

secessionist angels; between Raphael, one of "Christ's martyrs . . .
a white enthusiast still" and Satan, "A disciplined captain . . . old . . .
strong and hale" (4).[3] Yet it was as a personal, not a cosmic, allegory
that the War regenerated Melville and returned him to his life's
work. For ". . . battles can heroes and bards restore" (112)—if the
battle is between the Young Man (Pierre, Enthusiast Martyr) and his
Aging Adversary (Plinlimmon, Disciplined Betrayer) or between
between Young Fools of Faith and Duty, Northern and Southern
alike.

In *Moby-Dick* and *Pierre*, Melville gave the lie to the optimism of
the fifties, and no one listened. Now, as he spoke of "The shark [who]
Glides white through the phosphorus sea" (115) and of young men
irredeemably "enlightened by the vollied glare" (11), he spoke of
the hidden vulturism none could deny. Indeed, it is only when he
sings of initiation in a national context, as in "Chattanooga," that he
bursts into eloquence. In the first six stanzas of this poem Grant's
Young Men—young Enceladans—are seen climbing "the primal wall"
to the enemy stronghold; in the last stanza, those who survive the
Southern barrage reach the top—but only Death, ironically, is there
to greet them:

But some who gained the envied Alp,
　　And—eager, ardent, earnest there—
Dropped into Death's wide-open arms,
　　Quelled on the wing like eagles struck in air—
Forever they slumber young and fair,
　　The smile upon them as they died;
　　Their end attained, that end a height:
Life was to these a dream fulfilled,
　　And death a starry night. (61)

The Civil War was "man's latter fall" (4); Chaos had come again.

In his country's tragic waste Melville thought he saw reflected the
"misspent" energy of his youthful art, and the War confirmed, renewed, and redoubled his reverence for Pattern and belief in salvation through Law:

Dupont's Round Fight

In time and measure perfect moves

All Art whose aim is sure;
Evolving rhyme and stars divine
Have rules, and they endure.

Nor less the Fleet that warred for Right,
    And, warring so, prevailed,
In geometric beauty curved,
    And in an orbit sailed.

The rebel at Port Royal felt
    The Unity overawe,
And rued the spell. A type was here,
    And victory of LAW. (15)

And, therefore, one might almost say that Melville wrote the *Battle-Pieces* as a mode of self-discipline; or, in Captain Vere's words, as a celebration of "forms, measured forms," a celebration already begun in "Fruit of Travel Long Ago":

Greek Architecture

Not magnitude, not lavishness,
But Form—the Site;
Not innovating wilfulness,
But reverence for the Archetype. (248)

Not magnitude—*Moby-Dick*; not lavishness—*Mardi*; not wilfulness —*Pierre*. But reverence for the archetype—*Billy Budd*. The equivalences are of course inexact, but Melville's quatrain is nonetheless a palinode—can there be any doubt?—and how better to implement its spirit than by cherishing the restrictions of metered and rhyming verse? Formal encasement, then, reflects and is meant to reflect Melville's vision of the cosmos.

That vision, nowhere stated in so many words, suggests a universe from which the Creator has deliberately excluded Himself, a universe which may be inferred from a multiplicity of hints:

NONE WAS BY
WHEN HE SPREAD THE SKY; (7)

and retreated beyond the cope of the unrendable heavens. The sky, in other words, is the barrier to the Absolute, and this is why, consciously or not, Melville's descriptions fasten on its impenetrability: "And the sky a sheet of lead" (8), *"The sky is dun"* (20), *"Under a sunless sky of lead"* (29), "With burning woods our skies are brass" (88). And at the bottom of the world? "What if the gulfs their slimed foundations bare?" (6) Melville asks—and answers:

> A silent vision unavowed,
> Revealing earth's foundation bare,
> And Gorgon in her hidden place. (106)

She who petrifies Pierre. . . .

This is the dream-vision of "America" personified as the sleeping "Mother"; "So foul a dream upon so fair a face" (106); the murderous beneath the maternal. In "America" she undergoes a four-fold metamorphosis, appearing first as the embodiment of pre-Civil War innocence:

> The children in their glee
> Were folded to the exulting heart
> of young Maternity. (105)

Then with the advent of battle and the active engagement of her sons,

> Valor with Valor strove, and died,
> Fierce was Despair, and cruel was Pride
> And the lorn Mother speechless stood,
> Pale at the fury of her brood. (106)

"Later," overcome with horror, she falls into a trance and discloses to the "watcher" the hidden Gorgon of her being. Unexpectedly, that is, the Mother reveals her true, her double identity—the Gorgon of the Unconscious beneath a tranquil exterior, as beneath the nation's apparent unity, the rebellious sons of the South. But the goddess whom Pierre failed to mollify is now appeased by blood sacrifice and yields her sway. For in the last and prophetic stanza Melville envisions his country cathartized by suffering, inoculated by pain; a country of maturest insight and tragic vision:

> But from the trance she sudden broke—
> The trance, or death into promoted life;
> At her feet a shivered yoke,

And in her aspect turned to heaven
  No trace of passion or of strife—
A clear calm look. It spake of pain,
But such as purifies from stain—
Sharp pangs that never come again—
  And triumph repressed by knowledge meet,
Power dedicate, and hope grown wise,
  And youth matured for age's seat—
Law on her brow and empire in her eyes.
  So she, with graver air and lifted flag;
While the shadow, chased by light,
Fled along the far-drawn height,
  And left her on the crag. (107)

Gorgon lies quiescent, the unconscious spectre, as America is "puri-fied" in the rush of consciousness and triumph of light. Youth, Strug-gle, Death, Rebirth: Melville extends the myth of regeneration into a cultural context, and the land, at least momentarily, is redeemed.

Thus from the sullen sky to the bottom of the earth, Man is en-capsulated and knows Him only in His "ominous silence" (4):

      God walled his power,
And there the last invader charged. (55)

And was, of course, repulsed in Melville's unflinching vision of Man, heroically alone in a godless world. But a different spirit—radically, irreconcilably different—also animates the *Battle-Pieces*, very like the Yea-saying Melville had once despised: of Man believing in a God who cares for His creatures. The idea reasonably derives from Mel-ville's deep concern for Law, but its expression is at once embarrass-ing and philistine:

But God is in Heaven, and Grant in the Town,
  And Right through might is Law—
  God's way adore. (89)

          or

Faith in America never dies;
Heaven shall the end ordained fulfill.
We march with Providence cheery still. (152)

As if America's Destiny were Manifest! In short, parts of *Battle-*

Pieces exhibit a dangerous complacency and an unexpected tender-mindedness.

But Melville was aware of his double vision and cleverly turned it to account: once, for instance, in "Donelson," in the dialogue between a lean Copperhead who flatly states "The country's ruined . . ." (23) and a solid merchant who disputes him (cf. the argument between the peglegged cynic and the Methodist minister in *The Confidence-Man*); but, most notably, in the most complex of all the Battle-Pieces, whose very title "The Conflict of Convictions" reflects Melville's skeptical dualism. Although the personified arguers ("YEA AND NAY") are not as well differentiated as Melville would have us believe, several "conflicts" between them clearly emerge nonetheless. On the nature of God: is He "old" (5), perhaps nearing senility; or is He, albeit "The Ancient of Days . . . forever . . . young"? On the direction of History and purpose of the Past: does History move in cycles, the Past a stepping-stone to a "happier world"; or is the movement of History linear, the present age *"The last advance of life/ . . . the rust on the Iron Dome/"*—words reminiscent of Donne's Age of Rusty Iron—and the Past nothing but "the Future's slave"? Third, on the kind of champion demanded by such parlous times: "Senior wisdom," which "suits not now" or the uncertain "light/. . . on the youthful brow"? Small choice indeed! And, finally, on the future of America:

> Power unanointed *may* come—
> Dominion (unsought by the free)
> And the Iron Dome,
> Stronger for stress and strain,
> Fling her huge shadow athwart the main. . . .(7)
> (Italics added.)

As in *Clarel*, the operative verb with which the poem ends is "may" (see below, p. 212); and as in *Clarel* where it is suggested that Western Civilization may be redeemed, so here it is intimidated that America may emerge from civil war politically reborn. One is thankful that in one of the major statements of this volume Melville foreswore certitude and espoused indeterminacy, the source, as *Moby-Dick* attests, of his profoundest power. And yet, as the mythic pat-

tern of "America" indicates, there is a certain harmony established in
Battle-Pieces, one based neither on blind faith, nor mystical intuition, nor rational assurance, which is, nonetheless, deeply felt and
convincing: one based on the process of Nature and the fullness of
Time. Robert Penn Warren speaks tellingly of this ultimate order,[4]
and what I should like to do now is direct his argument at one of
the *Battle-Pieces* and analyze it more carefully than has yet been
done:

Shiloh

Skimming lightly, wheeling still,	1
The swallows fly low	
Over the field in clouded days,	
The forest-field of Shiloh—	
Over the field where April rain	5
Solaced the parched one stretched in pain	
Through the pause of night	
That followed the Sunday fight	
Around the church of Shiloh—	
The church so lone, the log-built one,	10
That echoed to many a parting groan	
And natural prayer	
Of dying foemen mingled there—	
Foemen at morn, but friends at eve—	
Fame or country least their care:	15
(What like a bullet can undeceive!)	
But now they lie low,	
While over them the swallows skim,	
And all is hushed at Shiloh. (41)	19

"Shiloh" is Melville's finest requiem, a poem of great gravity, insistently in the lower register; for, like Ishmael's Epilogue, it cele-
brates the peace of exhaustion after the irruption of battle. In this
regard, its burden is perfectly consonant with its construction, and
Melville exhibits a subtlety in verse one might not have expected
from a prose poet. For who would expect a nineteen-line poem of
imperfect meter and inexact rhyme scheme to be intricately ordered?
But through certain patterns of repetition, "Shiloh" is.

First and most obviously, Melville repeats the image of the skimming swallow of the first line in the next to last, thereby counterpointing, as Hennig Cohen notes, the circular movement of the poem with the curving motion of the bird;[5] and, of course, Melville also repeats the name "Shiloh," using it at the outset (line 4), in the middle (line 9), and at the end (line 19). Second and less obviously, as in Milton's sonnet on a similar subject, "On the Late Massacre at Piedmont," Melville lets the long, open "o" sound resonate throughout, in its length and tone slowing and solemnizing the verse. Its presence in "swallow," "follow," "low," "over," "Shiloh," "lone," "echoed," "groan," "foemen," "so," and "solaced"—in all, more than fifteen times—is incrementally and hypnotically effective. The verbal network of "Shiloh," then, is inordinately dense—and we have not spoken of the mesh of assonance, consonance and duplication of word or phrase, instances of which can be discovered in almost every line.

Third and least obviously, there is a structural pattern in "Shiloh" which evidently results from Melville's quest for pattern, for it is too exact to be accidental. Accordingly, every fifth line from the second through the seventeenth—lines two, seven, twelve, and seventeen—is precisely five syllables long (no other line is less than seven); and the intervening lines—three through six, eight through eleven, and thirteen through sixteen—contain thirty-one, thirty-two, and thirty-two syllables respectively. The last words of lines two and seventeen rhyme, "fly low" with "lie low," whereas lines seven and twelve not only bear no relation to one another but are also devoid of any kind of verbal play. In other words, lines seven and twelve are essentially placed variants which separate the poem into thirds and which afford the reader an opportunity to disengage himself from the complex of similar sounds. Only one other line in "Shiloh" similarly disengages itself—(What like a bullet can undeceive!)"—and this apostrophe, after the rambling fifteen line sentence which precedes it, conveys the staccato and jarring effect of the undeceiving bullet.

Melville's ear was by no means infallible, and on those occasions in the *Battle-Pieces* when he writes in imitation of Poe, he frequently fails; the first few lines of "The Canticle" sufficiently illustrate this point:

O the precipice Titanic
   Of the congregated Fall,
And the angle oceanic
   Where the deepening thunders call—
      And the Gorge so grim,
      And the firmamental rim! (90)

But in "Shiloh" Melville eschews the jog-trot and gambol for a state-
lier rhythm, and his poem may not unjustly be compared with Milton's sonnet. "Shiloh" is a poem of great artifice surely, if not the
greatest art.

   The notion of ultimate harmony expressed here is first enunciated
in such shorter fiction as "The Encantadas" as an inherent principle
of the cosmic order, is regarded, in *Battle-Pieces*, as a principle of the
natural order, and, in *Billy Budd*, will be perceived as a principle of
the divine order; and this "rage for order" is the essential thread
that connects the Melville of the fifties with Melville of the nineties.
In several other respects, however, the special concerns of the novelist are absent in the poet of *Battle-Pieces*: for instance, there is neither
the quest for sex nor the sacramentalism of the Center and there is
little symbolism and little that is even faintly quasi-autobiographical.
To be sure, "In the Prison Pen" reminds us of "Bartleby":

Or, dropping in his place, he swoons,
   Walled in by throngs that press,
Till forth from the throngs they bear him dead—
   Dead in his meagreness. (78)

And "The Scout Toward Aldie," which recounts the quest of a band
of Northern soldiers for the elusive Captain Mosby and his troop of
Southern rangers, reminds us vaguely of *Moby-Dick*. Although the
differences between this poem and Melville's masterpiece in matters
of tone, style, setting, technique, and detail cannot be overestimated,
certain similarities are nonetheless apparent: the Northern "Leader"
and Captain Ahab both leave young wives behind them before setting
forth on the hunt—the only Melvillean questers who do; both men
are called "king"; Mosby, like Moby, is patterned on a figure from
the real world—their names are just accidentally alike; both escape
"through green dark," as "glides in seas the shark" (117); few men

have seen Mosby except "the maimed ones or the low" (117)—
which well describes Captain Ahab and his groundling crew; rumors
of Mosby's ubiquity abound, as of Moby's; neither is killed in the
final confrontation, whereas the "Leader" and Ahab *are* slain by the
prey they seek.

Still, in the absence of sex, symbolism, and sacramentalism, in the
espousal of narrative form and not wholly assimilated reportage (for
Melville, like Crane in *The Red Badge of Courage*, depended on
the newspapers for information), "The Scout Toward Aldie" perfectly symbolizes the position of *Battle-Pieces* in the Melville canon:
as much a fresh beginning as a pertinent extension of older themes.
For us, in retrospect, the wheel of Melville's career had spun halfway by 1860 and reached its nadir; only with *Battle-Pieces* did it begin to turn upward toward the completion of its cycle. As in *Typee-
Omoo*, in the beginning was the Fact, and Melville's use of unsymbolized fact in these poems reminds us of nothing so much as that
diptych—just as *Clarel*, his next book, where fact assumes symbolic
equivalence, reminds us of nothing so much as *Mardi*, and, as we shall
see, *Billy Budd* recalls *Redburn-White-Jacket*. In other words, even
as the second half of Melville's career completes the first, it parallels
it as well. But whether Melville saw the course of his own history as
cycle or whether, in 1866, he saw it as line—and the *Battle-Pieces* as
the coda to a career or the first notes of a new movement—are questions we doubt he himself could have answered.

Soon after the publication of *Battle-Pieces*, Melville began work on
Clarel (published 1876), the monumental consolidation of his later
thought, as *Mardi* had been of his earlier. But before we can discuss
Clarel directly, we must answer a deceptively simple question: why
did Herman Melville go to Jerusalem in 1856? His purpose, we must
realize, was not the casual sightseer's, nor just a matter of curiosity,
nor just a traveling rest cure (for why then go to the Near East?).
At bottom, it was a quest for Being—but not exclusively in the Christian sense. Melville went in order that he might experience the surge
of primitive sensibility in his deepest self, and, as a matter of fact,

he did record that in Joppa he got that "old Jonah feeling."[6] He
either knew or intuited that Jerusalem was not merely the seat of
Christian faith but that, in accordance with ancient legend, she was
also regarded as the Sacred Center of the earth, the World Navel
where life began. Mircea Eliade writes that

> Palestine, Jerusalem, and the Temple severally and concurrently
> represent the image of the universe and the Center of the
> World. . . .
>   To us, it seems an inescapable conclusion that *the religious
> man sought to live as near as possible to the Center of the World*
> . . . the Center is precisely the place where . . . space becomes
> sacred, hence pre-eminently *real*.[7]

As a deeply disillusioned communicant, Melville sought *holy* land,
and his archetypal quest well relates to all those quests for the Center
made by his protagonists.

     Although Melville may have had premonitions of failure (he had
just remarked to Hawthorne that he doubted the eternity of his soul),
he could not have been prepared, on one hand, for the filthy, flea-
ridden, leprous city he encountered and, on the other, for the Church
of the Holy Sepulchre, about which he summed the fullness of his
agony: "All is glitter & nothing is gold. A sickening cheat."[8] A statement even more important when we recall the symbolic property of
gold in the Melville vocabulary. Like Clarel, himself despairing of
faith, Melville penetrated the walls of the "holy" city and found no
god within.

     I have said that *Clarel* is reminiscent of *Mardi*, and it is in several
respects. Each book is based on a similarly extravagant, albeit antithetical, principle of construction: *Mardi*, written admittedly at the
dictates of the unconscious mind, is wildly rhetorical and formless;
Clarel, written obviously with as much conscious control as Melville
could muster, is 18,000 lines of inordinately constricted octosyllabic
verse. Each book imaginatively reconstructs Melville's own voyages
to the South Seas and the Near East, the two most important voyages
of his life. Each book is vastly ambitious, heroic in scope, overlong,
and, although occasionally distinguished by flashes of brilliant writing, terribly flawed. Each book is a symposium on such varied sub-

jects as American politics and the quest for God. Each book is a "guided tour" of fantastic or mythicized places. Each book, *Mardi* accountably but *Clarel* quite unexpectedly, is filled with imagery of the sea and sailing. And, most interesting of all, in each book Melville offers two surrogates of self: first, a young quester (Taji, Clarel) who fruitlessly loves an asexual maiden (Yillah, Ruth), who is silenced or confused by the disputation of his elders, and who leaves at journey's end on his own, to fend for himself where he will and find his faith as he may; second, Melville also offers an older and wiser surrogate, an intellectual (Babbalanja, Rolfe), who achieves an inner harmony the younger man can never attain.

Walter Bezanson, whose edition of *Clarel* is standard, has marshalled much evidence indicating that Rolfe is the product of imaginative self-portraiture: he is a veteran sailor who knows the "tale of a mariner wrecked once and later stove in by a whale"; and who recalls how, in his youth, he jumped ship in the South Seas, visited Tahiti, and "returned to civilization only to be haunted by the memory ever after." In consideration of these and other details, Bezanson concludes that "the general contours of Rolfe's appearance, manner, speech and mind, bear surprising resemblance to the outward image of Melville that letters and biographical data of the period 1845–1851 suggest."[9] Nevertheless, and crucially, Rolfe is no longer a young man; in fact, as I have already suggested, he more nearly embodies those attributes by which Melville characterizes that other middle-aged gentleman, Master Betty or the Fiddler (see above, p. 141). Possessing "a genial heart [and] . . . a brain austere" (99), Rolfe is "poised at self-center and mature. . . . (418). He is that rarest of men, the thoroughly balanced personality who not merely, like Ishmael, achieves a momentary enlightenment but who is stabilized to the center of his being.

For Rolfe, Melville hints, is more than man. In the tantalizing chapter entitled "Of Rama" he is inferentially compared with the Indian god, an avatar of Vishnu, who lives on earth but does not know that he is divine (107):

> Such natures [like Rama's], and but such, have got
> Familiar with strange things that dwell

Repressed in mortals; and they tell
Of riddles in the prosiest lot. (108)

Rama, that is, has managed to penetrate his Unconscious and has
"got/Familiar with strange things that dwell [therein]/ Repressed in
mortals." But can a man similarly co-ordinate his conscious and unconscious faculties? "Was ever earth-born wight like this" (109)?
"Ay," answers Melville, and "in the verse, may be, he is." Internal
evidence indicates that if this remark does apply to one of the characters in *Clarel*, there are only two possible candidates to whom it
could apply, and "the case for Rolfe," as Bezanson says, "is easily
the stronger."[10] Rolfe, in other words, has presumably brought his
conscious mind into an intimacy with his Unconscious, but even insofar as he has initiated this rather ambiguous individuation, he nonetheless represents a major breakthrough in the transpersonal development of the Quester who would depotentiate and transform the
feared realm of the Mothers. And, therefore, it is not entirely beside
the point to note that in Indian mythology Rama beheads his mother
with an axe and that Herman Melville's own mother died in 1872,
four years before the publication of *Clarel*.

Rolfe comes to Jerusalem because

Some lurking thing he hoped to gain—
Slip quite behind the parrot-lore
Conventional ... (100).

but, in fact, he gives (to Clarel, at least) much more than he gains,
although at first he scandalizes the novice by discussing the psychology
of religious belief:

'... long as children feel affright
In darkness, men shall fear a God;
And long as daisies yield delight
Shall see His footprints in the sod.
Is't ignorance? This ignorant state
Science doth but elucidate—
Deepen, enlarge. But though 'twere made
Demonstrable that God is not—
What then? it would not change this lot:
The ghost would haunt, nor could be laid.' (104)

The occasional thrusts at Science throughout Melville's work, from the coldblooded surgery in *Mardi* and *White-Jacket* to Ahab's destruction of the quadrant to the failure of the swamp-draining mechanism in "The Happy Failure," culminate in a series of remarks in *Clarel*, of which this one is representative: that Science demonstrates but does not convince.

To Clarel's further discomfiture, Rolfe proceeds to the subject of Comparative Religion:

'Phylae, upon thy sacred ground
Osiris' broken tomb is found:
A god how good, whose good proved vain—
In strife with bullying Python slain.
For long the ritual chant or moan
Of pilgrims by that mystic stone
Went up, even much as now ascend
The liturgies of yearning prayer
To one who met a kindred end—
Christ, tombed in turn, and worshiped *there*,'
And pointed—'Hint you,' here asked Vine,
'In Christ Osiris met decline
Anew?' (105)

This is, of course, precisely what Rolfe is hinting, and although he immediately denies it, his point is irretrievably made—for Clarel's edification and our own. And, interestingly, Rolfe's faith in God, a faith which is unshakable, emerges from the very argument that disdains Christ's uniqueness. In the 1850's Melville damned the Comparative Religionists but in the 1870's he recognized their value: Christ and Osiris are just two avatars of the god who redeems the world and is slain, Rolfe believes. But if there were such other incarnations before Osiris, why should there not be others after Christ? The time, in other words, is propitious for an Epiphany, and in some of the most fluent poetry in the volume, a poetry which paradoxically approaches the rhythms of prose, Rolfe compares his (and our) time with the world just before Christ's Advent:

'To Cicero,'
Rolfe sudden said, 'is a long way

From Matthew; yet somehow he comes
To mind here—he and his fine tomes,
Which (change the gods) would serve to read
For modern essays. And indeed
His age was much like ours; doubt ran,
Faith flagged; negations which sufficed
Lawyer, priest, statesman, gentleman,
Not yet being popularly prized,
The augurs hence retained some state—
Which served for the illiterate.
Still, the decline so swiftly ran
From stage to stage, that *To Believe*,
Except for slave or artisan,
Seemed heresy. Even doubts which met
Horror at first, grew obsolete,
And in a decade. To bereave
Of founded trust in Sire Supreme,
Was a vocation. Sophists throve—
Each weaving his thin thread of dream
Into the shroud for Numa's Jove.
Caesar his atheism avowed
Before the Senate. But why crowd
Examples here: the gods were gone.
Tully scarce dreamed they could be won
Back into credence; less that earth
Ever could know yet mightier birth
Of deity. He died. Christ came.
And, in due hour, that impious Rome,
Emerging from vast wreck and shame,
Held the fore-front of Christendom.
The inference? the lesson?—come:
Let fools count on faith's closing knell—
Time, God, are inexhaustible.—' (106)

Perhaps Rolfe is right; perhaps it is downright unreasonable to
suppose, with Nietzsche, that God is dead. But in our dry season, the
governing bust of Cicero still sits behind the Lawyer as he did in the
days of the Christlike Bartleby. For even if God *is* inexhaustible, the
Protestant dialogue with Him is at an end. Christ, Rolfe feels, was

the world's "last and best/Best avatar" of diety, but now, after "creeds, war, stakes,"

> Where stretched an isthmus, rolls a strait:
> Cut off, cut off! Canst feel elate
> While all the depths of Being moan? . . . (210)

Or in the words of another pilgrim, Mortmain, who also recognizes, in the disintegration of Christian symbols, the loss of faith in the Protestant god:

> Translated Cross, hast thou withdrawn,
> Dim paling too at every dawn,
> With symbols vain once counted wise,
> And gods declined to heraldries? (250)

Although Rolfe is Melville's central spokesman, a word should be said of the poem's narrator who never visibly appears but who is often the poem's "presiding intelligence" and "general arbiter of . . . point of view."[11] In this capacity, he pre-empts the chapter entitled "The High Desert" and discourses rhetorically on the fate of Faith:

> But in her Protestant repose
> Snores faith toward her mortal close?
> Nay, like a sachem petrified,
> Encaved found in the mountain-side,
> Perfect in feature, true in limb,
> Life's full similitude in him,
> Yet all mere stone—is faith dead *now*,
> A petrifaction? Grant it so,
> Then what's in store? what shapeless birth
> Reveal the doom reserved for earth?
> How far may seas retiring go? (292)

Echoing Arnold, anticipating Yeats, the narrator holds little hope for a revival of conventional Protestantism. But what then?

> . . . to redeem us, shall we say
> That faith, undying, does but range,
> Casting the skin—the creed. In change
> Dead always does some creed delay—
> Dead, not interred, though hard upon
> Interment's brink? (292–93)

This argument, as we have seen, is essentially Rolfe's, and therein lies his trust. The narrator, however, devilishly pushes the argument one step further:

> But if no more the creeds be linked,
> If the long line's at last extinct,
> If time both creed and faith betray,
> Vesture and vested—yet again
> What interregnum or what reign
> Ensues? Or does a period come?
> The Sibyl's books lodged in the tomb?
> Shall endless time no more unfold
> Of truth at core? (293)

What if there is no other faith? What if Truth has already unfolded to its inmost leaf? The narrator barely hints at remedy:

> Some things discerned
> By the far Noahs of India old—
> Earth's first spectators, the clear-eyed
> Unvitiated, unfalsified
> Seers at first hand—shall these be learned
> Though late, even by the New World, say,
> Which now contemns? (293)

Melville never specifies just what the Indian seers knew which might prove valuable to the West, but the very Eastward-turning of his mind is itself significant. Perhaps he is hinting at a system of yogic contemplation, of deliverance through "the final release and detachment of consciousness from all bondage to object and subject,"[12] an Eastern analogue as Jung tells us, of the end result of the individuation process, the birth of the Self in Western Man. For, as we have observed, one in whom the Self is born "is out of reach of intense emotional involvement and therefore safe from absolute shock; [his] . . . consciousness [has become] detached from the world."[13] Rolfe, who is "poised at self-center and mature," is Melville's first quester to undergo this "centreing of personality," although he hardly represents the individual Self—a state of "grace" which belongs pre-eminently to Billy Budd, who goes to his hanging serenely, his Christ-like "consciousness detached from the world" and who does not suffer a mortal orgasm so truly is he "safe from absolute shock. . . ."

There are three ways of approaching God in Melville, and Rolfe is an important figure in the canon because he embodies the third way. First there are those who would "strike through the mask," "rationalists" who would prove that the Transcendental deity exists. Created by post-Medieval men living in a dualized, desacramentalized universe, Melville's version of *Deus Absconditus* is sought through reason and ultimately monomaniacal overreason. Ahab of course is this kind of seeker, but by the time of *Battle-Pieces*, a notably godless book, only on rare and nostalgically recidivist occasions do young Pierre-like antagonists try to penetrate the murky skies in search of Him. And, in *Clarel*, only Derwent, a speciously optimistic cleric, accepts this now discredited approach. Seeing a door cut into a cliff, Rolfe wonders aloud, "thence will the god emerge, and speak?" Derwent suggests they investigate: "That portal lures me." But Rolfe rejoins:

'Nay, forebear. . . .
We'd knock. An echo. Knock again—
    Ay, knock forever; none require. . . .' (248)

The second or "primitivist" approach demands the exercise of primitive sensibility and the physical voyage to a Sacred Center. This mode of ontological quest concerns itself with timeless Being, not a temporary philosophical construct, and its chief representative is Ishmael, who enters the sacred enclosure of the Grand Armada and is illuminated in a charismatic moment of inner peace, joy, and self-realization. But the failure of Melville's own "primitivist" voyage to the holy city of Jerusalem signals the bankruptcy of this second approach.

The third or "archetypal" way is Rolfe's, but it can begin only after the transpersonal Quester has made significant progress toward individuation; after he has coordinated "head" with "heart" and assimilated into his conscious mind archetypal contents. Rolfe, however, who phylogenetically incorporates the struggles of his predecessors, is such a man, and that is why the state of "grace" he enjoys is much more solidly based (and, therefore, much more permanent) than, say, Ishmael's. Indeed, Rolfe is virtually semi-divine, for Melville

hesitantly equates him with the Indian Rama. And herein lies the
wisdom of the Indian seers, which the West may learn: that God is
neither in Heaven, nor on earth, but within man; that He is neither
transcendent, nor immanent, but a psychic fact; and that if we are to
discover His Kingdom, we shall have to discover it within ourselves
or not discover it at all.

James Baird observes that Pierre Loti traveled to India and specifically to Benares, another holy city,

> in search of escape from the intolerable state of the ego in its
> I-You relationship with God. . . . In the community of the sages
> of Benares he discovered the discipline of escape from self [that
> is, the ego] (whether he learned it or not): 'You can only desire
> that which is different from yourself, that which you have not;
> and did you but know that the things you seek are within you, for
> the Essence of all things is within you, then desire would melt
> away.' There he discovered Brahma, the creator, Brahma beyond
> the reach of all the theologies of man, 'Brahma, the ineffable—
> he of whom we cannot even think, and of whom no words
> may ever be spoken, and whose nature may only be expressed by
> Silence.'[14]

(We have already noted that from the outset of his career, in the
second "Fragment," Melville symbolized the Absolute by Silence.)
Baird concludes that Loti's *India*, from which these extracts are taken,
"is an equivalent of Melville's *Clarel* as an exploration of the possibilities for contemporary religious faith."[15]

Rolfe's fullness of being and centrality of vision permit him a cath-
olicity denied his fellow pilgrims, and, in consequence, his judgment
of or sympathy for them seems to us inevitably right. Nehemiah, for
instance, is an "enthusiast" (76), narrowly sectarian and evangeli-
cal, who is reminiscent of the early, illusioned Pierre. He acts out
Biblical injunctions which to less saintly men are literally, if not symbolically, meaningless with the retort that

> 'All things are possible to God;
> The humblest helper will he brook.' (175)

On one occasion, Nehemiah flings stones from his path in order to
prepare the "tilth . . . /For the second coming of Our Lord." Is he

"crazy"? as one of the pilgrims suggests. Rolfe's ultimate rejoinder is characteristically generous, subtle, modest, questioning:

> 'And shall we say
> That this is craze? or but, in brief,
> Simplicity of plain belief?
> The early Christians, how did they?
> For His return looked any day.' (176)

Nor is Rolfe incapable of comprehending the "madness" of Mortmain, who is of that line of disillusioned questers of whom the *late* Pierre is representative. Born a bastard of a "Medean" mother (158), Mortmain is presently haunted by the Furies, as he admits. What he has done to justify their anger (presumably in retribution for what he did in revenge for his bastardy) is impossible to say. But in his futile struggle to escape the Mother, Mortmain, like Pierre, is driven "mad," although with "madness" comes insight, and he is brilliantly able to catalogue the evils of the modern world and is, so to speak, redeemed by the brutal honesty and intensity of his vision. It is in tribute to this vision that Rolfe renders his final verdict:

> 'If mad,
> 'Tis indignation at the bad,'
> Said Rolfe; 'most men somehow get used
> To seeing evil, though not all
> They see; 'tis sympathetical;
> But never some are disabused
> Of first impressions which appal.' (267)

Until he dies, Mortmain maintains a running debate with Derwent, the Anglican cleric who, in Bezanson's phrase, "prefers gracefulness to grace,"[16] a kind, decent, and engaging religious who wears his faith lightly and who exasperates all others who would dive deep:

> 'Behead me—rid me of pride's part
> And let me live but by the heart!' (298)

The optimist Derwent assumes the perfectibility of man, the progress of the race, and the blessedness of Nature. Nor can he be shaken in his assumptions. The narrator calls him a "Templar" (142), and, in fact, he reminds us of the Bachelors of Paradise for whom Evil is superstition. But he also reminds us of the less honorable Plinlimmon in whom "youth in years mature [also] survived" (142), and in his dealings with Clarel, Derwent clearly emerges—as far as Clarel is concerned—as the Young Man's Aging Adversary. For he tries to persuade Clarel—out of the best, not the worst, of motives—not to quest:

> 'Alas, too deep you dive.
> But hear me yet for little space:
> This shaft you sink shall strike no bloom:
> The surface, ah, heaven keeps *that* green;
> Green, sunny: nature's active scene,
> For man appointed, man's true home.' (364)

"Paternally," he says, "my sympathies run" (361), for his advice *is* generous, and he does try to protect Clarel from intellectually insoluble arguments; but Clarel brusquely rejects him.

However, as Melville's attitude toward Plinlimmon is ambiguous, so it also is toward Derwent. For if Clarel fairly despises the priest, Rolfe astonishingly admits that he "likes" him (254). (I say "astonishingly" not because Derwent is not likeable; he is excessively likeable—but because characters in Melville almost never "like"; they may and often do "love," but liking is a remarkable passion that only the maturest and most humane enjoy.) Nor should it be forgotten that Rolfe, who is himself not unaccustomed to diving, once advises "best skim/Not dive" (210), only to hear Derwent, who "took no mislike to Rolfe" (210), rejoin "No, no. . . ."

Rolfe's sympathy for ideas honorably expressed and the men who express them extends as well to Roman Catholicism and the Dominican who is her eloquent spokesman. Both men realize that, with the fragmentation of Protestantism, Rome is the last stronghold of Christianity, and the priest's plea on her behalf is desperately heartfelt:

> 'If well ye wish to human kind,
> Be not so mad, unblest, and blind
> As, in such days as these, to try
> To pull down Rome. If Rome could fall
> 'Twould not be Rome alone, but all
> Religion. All with Rome have tie,

Even the railers which deny,
All but the downright Anarchist,
Christ-hater, Red, and Vitriolist.' (229)

And, of course, the Scientific Materialist, who is represented in this poem by Margoth, a geologer and apostate Jew. But Margoth is a comic fool (and foil), not a true advocate, and he spends most of his time blasphemously deriding religion and those who profess its necessity. Melville grants his proposals a kind of demonic humor—

'Lay flat the walls [of Jerusalem], let in the air,
That folk no more may sicken there!
Wake up the dead; and let there be
Rails, wires, from Olivet to the sea,
With station in Gethsemane'—(207)

although as Margoth leaves the pilgrimage, Rolfe forgives him his truly invincible boorishness:

'We do forgive thee now thy scoff,
Now that thou dim recedest off
Forever. Fair hap to thee, Jew:
Consolator whom thou disownest
Attend thee in last hour lonest!' (278)

One should not suppose, however, that because Rolfe is magnanimous he is without a critical temper; on the contrary, his critical faculty is formidable—although he is surely not as contentious as Mortmain or Ungar (the latter, a Civil War veteran, one of the "transcended rebel angels" by his own account [479]). But Rolfe also realizes that "Evil and good they braided play/Into one cord" (419), a perception forever denied Melville's monomaniacs, the absence of which leads them into overstatement and extremity. Rolfe may well decry the flatness and indifference of democratic life:

'We acquiesce in any cheer—
No rite we seek, no rite decline.' (127)

. . . .

' 'Tis the New World that mannered me,
Yes, gave me this vile liberty
To reverence naught, not even herself.' (234)

But it is Ungar who calls America a "harlot on horseback" (475), and
who lavishes his deepest rage on his Mother country:

> 'Know,
> Whatever happen in the end,
> Be sure 'twill yield to one and all
> New confirmation of the fall
> Of Adam. Sequel may ensue,
> Indeed, whose germs one now may view:
> Myriads playing pygmy parts—
> Debased into equality:
> In glut of all material arts
> A civic barbarism may be:
> Man disennobled—brutalized
> By popular science—Atheized
> Into a smatterer—' (483)

Ungar's savagery returns us to the immitigible hatred of *The Confidence-Man* and beyond that to "Sketch Seventh" of "The Encantadas" in which Melville seems cryptically to allegorize some of the
events of the Revolutionary War and punningly to rename America
as "Anathema."

As Rolfe, like Babbalanja, mildly quests for Truth—for "some
lurking thing . . . behind the parrot-lore/Conventional" the narrator
says, metaphorizing in the old Melvillean way—so Clarel, like Taji,
rather more intensely quests for Being and Love, for sacrament and
sex, and it is his quest that we must now observe. Our first glimpse of
the young divinity student comes ironically on the Vigil of Epiphany. Clarel sits brooding in his "tomb"-like chamber in the holy city.
The inn, in which he is resident,

> abutted on the pool
> Named Hezekiah's, a sunken court
> Where silence and seculsion rule,
> Hemmed round by walls of nature's sort,
> Base to stone structures seeming one
> E'en with the steeps they stand upon. (7)

But the pool is "dead," and Clarel, whose faith, if not dead, is dying
has penetrated the walls only to find—as Pierre found within the
sarcophagus-soul of man—vastness and vacancy.

Through Nehemiah, who guides him around Jerusalem, Clarel—himself "all but feminine" (3) and virginal (6)—meets Ruth, like Fayaway, Yillah, and Lucy, another incarnation of maidenly Innocence. They fall in love, but, almost immediately, circumstances conspire against them. Ruth's father, a convert to Judaism, is slain by Arabs, and, in accordance with Jewish law, Clarel is not allowed to visit her throughout a period of mourning. This is why he goes on the pilgrimage in the first place, but when he returns, he discovers that she has died of a broken heart. Their unconsummated love, however, is not as simple, nor Clarel's emotions as pure, as this telling indicates. First, as Walter Bezanson rightly reminds us,[17] Clarel, who is motherless, feels less at ease with Ruth than with her mother, Agar, whom he idealizes—a curious business surely!

> In Agar's frank demeanor kind,
> What charm to woman may belong
> When by a natural bent inclined
> To goodness in domestic play:
> On earth no better thing than this—
> It canonizes very clay:
> Madonna, hence thy worship is.
>   But Ruth. . . .
> That frame to foster and defend,
> Clarel, when in her presence, strove
> The unrest to hide which still could blend
> With all the endearings of their love. (125)

Furthermore, on the pilgrimage, Clarel falls in love with the shy Hawthornesque Vine:

> Ah, clear sweet ether of the soul
> (Mused Clarel), holding him in view.
> Prior advances unreturned
> Not here he recked of, while he yearned—
> O, now but for communion true
> And close; let go each alien theme;
> Give me thyself! (237)

. . . .

Thought he [Clarel], How pleasant in another

Such sallies, or in thee, if said
After confidings that should wed
Our souls in one:—Ah, call me *brother*!—
So feminine his passionate mood
Which, long as hungering unfed,
All else rejected or withstood. (238)

(One is irresistibly reminded of Melville's remark in his review of *Mosses from an Old Manse*: ". . . I feel that this Hawthorne has dropped germinous seeds into my soul.") But Vine rejects Clarel's offer of reciprocal love just as that other esthete Kenyon in *The Marble Faun* denies that the love of man may surpass that of man for woman:[18]

But for thy fonder dream of love
In man toward man—the soul's caress—
The negatives of flesh should prove
Analogies of non-cordialness
In spirit. (238)

Nevertheless, when Clarel compares the depth of his feeling for the woman he possesses with that for the man he does not, he is not at all sure that his deepest desire is not for the man:

How vaguely, while yet influenced so
By late encounter, and his glance
Rested on Vine, his reveries flow
Recalling that repulsed advance
He knew by Jordan in the wood,
And the enigma unsubdued—
Possessing Ruth, nor less his heart
Aye hungering still, in deeper part
Unsatisfied. Can be a bond
(Thought he) as David sings in strain
That dirges beauteous Jonathan,
Passing the love of woman fond? (395–96)

Nor would it be wise to dismiss Clarel's agony as mere Romantic *Sehnsucht*, since his relationship with still another man, an effeminate Lyonese, also indicates his bisexual tendencies. In Bezanson's words,

Clarel, the night they share a room, marks his 'Rich, tumbled,

chestnut hood of curls' and then in a surprising figure likens him
to a Polynesian girl eloping with her lover to feed 'on berries
and on love' (xxvi.255)—though Rolfe is the man of Polynesian
memories. Clarel's ambiguous dream that night involves 'clasping
arms' (xxvi.316), but whether they are Ruth's or the Lyonese's
we are not told. The next morning Derwent speaks to Clarel,
of 'the sweet shape' of *Bacchus* (xxvii.24), and when he
comments on the Prodigal's 'warm/Soft outline' brings 'a
scare/Of incredulity' to Clarel's eyes (xxvii.18). It is possible that
Clarel is afraid to return to Ruth because she may be dead [as
he clairvoyantly intuits], but also because she may not be.[19]

The easiest way for Melville to solve Clarel's sexual crisis is to kill
Ruth, which, in fact, he does, and romantic love again proves a condition of death, not life. But Melville is not entirely begging the issue
of Clarel's "complex passion," for the quest for sex is inextricably associated with the quest for sacrament, and as Clarel fails in one, he
fails in both. Upon learning that Ruth is dead, he denies the God who
never manifests Himself and moves intransigently toward nihilism:

art thou God?—But ye—
All swims, and I but blackness see.—

.   .   .   .

In bitter trial: take my curse!—
O blind, blind, barren universe! (513)

The sentiments—the doubt of God, the blackness of life, the curse,
the blind universe—all suggest Clarel's affiliation with the stricken
Pierre, who also sees all hope crushed, all love die, and the quest for
sacrament fail. Our last glimpse of Clarel is as ironic as the first: we
see him as he follows in Christ's steps along the *Via Crucis*.

Thus we must not make the mistake of supposing that Clarel's
agony can be explained purely in terms of bisexual behavior and that
a session with a psychiatrist would solve his problem. For Melville is
also investigating the spiritual neurosis of our time, the cultural dilemma for which we may offer no clinical etiology. It is true that, in
the Epilogue, the narrator offers Clarel a certain balm, suggesting from
his vantage point of quasi-ominiscience that Clarel's path "may" lead,
as it led Christ, to eventual resurrection:

> Then keep thy heart, though yet but ill-resigned—
> Clarel, thy heart, the issues there but mind;
> That like the crocus budding through the snow—
> That like a swimmer rising from the deep—
> That like a burning secret which doth go
> Even from the bosom that would hoard and keep;
> Emerge thou mayst from the last whelming sea,
> And prove that death but routs life into victory. (523)

But whatever balm the narrator extends, another fact, as Melville
well knew, remains: that his pilgrims did "Not from brave Chaucer's
Tabard Inn/ . . . pictured wend" (141):

> Another age, and other men,
> And life an unfulfilled romance.

Before, during, but especially after *Clarel*, Melville continued to
write poetry: counting neither verse published in the early novels
nor the seventy-two Battle-Pieces, we still find nearly one hundred and
fifty poems in the collected *Works*. And although it is impossible to
date the great majority with exactness—many, for instance, developed
through several recensions over long or short periods of time—we
may be guided by the fact that Melville did publish two volumes of
them and was preparing a third at his death. In analyzing what he
himself called his "spontaneous after-growth," we shall first concentrate on this flood of verse, then turn to the late prose sketches, and
conclude with the capstone of his career, *Billy Budd*.

If *Clarel* is a middle-aged man's recapitulation, *John Marr and
Other Sailors* (1888) is often an old man's reminiscence; and if there
are a multiplicity of questers who confront the natural world in
Clarel, there are a multiplicity of approaches to the attitudes concerning it in *John Marr*: collision with it, submission to it, flight from it;
but, most important of all, survival despite, and ultimately because
of, it, for these, respectively, are the themes on which *John Marr* begins and ends. Melville's prose prologue describes the titular protagonist—once, long ago, a seafarer, now a prairie dweller. Bereft of wife

and child, he "resolves never to quit the soil that holds the only be-
ings ever connected with him by love in the family tie" (160), although, in truth, it is the absence of his erstwhile comrades that he
really regrets. Marr tenaciously clings to life, but he has nothing to
live for but his dreams, for only in them are he and his former shipmates reunited:

> Since as in night's deck-watch ye show,
> Why, lads, so silent here to me,
> Your watchmate of times long ago?
>
> .   .   .   .
>
> I yearn as ye. But rafts that strain,
> Parted, shall they lock again?
> Twined we were, entwined, then riven
> Ever to new embracements driven,
> Shifting gulf-weed of the main!
>
> .   .   .   .
>
> To see you at the halyards main—
> To hear your chorus once again! (164–66)

"Bridegroom Dick," the longest representative of this nostalgic
strain, is rambling and digressive, an old man's "addled" (168)
memories and maunderings—one thinks of Oliver Wendell Holmes'
"The Boys," another poem that invokes the long-gone friends of
youth, the "memory traces" of comradeship (165). But Melville
really overdoes it here, and we read in embarrassment as Dick, an old
tar, addresses his wife by a battery of sentimentalized nicknames:
"blessed heart alive," "Bonny Blue," "old lassie," "little girl," "old
aunty," "old wifie," "Sweet Wrinkles," etc., etc., etc. Nevertheless, in
his better poems of imaginative reminiscence, Melville cuts through
the contaminations of rhetoric and plunges to the heart of his primal
myth:

The Enviable Isles

> Through storms you reach them and from storms are free.
>   Afar descried, the foremost drear in hue,
> But, nearer, green; and, on the marge, the sea
>   Makes thunder low and mist of rainbowed dew.

But, inland, where the sleep that folds the hills
A dreamier sleep, the trance of God, instills—
    On uplands hazed, in wandering airs aswoon,
Slow-swaying palms salute love's cypress tree
    Adown in vale where pebbly runlets croon
A song to lull all sorrow and all glee.

Sweet-fern and moss in many a glade are here,
    Where, strown in flocks, what cheek-flushed myraids lie
Dimpling in dream—unconscious slumberers mere,
    While billows endless round the beaches die. (204)

As a young man, Melville had written (in *Moby-Dick*) that

> . . . as this appalling ocean surrounds the verdant land, so in the
> soul of man there lies one insular Tahiti, full of peace and joy,
> but encompassed by all the horrors of the half known life.   God
> keep thee! Push not off from that isle, thou canst never return![20]

In middle age (in "Fruit of Travel Long Ago") he had pictured
himself as one who had irrevocably cast off:

> I have swum—I have been
> Twixt the whale's black flukes
>   and the white shark's fin. . . .[21]

Now in old age he had fought his way back to the sacred shore. There
is, in other words, a cycle in Melville's art which surely reflects a
rhythm in his life, and "The Enviable Isles" well suggests that its
author's life would indeed be rounded with a sleep.

As William Bysshe Stein asserts, certain poems in *John Marr* "reveal what can only be defined as a search for psychic balance," for
nothing less than "individuation," and Stein uses this term with an
undoubted awareness of its Jungian context.[22] In *Clarel*, as we have
seen, Rolfe achieves the reconciliation of head and heart, and Melville ambiguously and furtively suggests that he may have achieved
an intimacy with his Unconscious as well. That intimacy is undoubtedly attained in "The Enviable Isles," where the quester penetrates
the pleromatic round and wins, in symbol, the prize for being individuated, the prize Ahab (for example) fails to win—union with
the depotentiated Mother. For as Jung tells us: ". . . the classical indi-

viduation process ['closes'] . . . with the symbol of the *hieros gamos*, the marriage of the son with the mother-bride."[23]

Similarly, there seems little doubt that a conscious alliance with the unconscious realm of the Mothers is symbolized in "The Maldive Shark":

> About the Shark, phlegmatical one,
> Pale sot of the Maldive sea,
> The sleek little pilot-fish, azure and slim,
> How alert in attendance be.
> From his saw-pit of mouth, from his charnel of maw
> They have nothing of harm to dread,
> But liquidly glide on his ghastly flank
> Or before his Gorgonian head;
> Or lurk in the port of serrated teeth
> In white triple tiers of glittering gates,
> And there find a haven when peril's abroad,
> And asylum in jaws of the Fates!
> They are friends; and friendly they guide him to prey,
> Yet never partake of the treat—
> Eyes and brains to the dotard lethargic and dull,
> Pale ravener of horrible meat. (200)

Tiny pilot fish swim fearlessly "before . . . [the Shark's] Gorgonian head," and, more incredibly, "are [his] friends"—which surely indicates the plenum of ego-consciousness in the symbolic fish. And although their friendship should be apprehended in several senses—Melville himself supplying "an asylum in jaws of the Fates!"—one of those senses should indicate a reconciliation with the Gorgonish Parent, who is no longer a cannibal to be feared, combated, and overcome. Thus the latest stage in the transpersonal history of Melville's Quester reveals a quester who has given up the quest!

But *John Marr* is not so uniform in temperament that all the poems in it espouse the same *parti pris*, any more than "America" and "The Conflict of Convictions" prophecy the same fate for the Mother Country. "The Berg," for instance, describes how

> . . . a ship of martial build . . .
> Directed as by madness mere

Against a stolid iceberg steer,
Nor budge it, though the infatuate ship went down.
·   ·   ·   ·   ·   ·   ·   ·   ·   ·   ·   ·   ·   ·   ·   ·

Hard Berg (methought), so cold, so vast . . .
Impingers rue thee and go down,
Sounding thy precipice below,
Nor stir the slimy slug that sprawls
Along thy dead indifference of walls. (203–4)

That this poem is subtitled "A Dream" is significant, for the event it
describes is reserved for the play of the untutored imagination, resur-
recting as it will, an ancient pattern: of the maddened quester crashing headlong against the indifferent, impenetrable walls of Secular
Reality.

Unlike "The Berg," which relates the impersonal wilfulness of a
ship at sea, "The Haglets," aspiring rather toward irony than horror,
recounts an accidental sinking with all hands on board. But the disaster is doubly ironic: first because the ship has just won an important
battle against a human foe and escaped unscathed; and second because part of the booty collected in that triumph is itself "responsible"
for the shipwreck (swords, beneath deck, invert the compass). Melville describes the triumphant ship in terms of sexual potency:

The eddying waters whirl astern,
The prow, a seedsman, sows the spray;
With bellying sails and buckling spars
The black hull leaves a Milky Way. . . . (186)

And the pride of sex is matched only by the promise of rebirth, for
victory comes on the last night of the "Old Year":

But shall the New
Redeem the pledge the Old Year made,
Or prove a self-asserting heir?

But the questers are never reborn, for the celebrant ship goes down.
Witnesses are three, three pursuing haglets, inscrutable monitors, hags
of Fate, who, like the three sisters, weave Man's destiny:

Like shuttles hurrying in the looms

Aloft through rigging frayed they ply—
Cross and recross—weave and inweave,
Then lock the web with clinching cry
Over the seas on seas that clasp
The weltering wreck where gurgling ends the gasp. (193)

Yet Death offers more than a final disengagement; it offers a sweet dream of peace and the ultimate harmony of Nature and God:

And up from ocean stream
And down from heaven far,
The rays that blend in dream
The abysm and the star. (194)

Much more poignant than "The Berg" or "The Haglets" is "The Figure-Head" which concerns itself not with death through madness or misfortune but with diminution through natural decay, diminution of love, perhaps, and of sexual energy:

The *Charles-and-Emma* seaward sped,
(Named from the carven pair at prow,)
He so smart, and a curly head,
She tricked forth as a bride knows how:
    Pretty stem for the port, I trow!

But iron-rust and alum-spray
And chafing gear, and sun and dew
Vexed this lad and lassie gay,
Tears in their eyes, salt tears nor few;
    And the hug relaxed with the failing glue.

But came in end a dismal night,
With creaking beams and ribs that groan,
A black lee-shore and waters white:
Dropped on the reef, the pair lie prone:
    O, the breakers dance, but the winds they moan! (197–98)

One should not fail to observe the subtle modulations through which the poem develops: from youth to middle age to old age, from innocence to maturity to death, from embarkation to sailing to reefing; from day to night, light to darkness, color to non-color. In the splendid last stanza one should particulary observe the ambiguity of "creaking beams" and of "ribs that groan"; of the personification of winds that "moan"; and, finally, of the victory dance of the gleeful breakers, for Nature has triumphantly broken the human bond.

Perhaps the only other lines in *John Marr* that can rival the excellence of this stanza is the quatrain "The Tuft of Kelp," a nugget of gnomic wisdom: like "The Aeolian Harp" and "Far Off Shore," poems in which a wrecked ship and raft aimlessly float but will not sink, "The Tuft of Kelp" is also, in symbol, about survival, the perennial ascent of Ishmael:

> All dripping in tangles green,
>   Cast up by a lonely sea
> If purer for that, O Weed,
>   Bitterer, too, are ye? (199)

One should notice Melville's equivocal regard for the Sea of Life— life-dealing and death-dealing, purifying and embittering; the paradoxical structure of the first line which opposes that which drips with that which is tangled; and the nice antithesis between "purer" and bitterer" which culminates in a question mark. And yet Melville's final word, the poem which concludes *John Marr*, stresses the redemptive aspect of Ocean, not merely survival but secular baptism:

Pebbles [No. VII]

> Healed of my hurt, I laud the inhuman Sea—
> Yea, bless the Angels Four that there convene;
> For healed I am even by their pitiless breath
> Distilled in wholesome dew named rosmarine. (206)

As he had done with *John Marr*, Melville published *Timoleon* (1891) in a limited and private edition of twenty-five copies. I have already discussed the last third of this volume, the "Fruit of Travel Long Ago," and will not return to it here, although I would point out that the major and title poem, "Timoleon," is—if only in a figurative sense—another such Fruit; for although it was written sometime after 1877, the spirit that animates it is more reminiscent of *Pierre* (and Melville's early life) than any later work. It is set in ancient Greece where the titular protagonist and his elder brother, Timophanes, live in their mother's home (no mention is ever made of an earthly father). This woman, who would become "an envied dame of power, a social queen" (211), is obviously another version of Mrs. Glendinning and perhaps finds her origin in Melville's own mother who, as we know, was terribly conscious of the social status she lost after her husband's death. The white hope of the remaining Melvilles was not Herman, but his elder brother, Gansevoort (who died at thirty), and it is clear from family documents, as Leon Howard notes in relation to this poem, that Gansevoort was the favored son, the one who might yet recoup the family fortune.[24] Herman, regarded in his youth as rather slow and docile, could not be so relied on. In other words, the relationship of Herman, Gansevoort, and Maria Melville, however foreshortened and exaggerated, still bears a certain resemblance to that of Timoleon, Timophanes, and their mother:

> Timophanes was his mother's pride—
> Her pride, her pet, even all to her
> Who slackly on Timoleon looked:
> Scarce he (she mused) may proud affection stir.
>
> .   .   .   .
>
> When boys they were I helped the bent;
> I made the junior feel his place,
> Subserve the senior, love him, too;
> And sooth he does, and that's his saving grace.
>   But me the meek one never can serve,
> Not he, he lacks the quality keen
> To make the mother through the son
> An envied dame of power, a social queen. (211)

At first, as children, the brothers are "playfellows," but as they mature, "develop into variance wide in span"; then sibling rivalry evolves into active enmity, for Timophanes becomes the tyrant lord of Corinth, and Timoleon, whose heart is "just . . . and humane," whose love of justice is unexampled, and who is a "loyal son [and] . . . patriot true," feels "profound . . . hate" for his brother. Timoleon pleads with him to foreswear tyranny, but Timophanes literally laughs in his face. Thus, like fatherless Pierre, subject as well to a domineering mother, Timoleon resolves to act on behalf of the Olympian Father gods, scorning and chancing the scorn of the chthonic Mother deities:

In evil visions of the night
He sees the lictors of the gods,
Giant ministers of righteousness,
Their *fasces* threatened by the Furies' rods.
    But undeterred he wills to act,
Resolved thereon though Ate rise;
He heeds the voice whose mandate calls,
Or seems to call, peremptory from the skies. (212)

Timoleon kills his brother, "and Right in Corinth reassumes its place." (Pierre's murder of his cousin, Glen Stanly, provides a salient parallel.) But, of course, no reader should be fooled into supposing that Timoleon's motive is so disinterestedly high-minded and pure: for his self-righteousness and the absolute villainy of Timophanes strain all credible limit, even though Melville elevates the dialogue beyond familial jealousy onto the plane of abstract ideas:

. . . where dread stress inspires
A virtue beyond man's standard rate,
Seems virtue there a strain forbid—
Transcendence such as shares transgressions' fate? (209)

But it is as impossible to regard "Timoleon" as it is to regard *Pierre* solely on this level of discourse; the rationalizations of brother hatred constantly intrude. In short, like Pierre, Timoleon is a victim of self-deception, as Melville knows and makes perfectly clear by impugning his otherwise unimpeachable injunction:

He heeds the voice whose mandate calls,
Or seems to call, peremptory from the skies. (212)
                                              (Italics added.)

Pierre, of course, ultimately discovers that his "divine" mandate is of earthly fabrication, that sexual desire is as much as, if not more, his cue for passion as abstract love; Timoleon, on the other hand, never discovers that fraternal hatred no less than abstract justice is his hidden spring. But Timoleon does learn, by innocently trying to assert the Right, that the Right is not as uncomplex as he had supposed, that killing a hated and evil brother is no easy matter even if one's cause is entirely just. For "heavy," indeed, is a mother's ban— the revenge of the Furies—and captious, "the whispering-gallery of the world," but even more disagreeable is the force of remorseless conscience:

> Reaction took misgivings' tone,
> Infecting conscience, till betrayed
> To doubt the irrevocable doom
> Herself had authorized when undismayed. (213)

Timoleon first contemplates suicide, then "won from that," becomes an exile, although wherever he goes, he cannot elude "his playfellow's reproachful face." The high seriousness of Melville's argument cannot be doubted: that a man cannot serve both a god of spirit and a god of blood, and that if he must choose between them, he is trapped, a victim of conflicting claims:

> Estranged through one transcendent deed
> From common membership in mart,
> In severance he is like a head
> Pale after battle trunkless found apart. (214)

Again like Pierre, Timoleon is a kind of spiritually mutilated Enceladus, and he too finally loses all patience with the Father gods and arraigns "heaven as compromised in wrong":

> To second causes why appeal?
> Vain parleying here with fellow clods.
> To you, Arch Principals, I rear
> My quarrel, for this quarrel is with gods.
> Shall just men long to quit your world?
> It is aspersion of your reign;
> Your marbles in the temple stand—
> Yourselves as stony and invoked in vain?
> Ah, bear with one quite overborne,
> Olympians, if he chide ye now;
> Magnanimous be even though he rail
> And hard against ye set the bleaching brow.
> If conscience doubt, she'll next recant.
> What basis then? O, tell at last,
> Are earnest natures staggering here
> But fatherless shadows from no substance cast?
> Yea, *are* ye, gods? Then ye, 'tis ye

Should show what touch of tie ye may,
Since ye, too, if not wrung are wronged
By grievous misconceptions of your sway.
    But deign, some little sign be given—
Low thunder in your tranquil skies;
Me reassure, nor let me be
Like a lone dog that for a master cries. (214–15)

Recalling the spirit and rhetoric of Pierre and the invocation of Clarel, Timoleon implores the gods who, needless to say, give no signs.

Therefore, if Timoleon ultimately thrives in exile, it is not because he is able to reconcile himself to a silent heaven but because, unlike Pierre, he is somehow able to mollify the Furies. For he is eventually absolved of his crime and would indeed be welcomed home a hero. That is to say, he simply outlasts the revenge of the Mother country and survives the revenge of the Mother goddesses—although hardened beyond forgiveness, he scorns his native land. Thus as the early "Fragment" records a *Pierre*-like prelude to Pierre's struggle with the mother, so the late "Timoleon" records a *Pierre*-like aftermath. Timoleon's last years are spent in Sicily as "the Isle's loved guest," a fate which braids victory with martyrdom—Timoleon, "crowned with laurel twined with thorn. . . ."

As poetry, *John Marr* may have a greater claim to our attention than *Timoleon*, but as far as the themes of the volumes go, it is *Timoleon* that recalls Melville's greatest work. Both, however, are absolutely essential for, and together provide the gateway to, the sensibility of *Billy Budd*: the former by establishing the principles of ultimate harmony and reconciliation; the latter, the collision of irreconcilable alternatives. For this is the implicit theme not only of the title poem but of at least ten other poems in the volume as well.

For instance, in "After the Pleasure Party," a female astronomer suffers the agony of sexual frustration and blames it on the counterdemand of intellectual desire:

And kept I long heaven's watch for this,
Condemning love, for this, even this?
O terrace chill in Northern air,

O reaching ranging tube I placed
Against yon skies, and fable chased
Till, fool, I hailed for sister there
Starred Cassiopea in Golden Chair. (217)

In youth she spurned the god of love; now, in middle-age, she herself
is spurned. Although it has been demonstrated that her emotions are
bisexually oriented,[25] still, as in *Clarel*, given the context in which
the poem was written—the desires of self and the strictures of society
—her suffering is not entirely attributable to psychoneurosis. Her
plight is not only real but seemingly inevitable.

In "The Ravaged Villa" Melville draws a more complex set of
antitheses:

In shards the sylvan vases lie,
    Their links of dance undone,
And brambles wither by thy brim,
    Choked fountain of the sun!
The spider in the laurel spins,
    The weed exiles the flower:
And, flung to kiln, Apollo's bust
    Makes lime for Mammon's tower. (222)

. . . the Spiritual and the Material, the Cultural and the Industrial,
the Hellenic and the Christian, the Sylvan and the Citified, the Whole
and the Fragmentary, the Cultivated and the Wild, the Ancient and
the Modern. (Similarly, "The Age of the Antonines" contrasts Ancient
with Modern, more specifically Roman with American.)

Five other poems recall antinomies familiar to all readers of Melville's early work: "Lamia's Song" opposes the Alp with the Valley,
the life of challenge with the life of ease; and "The Night March,"
the lonely Individual with the Mass, the Leader with the Followers.
In "The Weaver" Melville again makes it thoroughly clear that
man cannot serve two masters, himself and his God, a lesson Father
Mapple well knew; and in "The Enthusiast" he counters discretion
and "conform[ity]" with a Pierre-like devotion to Truth—he will not
declare so wholeheartedly for the latter in *Billy Budd*. "In a Garret"—

Gems and jewels let them heap—
    Wax sumptuous as the Sophi:

> For me, to grapple from Art's deep
>   One dripping trophy!— (228)

contrasts land-sense with sea-sense, the narrowly perfected *objet d'art* with the work of uncalculated creative energy, and (inferentially) Classical taste with Romantic, and the Conscious Mind with the Unconscious.

In *Timoleon* the irreconcilable contradictions of life are resolvable only through Art, an act of human possibility—not as in some of the other verse, through Time, Nature, Death, or Religion:

Art

> In placid hours well-pleased we dream
> Of many a brave unbodied scheme.
> But form to lend, pulsed life create,
> What unlike things must meet and mate:
> A flame to melt—a wind to freeze;
> Sad patience—joyous energies;
> Humility—yet pride and scorn;
> Instinct and study; love and hate;
> Audacity—reverence. These must mate,
> And fuse with Jacob's mystic heart,
> To wrestle with the angel—Art. (231)

But the sanitive powers of Art are temporary, not permanent, as the female astronomer well knows and regretfully admits: "For never passion peace shall bring, / Nor Art inanimate for long / Inspire" (221). The fact is that throughout *Timoleon* Melville puts "the torch to ties though dear, / If ties but tempters be" (231). Thus, in "C[oleridge]'s Lament" he refuses to succumb to the Tahiti of nostalgia and sentiment; the "lovers' quarrel" between himself and life— the phrase originally is Melville's, not Frost's—came in youth and youth only, and now he is old. Nor will the god who came when the world was young come again; in "The Margrave's Birthnight" Christ, who marred his grave, will not partake of a second supper, though many guests have been received and wait expectantly. But perhaps the poem which best expresses the relentless pessimism of this volume is "The Garden of Metrodorus," for here Melville re-institutes the green interior close—his master symbol—but in such an ambiguous way as to impugn its holiness:

The Athenians mark the moss-grown gate
And hedge untrimmed that hides the haven green:
    And who keeps here his quiet state?
    And shares he sad or happy fate
Where never foot-path to the gate is seen?

Here none come forth, here none go in,
Here silence strange, and dumb seclusion dwell:
    Content from loneness who may win?
    And is this stillness peace or sin
Which noteless thus apart can keep its dell? (225)

Save an occasional stanza in newspaper or novel and the four volumes of verse we have already discussed, Melville published no other poetry during his lifetime, although he was preparing a fifth volume as death interceded. The first and larger section of it is entitled *Weeds and Wildings*, the second and slimmer, "A Rose or Two," and, taken singly or together, they announce an unexpectedly horticultural attitude. Dedicated to a devoted wife of forty-four years, it revels in that floral imagery Melville never quite eshewed but never, on the other hand, as totally embraced since the halcyon honeymoon days of *Mardi*. Indeed, one may well cull from it a pretty anthology of flowers: rose, iris, pink, clover, aster, holly, buttercup, dandelion, aloe, lilac, willow, syringa, magnolia, hollyhock, sweet-briar, violet, daisy, pansy, and posy. *Weeds and Wildings* is, in the main, playful, pensive and poignant, and it would be foolish to doubt the obvious serenity of a volume whose latitude is Eden's, although it might be suggested that, as in *Billy Budd*, the serenity is not unqualified:

... here by Eden's gate I linger
Love's tryst to keep, with truant Eve. (265)

But, in point of fact, the lovers "languish" outside the gate, "with the secret desire for the garden of God," the sacred garden of Melville's myth.

Thus the redaction of the quest for sacrament may metamorphose, but it never really dies, as the most important poem in the volume,

"The Rose Farmer," affirms. (Melville himself, we might add, became in later years a superb cultivator of red roses; like white whales, but in a minor key, they too unite the beautiful with the dangerous.) The farmer of our poem is an old man, one of those

> . . . who after ragged scrambles
> Through fate's blessed thorns and brambles
> Come unto our roses late— (303)

Roses, then, evidently symbolize peace and ease, and devotion to them, a kind of natural religion, an allegory of love. But notice—they are not the farmer's by right of lineal inheritance:

> A corpulent grandee of the East,
> Whose kind good will to me began
> When I against his Rhamadan
> Prepared a *chowder* for his feast,
> Well dying, he remembered me. . . . (304)

Through the disguise one recognizes Queequeg in his last incarnation, Queequeg, who once bequeathed to Ishmael the gift of life.

The farmer's dilemma is whether to gather his flowers in beautiful heaps or scimitar them in order to distill "some crystal drops of Attar," and the problem, as we shall see, strikes to the heart of a perennial Melvillean dilemma. The farmer seeks the advice of a sybaritic Persian who unequivocally tells him to heap the flowers:

> 'Every way—for wise employment,
> Repute and profit, health, enjoyment,
> I am for roses—*sink* the Attar!' (309)

As for distillation,

> '. . . Go ask the Parsee yonder.
> Lean as a rake with his distilling,
> Cancel his debts, scarce worth a shilling!
> How he exists I frequent wonder.
> No neighbor loves him. . . . ' (307)

Thus Melville roughly establishes an opposition between Queequeg and the Parsee, Fedallah (and, by implication, Ahab), just as he had done in *Moby-Dick*; between the submissive accepter of roses as they are and their aggressive destroyer who would transform them; between one who would cultivate his garden and one who would quest for its "mummified quintessence" (307); between one satisfied with Secular Reality and one who demands the Absolute. And, discouragingly enough, the market for roses and attar is very much like that for *Typees* and *Moby-Dicks* respectively; says the Persian:

'I give away, but more I sell,
In mossy pots, or bound in posies,
Always a market for my roses.
But attar, why, it comes so dear
Tis far from popular, that's clear.' (307)

The farmer leaves the sybarite as much in doubt as he was before, wondering if, perhaps, the easiest way of life, the way which denies the "transcendental essence," is not the best, but resolved, in any event, not to argue an insoluble proposition:

Discreet, in second thought's immersion
I wended from this prosperous Persian
Who, verily, seemed in life rewarded
For sapient prudence not amiss,
Nor transcendental essence hoarded
In hope of quintessential bliss:
No, never with painstaking throes
Essays to crystallize the rose.
But here arrest the loom—the line.
Though damask be your precious stuff,
Spin it not out too superfine:
The flower of a subject is enough. (309–10)

As Melville had spoken symbolically of the quester as ship and fish in the nautical *John Marr*, so in the pastoral *Weeds and Wildings* he speaks of him as plant (recalling, of course, the sea-plant tuft of kelp). In "The American Aloe on Exhibition," for instance, the aloe apparently symbolizes the late-blooming poet and the "bon-bons" of the first stanza, instantly attractive but impermanent literature:

But few they were who came to see
    The century-Plant in flower:

Ten cents admission-price you pay
  For bon-bons of the hour.

In strange inert blank unconcern
  Of wild things at the Zoo,
The patriarch let the sight-seers stare—
  Nor recked who came to view.

But lone at night the garland sighed
  While moaned the aged stem:
'At last, at last! but joy and pride
  What part have I with them?'

Let be the dearth that kept me back
  Now long from wreath decreed;
But, Ah, ye Roses that have passed
  Accounting me a weed! (278–79)

Melville implies in the middle stanzas that his seeming uninterest in popular success—his "strange inert blank unconcern"—is the facade of truer feelings, but that, after a lifetime of popular disregard, recognition has come too late to do him any good. In this respect, the poem seems to be an ironic commentary on those foreign readers who discovered Melville, read him assiduously, and at least from 1884 expressed in their letters admiration for his unsung genius—from England, James Billson, W. Clark Russell, and J. W. Barrs; from Canada, Archibald MacMechan, Munro Professor of English at Dalhousie University, the first academic to show real interest.

In "Time's Betrayal" Melville again seems to be symbolizing himself; in the praescript to the poem he writes that

> . . . systematically to bleed the immature trunk, though some
> sugar-makers, detected in the act on ground not their own, aver
> that it does the sylvan younker a deal of good, can hardly contrib-
> ute to the tree's amplest development or insure patriarchal long
> life to it. Certain it is, that in some young maples the annual
> tapping would seem to make precocious the autumnal ripening
> or change of the leaf. (273)

It would seem that Melville is alluding to his own early and over-rapid career—*Typee* through *Pierre*, seven books in seven years—a phase that ended, as he well knew, when he reached his "inmost leaf." And yet, although the tree does age prematurely, "such premature change would seem strikingly to enhance the splendor of the tints":

> In season the leafage will tell,
> Turning red ere the rime [i.e. hoar frost]
> Yet, in turning, all beauty excell [*sic*]
> For a time, for a time! (274)

Perhaps this is how Melville conceived the fruits of his "spontaneous after-growth," which blossomed forth not only in these poems but also, just before the final frost, in *Billy Budd*.

Perhaps the most curious section of *Weeds and Wildings* is "Rip Van Winkle's Lilac," for one would not have expected Melville to collaborate with that "happy Shade," Washington Irving; one recalls Melville's obliquely pejorative allusions to Irving in his review of *Mosses from an Old Manse* and in "Bartleby" as well as his astringent comment in an 1851 letter to Evert Duyckinck that "Irving is a grasshopper" compared with Hawthorne.[26] Nevertheless, as Melville retells the tale, we begin to realize the unsuspected affinity that binds them. For Rip, like Tommo, seeks and finds sleep, unconsciousness, in "an innermost hollow of . . . mountains" (281); the Catskills are Rip's sacred glade and "insular Tahiti." We meet him as he starts his uncertain way home "in his picturesque resurrection" (290), for the tale, "happily told by happiest Irving" is indeed one of temporal rebirth, the defeat of death. Melville is in full sympathy, and even adds a symbolic detail: the weeping willow Rip left at his doorstep is, upon his return, a laughing lilac.

After his retirement from the New York City Custom House in 1885, Melville probably revised, but never published, a series of sketches he had begun nine or ten years earlier about two members of the fictional Burgundy Club, a rather Addisonian constituency, the Marquis de Grandvin and his disciple Jack Gentian. (Melville, of course, is punning on names again: Burgundy red, Grand vin,

Gentian purple.) The Marquis is a Frenchman, Jack is an American, but both are cordial, gallant, and gracious; indeed, they are non-questing Bachelors of Paradise. In the six short chapters he devotes to them, Melville tells us little of the Marquis but discourses at comparative length on his companion, who bears some resemblance, literally and psychologically, to the author himself. For instance, we are told that Gentian is a man of "impulsive straightforwardness" and that he is known for an "occasional unlicensed emphasis in his talk," although neither characteristic is ever revealed in the text. Of "double Revolutionary descent," Jack wears the order of the Cincinnati (a badge of honor worn only by descendants of officers of the Revolution), and although, in consequence, he fancies himself something of an aristocrat, he is, in fact, at "heart," a "democrat." He was graduated from Harvard (the whaleship was Ishmael's Harvard and Yale), fought on the Northern side in the Civil War and became a Major, as did one of Melville's own grandfathers in the Revolution (the other becoming a General). And as Major Melville continued to wear military garb long after the war (he is properly enshrined in Oliver Wendell Holmes' "The Last Leaf"), so Jack Gentian is an apostle of the bygone. Engaged in nostalgic reminiscence, he adverts to a casual acquaintance of Melville's prime, the minor poet Charles Fenno Hoffman; and, on another occasion, the narrator reminds Jack of Nathaniel Hawthorne's English devotional, *Our Old Home*, which he (or, perhaps, Melville himself) misremembers as *Our Old Name*.[27]

Grandvin and Gentian are poets as well as gentlemen, and Melville attributes to them two poems he may have originally written soon after his Mediterranean tour of 1856–1857. "At the Hostelry," assigned to Grandvin, records the conversation of such genial seventeenth century Dutchmen and Flemings as Van der Velde, Douw, Steen, and Brouwer on the subject of the Picturesque, while Teniers (about whom Melville wrote "The Bench of Boors") is praised because he "beautifies the grime. . . ." (323). Far more interesting, however, is the silence of those who do not speak than the chatter of those who do. Claude, Rembrandt, Velasquez, Durer, Poussin, Da Vinci and Michelangelo (among others) wordlessly listen, while

Tintoretto, speaking as if for them all, remarks that he has little use for the Picturesque.

The difference between the pigmy Van der Velde and the giant Rembrandt is approximately the difference between *Israel Potter* (in which Melville leans as heavily as he ever does on the Picturesque) and *Moby-Dick*; or between Washington Irving, that most picturesque of American writers, and Melville himself at his best; or, as Melville construed it, between the tempting Valley of ease and the rigorous Alp of challenge. And, therefore, it is not without significance that Melville's ultimate mellowing led him to a tentative conciliation with Irving; and "Rip Van Winkle's Lilac" records how an itinerant artist paints the flower emergent from rotted boards and willingly acknowledges how moved he is by the picturesqueness of the scene.

As "At the Hostelry" illuminates Melville's ideas, so "Naples in the Time of Bomba" illuminates the man. For its "author" is Jack Gentian, Melville's surrogate, and in it, as in "Timoleon" and "The American Aloe on Exhibition," a well-deserved but entirely unsolicited recognition is paid the protagonist who, inevitably, finds such praise gratuitous:

> But I, Jack Gentian, what reck I,
> The popular hero, object sole
> Of this ovation! (341)

Again, one must consider that "knot of 'Melville readers,' " most of whom were Englishmen, some of whom corresponded with the author. And they admired most of all, it would seem, some of the least approachable books. J. W. Barrs, for example, claimed "a very deep rooted fondness for Babbalanja. . . ." "Time, which is the solver of all riddles," Melville wrote his father-in-law in 1849, "will solve 'Mardi' " [*sic*]; and Barrs added that " 'Pierre' [*sic*] I have always liked. . . ." Archibald MacMecham mentioned that he had "for a number of years . . . read and reread 'Moby Dick [*sic*] with increasing pleasure on every perusal. . . ." And W. Clark Russell in an article in "America," a Chicago weekly, stated flatly that

There is no name in American letters that deserves to stand

higher [than Melville's] for beauty of imagination, for accuracy of reproduction, for originality of conception, and for a quality of imagination that in 'Moby Dick,' for instance, lifts some of his utterances to such a height of bold and swelling fancy as one must search the pages of the Elizabethan dramatists to parallel.[28]

Although Melville probably never saw Russell's article, he was aware of Russell's profound admiration and must have suspected at the end—as he must have doubted during the years in which his works went unattended—that he would not be forgotten.

But, however we regard it, Melville's dialogue with Fame was an ambiguous one; for even as he desired recognition, he flirted with anonymity. At the outset of his career, he signed the "Fragments" L. A. V. In his prime, he published his review of the *Mosses* "By a Virginian Spending July in Vermont," offered to publish *Pierre* anonymously, or *"By a Vermonter,"* or *"By Guy Winthrop,"* and first published "The Encantadas" in *Putnam's Monthly* under the pseudonym Salvator R. Tarnmoor. Near the end, he would have published *Clarel* (and did publish *John Marr*) anonymously and did not attempt to publish *Billy Budd* at all. As a youth, he was signed aboard the *St. Lawrence* as Norman Melville; in his prime, there were those who insisted that "Herman Melville" was really an alias; at the end, the New York *Times* reported the death of Henry Melville.[29] The public man enjoyed his early fame, relished philosophical conversation, and was a good friend; in fact, two of his shipmates named children after him. But the private man embraced solitude and would not talk about his work. Like Ishmael, Melville could tell tall and ingratiating tales, but "Ishmael," as everyone knows, is a pseudonym.

A ffiliated with the floral poetry of Melville's later career is the short prose sketch "Under the Rose," which purports to be "an extract from an old MS. entitled 'Travels in Persia. . . .' "[30] Although in a barren pseudo-seventeenth century style, it interests us nonetheless because Melville once again appropriates the symbolism of the wall. The narrative centers upon a beautiful amber vase in which tiny insects are embedded and onto which a "round device of sculpture on

one side" is attached; this "relievo" portrays two angel-like figures
approaching a "Job-like" man who sits near a tomb. However, when
the vase is filled with downhanging roses, both the insects and the
iconography are concealed. Enthralled by the vase, a great Persian
composed an allegorical poem, which, suitably translated, reads as follows:

> Specks, tiny specks, in this translucent amber,
> Your leave, bride-roses, may one pry and see?
> How odd! a dainty little skeleton-chamber;
> And—odder yet—sealed walls but windows be!
> Death's open secret.—Well, we are;
> And here comes the jolly angel with the jar! (344)

Dorothee Metlitsky Finkelstein, one of the few critics to take this
sketch seriously, observes that

> In "Under the Rose" the symbol [of insects trapped in amber]
> re-iterates the tragic predicament of mortal man trapped in an
> enigmatic substance which is both life-in-death and death-in-life.
>   The owner of the vase is called the "Azem." It is obvious [even
> from his relatively scant knowledge of transliterated Arabic]
> that Melville knew the meaning and usage of the Arabic word
> al-'Azim, the Great, as one of the attributes of God.[31]

The figures on the relievo who approach suffering Man, she continues,
are "two angels of Islamic tradition": one carries a spade and a pot
of roses and "suggests a grave-digger"; the other, "the jolly angel with
the jar," is a "wine-bearer," but "[h]e, too, in the final analysis, represents death. . . ."[32] We should only add that, like his greatest mentor,
Melville also regards Man as but a fly to the gods, a Job-like sufferer,
yet not one without an insight into his final condition. Man not only
patiently waits for Death but also sees, through the impenetrable
wall of Secular Reality suddenly made translucent, the instruments of
God approach.

  This reading of "Under the Rose" accords well with another of
Melville's last sketches, "Daniel Orme."[33] Daniel is a gruff, old sea-
dog who, it is suggested, was once a buccaneer (that is, a quester);
retired now but living in a hotel "hard by the waters," he becomes
a cynosure through "a singularity in his habits. . . ."

At times, but only when he might think himself quite alone, he would roll aside the bosom of his darned Guernsey frock and steadfastly contemplate something on his body. If by chance discovered in this, he would quickly conceal all and growl his resentment. (119)

Superstitiously eager to discover his secret, several fellow lodgers drug his tea one evening, and, as he sleeps, an old-clothesman examines him and reports to the others what he has seen:

> . . . a crucifix in indigo and vermillion tattooed on the chest and on the side of the heart. Slanting across the crucifix and paling the pigment there ran a whitish scar, long and thin, such as might ensue from the slash of a cutlass, imperfectly parried or dodged. (120)

According to William Braswell, who recognizes in the sketch "a symbolical self portrait" of the author, "these few sentences ['compress . . .'] the most moving part of . . . [Melville's] own religious history."[34] The residents of the hotel cry for Orme's eviction, but they are denied by the hotel-mistress, who resolutely stands by her tenant. She is, in effect, the mother who protects her child, and theirs is the alliance of the individuated hero.

On Easter Day Orme dies—sitting on a terrace, his opened eyes turned toward Ocean; his pipe smoked to the full, then broken. He dies with his life fulfilled and with the dignity men would deprive him of. His last thoughts, Melville hints, are of "many a far-off scene of the wide world's beauty dreamily suggested by the hazy water before him" (122)—thoughts of a sea-rover which include, we may be sure, the Enviable Isles and the sacred glen. As in "Rip Van Winkle's Lilac" and "Under the Rose," so in "Daniel Orme": even as Man nears death, he becomes aware of eternal life.

Although, as we have said, the women of Melville's fiction from "Cock-A-Doodle-Doo!" through "Fruit of Travel Long Ago" are not of literary importance, it *is* significant that almost all of them may be characterized in one of three ways: as humble and passive victims

(Hunilla, Marianna, Merrymusk's wife, and the exploited virgins of "The Tartarus of Maids"); as Good "Mothers" lavishing affection (Silvio's "maternal" daughter in "Pausilippo," the girl who tends Jimmy Rose in his last illness, the Negress who suckles her child in "Benito Cereno," and the quester's wife in the "Envoi"); and as shrewish parodies of the Terrible Mother (the wives in "I and My Chimney" and "The Apple-Tree Table"). The point is that Melville deliberately eschewed formidable images of the Terrible Mother—another way of saying that he did not permit his protagonists to quest. But with "America" of the *Battle-Pieces*, the Dread Mother (or, as she is occasionally symbolized, the Mother Country) reenters the fiction, for if the process of individuation is to continue, the Quester (the ego become the Self) must fulfill his destiny in relationship to her and to the unconscious realm she represents. But now the savagery of Ahab and Pierre has been attenuated and become a tangentially minor strain. If it is true that Mortmain and Ungar still hate the Mother, it is also true that Rolfe, the mature and central consciousness of *Clarel*, has made his peace with her. If it is true that Timoleon scorns her, it is equally true that she forgives him, that in "America" the Sons and the Mother have effected a reconciliation, and that in "The Enviable Isles," "The Maldive Shark," and "Daniel Orme" there is a real harmony between them.

Thus it is fascinating to observe that of the sixteen books Melville wrote, he dedicated only one, the last, to a woman. All the others went to male relatives, male friends or acquaintances, the Union dead, or went undedicated—except for *Pierre* which was addressed to Mr. Greylock, and *Israel Potter* which was addressed to the Bunker Hill Monument. For it is only after the little fish have made their peace with the depontentiated Parent and Daniel Orme has reunited himself with the maternal protectress that Melville can dedicate *Weeds and Wildings* to his wife, the "Madonna of the Trefoil" as he now calls her, the Holy Mother. The curve of his love for Elizabeth, in other words—it is, roughly, the same sort of curve for Hawthorne and, in a less intense spirit, for Duyckinck—carried him from an initial burst of enthusiasm, through a period of alienation, to this ultimate renewal of sentiment. There is no doubt that Melville was deeply in love with the idealized sister-bride, the Yillah of his dreams, and, in fact, one would imagine that most of the letters Elizabeth cherished all her life and which were destroyed on the day of her death[35] date from these early years, from, let us say, their courtship (1847) to Herman's return from England (1850) where, as his *Journal* records, he suffered pangs of homesickness.

But, soon after his return, he seems to have undergone a growing disillusion with marriage and sex to judge from his suggestive scoring and underscoring (1851) of a passage in "The Maid's Tragedie":

> For aught I know, all husbands are like me;
> And every one I talk with of his wife,
> Is but a well dissembler of his woes
> As I am; would I knew it, for the rareness afflicts me now....[36]

From such bitter remarks in *Pierre* (1852) about marriage as this one:

> That nameless and infinitely delicate aroma of inexpressible
> tenderness and attentiveness which, in every refined and honor-
> able attachment, is cotemporary with the courtship, and precedes
> the final banns and the rite . . . like the *bouquet* of the costliest
> German wines, too often evaportates upon pouring out to drink, in
> the disenchanting glasses of the matrimonial days and nights.[37]

As well as from that horrible little tale of mechanical love, "The Tartarus of Maids" (1855). Nevertheless, at least from the time of the "Envoi" (c. 1858), where the quester gratefully accepts domestic confinement, Melville seems to have gradually reaffirmed his love for Elizabeth until, as his tributary dedication implies, she had become for him a version of the archetypal Mother. It was from her terrible arms, in *Typee*, that the phylogenetic Hero had wrestled himself free; it was to her merciful arms that he voluntarily returned.

I have called *Billy Budd* the capstone of a career, and, like *The Tempest*, with which it has been compared, it makes a work of art of the canon and the life, affording both a wholeness and a harmony. In retrospect, we see that Melville had to write *Billy Budd* for at least four reasons, and in each case his conscious choice brilliantly affirmed his unconscious "urge towards self-realization." First, after the ferocious but necessary combat with the Great Mother, the Quester, in his transpersonal progress toward individuation, gradually begins to disengage himself from the quest: the soldiers in *Battle-Pieces* are less involved in questing than Pierre; Rolfe is less involved than the soldiers; the tiny pilot fish less involved than Rolfe; Daniel Orme less than the pilot fish. This sequence reaches its natural and inevitable conclusion with Billy Budd, the ultimate non-quester.

Second, although the quest for the Father is, on the whole, less harrowing than the quest for the Mother, it is no less persistent .Thus we realize that Redburn's secret sympathy for Jackson on the voyage out does not result from homosexual desire but from the longing of a timid child for a parent-figure; and that White Jacket's affection for Jack Chase does not constitute a homosexual allegiance but rather hero worship of a son for an ideal father. And in their separate ways, Ahab, Pierre, Bartleby, Clarel, and Timoleon all seek to embrace the Father whom they simultaneously affirm and deny. Billy, however, does not emerge from the main line of Melvillean protagonists and, therefore, his *foremost* predecessors are not to be found in the matriarchal novels—*Typee*, *Mardi*, *Moby-Dick*, and *Pierre*—but rather as the titular heroes of the partriarchal ones, *Redburn* and *White-Jacket*. But only in his last book does Melville finally achieve the "elemental"[38] and sacramental mergence of Father and Son, and only then does he dedicate a book to Jack Chase.

Third, as we have already mentioned on several occasions, Billy incarnates the final stage of individuation, the emergence of the Self. But this emergence, says Jung, is in a sense foreordained, because the symbol of

> . . . the *hieros gamos* in the pleroma . . . implies . . . the future birth of the divine child, who, in accordance with the divine trend toward incarnation, will choose as his birthplace the empirical man. The metaphysical process is known to the psychology of the unconscious as the individuation process.[39]

In Melville we may discern this metaphysical and psychological sequence in the relationship between "The Enviable Isles," wherein the

pleromatic union is symbolized, and *Billy Budd*, wherein the Christ-
like, "child-man" is rendered incarnate in "Baby" Billy.

Finally, with *Billy Budd* Melville completed the recapitulation of
the first phase of his career, a recapitulation he had unconsciously begun in *Battle-Pieces* and, as if obsessively, continued in *Clarel*. For
as these books bear certain rough equivalence to *Typee-Omoo* and
Mardi respectively, so *Billy Budd* is noticeably reminiscent of *Redburn-White-Jacket*. (These affinities—*White-Jacket*, in particular,
seems to have been a "source"—are so well known that there is no
need to catalogue them in the text.)[40] In sum, we may say that with
Billy Budd Melville seized an opportunity for putting his life and his
art into a final order.

As Billy Budd, newly impressed aboard the *Bellipotent*, leaves his
former ship, he waves good-bye to his comrades and then makes "a
salutation as to the ship herself, 'And good-bye to you too, old *Rights-
of-Man.*' " Melville's irony—not Billy's—is obviously intentional and
perhaps too, as John Noone suggests, he is also implying a symbolic
removal from the world of Rousseau to the world of Hobbes.[41] Of
one thing we may be sure: Billy is "twenty-one" (44), technically a
man, and since he has attained his chronological majority, he may no
longer live as a prelapsarian Adam. Nor am I now—nor was Melville—employing a facile metaphor: we are meant to understand that
aboard the *Rights* Billy symbolizes Adam before the Fall, as the incident of his fight with the Red Whiskers makes perfectly clear. Captain
Graveling describes Billy to the impressing officer, Lieutenant Rat-
cliffe, as one loved by all save "the big shaggy chap with the fire red
whiskers":

> He indeed, out of envy, perhaps, of the newcomer, and thinking
> such a 'sweet and pleasant fellow,' as he mockingly designated
> him to the others, could hardly have the spirit of a gamecock,
> must needs bestir himself in trying to get up an ugly row with
> him. Billy forebore with him and reasoned with him in a pleasant
> way—he is something like myself, Lieutenant, to whom aught like
> a quarrel is hateful—but nothing served. So, in the second dog-
> watch one day, the Red Whiskers in presence of the others, under
> pretense of showing Billy just whence a sirloin steak was cut—

for the fellow had once been a butcher—insultingly gave him
a dig under the ribs. Quick as lightning Billy let fly his arm. I dare
say he never meant to do quite as much as he did, but anyhow
he gave the burly fool a terrible drubbing. (47)

Like the villainous Claggart, the scurvy Red Whiskers is envious of
Billy, envious of his popularity with the crew and perhaps angered
by his invincible innocence as well. And, therefore, again like Claggart and in the same language, he too mocks Billy's most apparent
defect: his effeminacy. Both euphemistically call him a "sweet and
pleasant [young] fellow," and there is no doubt that Billy is seemingly effeminate:

He was young; and despite his all but fully developed frame, in
aspect looked even younger than he really was, owing to a
lingering adolescent expression in the as yet smooth face all but
feminine in purity of natural complexion. . . . (50)

Little did Billy "observe that something about him provoked an ambiguous smile in one of two harder faces among the bluejackets"
(51). Billy, thinks the Red Whiskers, "could hardly have the spirit
of a gamecock"—a standard Melvillean pun—but then the Red
Whiskers goes too far, and "insultingly gave him a dig under the
ribs." A simple elbow under the rib should hardly call forth such retribution as a terrible drubbing, but the Red Whiskers has really
done much more: he has elbowed Billy in the sex—in the sir (male)
loin (genital), and the genital of prelapsarian Billy may very well be
the place from which Eve was born—the rib, not the groin, just as
the blow to the side may also suggest the spear Christ Himself ultimately suffers.

Indeed, this episode aboard the *Rights* is prefiguratory in several
senses and should not be, as it usually is, casually disregarded; for,
in Captain Vere's cabin, most of its elements will reappear intensified
or transformed. The man Red Whiskers will become the Satanic antagonist Claggart; the symbolic blow to Billy's sex will assume the
proportion of symbolic "impotence"; and the symbolic Billy as Adam
who suffers it will become the symbolic Billy as Christ crucified. But
we shall discuss the fatal event aboard the *Bellipotent* in due course.

"By his original constitution aided by the co-operating influences of his lot, Billy in many respects was little more than a sort of upright barbarian, much such perhaps as Adam presumably might have been ere the urbane Serpent wriggled himself into his company" (52). But soon after Billy climbs aboard Captain Vere's ship, he falls, for despite his innocence, he is now revealed to be imperfect—he suffers from the tongue-tie, "a striking instance that the arch interferer, the envious marplot of Eden, still has more or less to do with every human consignment to this planet of Earth" (53). Like the Red Whiskers and Claggart, Satan himself is motivated, in part, by envy, and before long his urbane representative wriggles himself into Billy's company.

John Claggart is a man in whom reason has run riot, and for reasons not even "psychologic theologians" can comprehend. That he suffers, at bottom, from "a phenomenal pride" conditioned by a "Natural Depravity" is easily ascertained, but such words hardly elucidate that "mystery of iniquity" wherein lurks the ultimate cause of his "elemental evil." The immediate cause, however, the event that irrevocably confirms the direction of his "monomania" (90), is somewhat easier to understand and helps explain why Claggart, like maddened Ahab, singularly devotes himself to hunting down an unselfconscious prey. (I fasten here on some of the similarities between the questers; the overwhelming differences are obvious to all.) Just as Ahab, after Moby Dick bites off his leg, comes to believe that the Whale personifies all Evil and is consciously malicious, so Claggart, after Billy spills his soup pan before him, comes to believe that Billy bears him "malice" (80) and that the apparently trivial spilling is an act of direct mockery (78). But, like the elbow under the rib, it is not as trivial as it seems, to the man who suffers it.

The "greasy liquid" that streams across Claggart's path has long since been understood as symbolic sperm,[42] and it is—at least as far as Claggart is concerned. To Billy the spilling is pure accident, but to the Master-at-Arms it is a deliberate provocation, a stream flung across his path as if it were a gauntlet, a brazen yet backhand tease by one who has presumably discovered his secret. And, in fact,

> pausing, he was about to *ejaculate something hasty* at the sailor, but checked himself, and pointing down to the streaming soup,

playfully tapped him from behind with his rattan, saying in a low musical voice peculiar to him at times, 'Handsomely done, my lad! And handsome is as handsome did it, too.' (72) (Italics added.)

Thus Melville exposes Claggart, as he does also on those other occasions

When Claggart's unobserved glance happened to light on belted Billy rolling along the upper gun deck in the leisure of the second dogwatch, exchanging passing broadsides of fun with other young promenaders in the crowd [;] that glance would follow the cheerful sea Hyperion with a settled meditative and melancholy expression, his eyes strangely suffused with incipient feverish tears. Then would Claggart look like a man of sorrows. Yes, and sometimes the melancholy expression would have in it a touch of soft yearning, as if Claggart could even have loved Billy but for fate and ban. (87–88)

Like Captain Ahab—and Jim Conklin and Joe Christmas—John Claggart is also a "man of sorrows." But he does not bear a descriptive of Christ and His initials because Melville is making a sly joke in an "inside narrative"; and certainly not because he is engaging in blasphemy. Melville, rather, is symbolizing the theological and psychological interdependence of Claggart and Billy, for "if we see the traditional figure of Christ as a parallel to the psychic manifestation of the self, then the Antichrist would correspond to the shadow of the self, namely, the dark half of the human totality, which ought not to be judged too optimistically"[43]—a description which neatly fits the man who hates himself for loving, whose yearning for Billy is always "an evanescence, and quckly repented of. . . ." (88). In W. H. Auden's words,

Claggart, as the Devil, cannot . . . admit a sexual desire, for that would be an admission of loneliness which pride [and Claggart's is 'phenomenal'] cannot admit.

For

Absolute pride denies that the six other deadly sins are its children and despises them as weakness, being incapable of seeing that it is the source of all weakness. The Devil, therefore, cannot himself be lustful, gluttonous, avaricious, envious, slothful, or angry, for his pride will not allow him to be anything less than proud.[44]

But even if Claggart's homosexual motive is "half-stated only to be withdrawn" because the Devil "cannot himself be lustful," the effects of the motive linger long enough to determine the course of Claggart's behavior.

Thus, three times after the soup-spilling, Melville re-introduces the episode as evidence that impels Claggart to believe, quite sincerely, that Billy is less innocent than he seems; that, in Claggart's words to Vere, "A mantrap may be under the ruddy-tipped daisies" (94). For, like Ahab, Claggart insists that the world of Appearance is deceptive. Look to "the little lower layer," Ahab counsels Starbuck—like "Starry" Vere, a courageous man, sterling but not brilliant. Look to the mantrap beneath, Claggart echoes. And since neither Claggart nor Ahab can believe that his prey is exactly what he seems to be— a childlike man, a dumb beast—he ends by finding an enemy where none is. For Claggart "can really form no conception of an unreciprocated malice" (80), and, therefore, he projects upon the object of his quest the hatred *he* feels and fancies, all the while, that he is the one hated. The result of such madness is fatal: in final confrontation the hunted turns upon and assails the hunter. As the Whale smashes the *Pequod*, so Billy—like Moby Dick, unspeakably silent, desperately harrowed, unable to respond except through violence—kills Claggart with a blow.

Like Starbuck, Captain Vere watches in horror unable to prevent the final assault, and from this point in the novella he becomes its major protagonist. Recent *Billy Budd* scholarship has, in fact, particularly dwelt upon his character, and now there are as many cases "against" the Captain as there once were "for" him. For Vere is deeply ambiguous—his decision to hang Billy, greatly disputed—and he has been, with as much vigor, attacked as a murderer as he has been defended as a savior.[45] Clearly, then, we must approach him with much caution.

"A bachelor of forty or thereabouts," Captain Vere may be Billy's natural father—or he may not be, just as he may be God the Father or merely a fatherly man. Although modest and unobtrusive aboard ship, he is resolute, "never tolerating an infraction of discipline" (60), which is to say that he is just but not merciful. Regarded as "a sailor of distinction," he is "intrepid to the verge of temerity, though never injudiciously so" (60); and although earnest, without humor, and, in the main, practical, yet he must "at times betray a certain dreaminess of mood . . . absently gaze off at the blank sea" (61): hence his nickname "Starry." Vere has a "marked leaning toward everything intellectual" (62), although he prefers "unconventional writers like Montaigne, who, free from cant and convention, honestly and in the spirit of common sense philosophize upon realities" (62); yet he is not without a streak of unconscious pendantry and is fond of citing "some historic character or incident of antiquity as he would be to cite from the moderns" seemingly "unmindful of the circumstance that to his bluff company such remote allusions, however pertinent they might really be, were altogether alien to men whose reading was mainly confined to the journals" (63). Like so many other characters in the canon, Vere is an "isolatoe," although never called by that name.

As a social thinker, Vere is deeply conservative, yet from principle, not the hope of personal gain: "While other members of that aristocracy to which by birth he belonged were incensed at the innovators [the time of *Billy Budd* is 1797] mainly because their theories were inimical to the privileged classes, Captain Vere disinterestedly opposed them not alone because they seemed to him insusceptible of embodiment in lasting institutions, but at war with the peace of the world and the true welfare of mankind" (62-63). It is, then, to this discreet but honorable gentleman that Claggart, "like the scorpion for which the Creator alone is responsible," approaches with an insidious tale of malfeasance aboard the *Bellipotent*.

At first glance Vere is vaguely repelled by his Master-at-Arms but, thereafter, is angered by his lengthy and calculated indirection and his presumption in alluding to the Nore Mutiny; Claggart's manner reminds Vere of how, at a previous meeting, "Claggart had somewhat irritated him as appearing rather supersensible and strained":

Furthermore, something even in the official's self-possessed and
somewhat ostentatious manner in making his specifications
strangely reminded him of a bandsman, a perjurous witness in a
capital case before a court-martial ashore of which when a
lieutenant he (Captain Vere) had been a member. (94)

And, therefore, when Claggart tells him that he suspects Billy of
malignant designs, Vere feels so little reliance "in the informer's good
faith" that he cuts him short with "Do you come to me, Master-at-
Arms, with so foggy a tale?" Claggart, however, will not be intimidated, and

> circumstantially alleged certain words and acts which collectively,
> if credited, let to presumptions mortally inculpating Budd.
> And for some of these averments, he added, substantiating proof
> was not far. (96)

Vere's first thought is to summon whatever evidence Claggart claims
he can produce, and if Vere had demanded proof, Claggart would
have been trapped. "But such a proceeding would result in the matter
at once getting abroad, which in the present stage of it, he thought,
might undesirably affect the ship's company" (96). But notice that
the idea of secrecy is directly attributed to Vere, who does not realize
that he is being unnecessarily cautious. He well exemplifies an apo-
thegm Melville devised for his contemporary sketch "Rammon": ". . .
isolation is the mother of illusion."[46] For as the isolate Captain under-
estimates his company's loyalty, he unwittingly succumbs to an illusion, and orders Billy to his cabin.

When Billy recognizes the charge of his Satanic adversary, he undergoes two parallel transformations. A symbol, from his arrival
aboard the *Bellipotent*, of postlapsarian Adam, he now becomes symbolic of the suffering Christ. At first he stands "like one impaled,"
then like one "transfixed," and, finally, at the height of his agony,
his face bears an expression which is "as a crucifixion." Similarly,
Billy undergoes a sexual transformation, as Melville employs the symbolism of impotence as well as an outright pun: at first he stands
"like one . . . gagged," then like one "in the first struggle against suf-
focation" (which Melville, metaphorically, calls "impotence") and,

finally, at the height of his agony, in "paralysis" (98–99). "The next instant," as when his arm flew like "lightning" against the Red Whiskers, Billy answers Claggart with his fist: ". . . quick as the flame from a discharged cannon at night, his right arm shot out. . . ." (99). And the discharged cannon by which Billy gives the lie to his accuser symbolizes that sexual potency he is thought not to possess.

As elements of the fight on deck of the *Rights-of-Man* prefigure this confrontation aboard the *Bellipotent*, so elements of this confrontation prefigure—again in a form intensified and transfigured— the events of Billy's hanging. Once prelapsarian Adam, now Man, having fallen, become the suffering Christ, at the yardarm Billy completes his spiritual journey and becomes the redeemed and redemptive God. Similarly, once suffering from a sexual blow under the ribs, here rendered momentarily impotent, at the yardarm Billy dies without sex entirely. Thus manhood becomes the price of divinity.

Thoroughly drubbed, the Red Whiskers comes to love Billy, for Billy has convincingly demonstrated his masculinity. The Red Whiskers' truest antecedent is the red-whiskered polygamous Max the Dutchman of *Redburn*, and the symbolic heterosexualism of his fiery beard helps us account for the terms in which he teases his apparently epicene victim. Claggart, on the other hand, is "beardless" (64), which indicates that he, like "smooth"-faced Billy (50), is without heterosexual desire. Claggart is drawn, in part, from that other devilish Master-at-Arms Bland in *White-Jacket* who, in turn, as Hayford and Sealts tell us,[47] is based on a real life Master, one Sterritt, who was a castrate. But Claggart, who "was about to ejaculate something hasty at" Billy before tapping him from behind instead, is evidently not such a man: he is naturally without a beard, never shorn of one. Furthermore, after Billy kills him, Melville begins to pun heavily on his loss of life as a loss of sexual energy. His "body fell over lengthwise"—Satan is, after all, a fallen angel—"like a heavy plank tilted from erectness" (99). And we shall see in a moment what happens to his "erectness."

Vere enjoins Billy to help him revive Claggart, and

> The twain raised the felled one from the loins up into a sitting position. The spare form flexibly acquiesced, but inertly. It was

like handling a dead snake. They lowered it back. Regaining
erectness, Captain Vere with one hand covering his face stood to
all appearance as impassive as the object at his feet. (99)

Indeed, raising Claggart "from the loins up," his spare form flexibly
acquiescent! E. L. Grant Watson first recognized the suggestiveness
of the "dead snake" image,[48] after which, we notice, Melville refers
to Claggart in the neuter, not the masculine, gender. To stimulate his
sex, in effect, is to awaken his life, but Vere and Billy fail, and, therefore, there is nothing left for Vere to do except regain his "erectness"
—Claggart's, of course. Exactly the same situation obtains when Billy
dies. As Richard Chase has observed,[49] it is not Billy who experiences
an erection but Captain Vere:

> At the pronounced words and the spontaneous echo that
> voluminously rebounded them, Captain Vere, either through
> stoic self-control or a sort of momentary paralysis induced by emo-
> tional shock, stood erectly as a musket in the ship-armorer's
> rack (123–24).

(Again Melville resorts to the language of weaponry to symbolize
sexual power.) The Lord made Christ and He made Satan, and as He
gave them sexual energy, so He takes it away. And regains it.

Since Vere decides that Billy must hang the instant after Claggart
is pronounced dead, we must try to understand what aspects of temperament and conviction lead him to such an immediate judgment.
In the first place, as we know, Vere strictly adheres to the military
code, refusing ever to tolerate an infraction of discipline:

> 'In wartime at sea a man-of-war's man strikes his superior in
> grade, and the blow kills. Apart from its effect the blow is, accord-
> ing to the Articles of War, a capital crime.' (111)

As the cynical Dansker reminds Milton Stern of the GI who "knows
'the score,' "[50] so we may say that Vere reminds us of his superior officer who rules "by the book." The two, in fact, unknowingly conspire to doom Billy. Vere, however, is able to generalize his argument
and grace it with mythological example:

> 'With mankind . . . forms, measured forms, are everything; and
> that is the import couched in the story of Orpheus with his lyre

spellbinding the wild denizens of the wood.' And this he once ap-
plied to the disruption of forms going on across the Channel
and the consequences thereof—(128)

a disruption we know he disinterestedly opposes. Furthermore, he insists, if the forms are not maintained, the crew will mutiny, for it
expects a murderer to hang:

> 'Even could you explain to them—which our official position for-
> bids—they, long molded by arbitrary discipline, have not that
> kind of intelligent responsiveness that might qualify them to
> comprehend and discriminate. No, to the people the foretopman's
> deed, however it be worded in the announcement, will be plain
> homicide committed in a flagrant act of mutiny. What penalty
> for that should follow they know. But it does not follow. Why?
> they will ruminate. You know what sailors are. Will they not
> revert to the recent outbreak at the Nore? Ay.' (112)

Thus the drumhead court itself, which Vere knowingly prejudices—
by testifying from the ship's weather side (thereby not "sinking his
rank") (105) and by exercising what the court suspects is "prejudg-
ment" (108)—is obviously *pro forma* and nothing more; for Vere
has decided to hang Billy before he convenes it.

Vere's reliance on measured forms is predicated on the assumption that transcendental categories are unknowable. Like Bartleby
staring at the blank wall, Vere often stares at the blank sea. ("Blank,"
of course, is one of Melville's favorite descriptives of Secular Reality;
"lurks," which is used frequently in this novella and throughout the
canon, is one of his favorite descriptives of the Absolute. But in *Billy
Budd* nothing, as far as Vere can tell, lurks behind the blankness of
Nature.) Therefore, he feels that, however much he himself dreams
of and yearns for Essence, he must suffer and accept the world of
Sense, for the two never interpenetrate. As for Billy's crime, "At the
Last Assizes it shall acquit," but here "We proceed under the law of
the Mutiny Act" (111).

"In the feature no child can resemble his father more than that
Act resembles in spirit the thing from which it derives—War," and
"War looks but to the frontage, the appearance." Captain Vere is
also a son of War, nursed in isolation, and he too looks but to the

frontage, the appearance, the illusion. Thus from principle, no less than practice, Vere believes that Billy must hang, although one cannot emphasize too strongly his real love for Billy, his agony at what he must do, the divine magnanimity each feels for the other in their private interview, and the absence of any remorse in Vere even on his deathbed.

Now the argument as recounted here, on which Captain Vere's decision depends, is assailable at three points—despite the enormity of his good will. First, even if the maintenance of forms is, in general, a necessary bulwark against anarchy, one must question whether it is rational to maintain one particular form (the death penalty) at this one particular time (in consideration of the innocence of the slayer, the guilt of the slain, and such other mitigating factors as the relative nearness of the fleet). Although the Captain does not doubt his own sanity, the surgeon does, speculating that Vere may be "unhinged" (102). In fact the narrator himself is unsure:

> Who in the rainbow can draw the line where the violet tint ends and the orange tint begins? Distinctly we see the difference of the colors, but where exactly does the one first blendingly enter into the other? So with sanity and insanity.
>
> .   .   .   .
>
> Whether Captain Vere, as the surgeon professionally and privately surmised, was really the sudden victim of any degree of aberration, every one must determine for himself by such light as this narrative may afford. (102)

But the narrative affords only the most ambiguous half-light.

Similarly, as we are led to believe that Vere may not be entirely sane in his stubborn insistence on forms, so we are led to suppose that his understanding of his company's mind is erroneous. For there is not a single shred of evidence that would support Vere's contention that mutiny would ensue if Billy were not hanged, whereas on three separate occasions there are mutinous rumblings among the crew because he *is* hanged. Howsoever conditions may be elsewhere, there is absolutely no justification aboard the *Bellipotent* for distrusting the crew. Furthermore, Melville makes it clear, by indirectly contrasting Vere with Lord Nelson, that even if Vere had reason to doubt his crew, hanging one of them as an example to the others is the work of little men:

> In the same year with this story, Nelson, then Rear Admiral Sir
> Horatio, being with the fleet off the Spanish coast, was directed by
> the admiral in command to shift his pennant from the *Captain*
> to the *Theseus*; and for this reason: that the latter ship having
> newly arrived on the station from home, where it had taken part
> in the Great Mutiny, danger was apprehended from the temper
> of the men; and it was thought that an officer like Nelson was the
> one, not indeed to terrorize the crew into base subjection, but to
> win them, by force of his mere presence and heroic personality,
> back to an allegiance if not as enthusiastic as his own yet as true.
> (59)

It is Vere who terrorizes his crew into base subjection by hanging an innocent man. Again this is not to say that he does not have his reasons, and Vere's judgment is the wisest he can honestly imagine. But the unobtrusive Captain clearly lacks "presence and heroic personality"—this man "who whatever his sterling qualities was without any brilliant ones. . . ." (61). Compared with Nelson, Vere is the lesser man and, tragically, he can only make the lesser determination. There is no doubt that Billy would not have been hanged aboard a ship captained by Nelson, a man able to rise beyond regulation and form when circumstances demand, "the greatest sailor since our world began" (58).

Finally, one must challenge the theoretical underpinning of Vere's decision, that the natural and transcendental spheres never interpenetrate, that the world of Nature invariably presents itself as a blank counter to the world of God. Vere does, "in the spirit of common sense philosophize upon realities," but how much is common sense, how much is cosmic naturalism, worth in comprehending Billy Budd? Vere lacks vision, and without vision the best of people perishes. For even as Billy is hanged,

> the vapory fleece hanging low in the East was shot through with
> a soft glory as of the fleece of the Lamb of God seen in mystical
> vision, and simultaneously therewith, watched by the wedged
> mass of upturned faces, Billy ascended; and, ascending, took the
> full rose of the dawn.

> In the pinioned figure arrived at the yardend, to the wonder of
> all no motion was apparent, none save that created by the slow
> roll of the hull in moderate weather, so majestic in a great ship
> ponderously cannoned. (124)

Melville, of course, is deliberately speaking in simile—"as of the
fleece of the Lamb of God"—just as he does later when he tells us
that to Billy's comrades a chip of the yardarm "was as a piece of the
Cross" (131). By the same strategy the motionlessness of the hanged
body is no more than "apparent." But these qualifications are sops—
and should be recognized as such—sops to disarm the rationalist non-
believers. For Melville is dramatizing that difference between scientific and religious truth he had enunciated in Clarel: the surgeon
demonstrates the insufficiency of natural cause to account for the absence of spasm in Billy, but the vision of the motionlessness of the
figure pinioned in the full rose of the fleecy dawn *convinces* us, as it
surely convinced the commonsensical Vere, that a miracle is taking
place. The refusal of the scientist to acknowledge the category of the
miraculous when, in fact, no other category will suffice, fails to restrain
us from believing what the ambiguous evidence of sense and simile
would have us deny—that human experience is numinous whenever
the charisma of God is released in the mind of man.

In the *Anatomy of Criticism* Northrop Frye describes the four
mythoi or "narrative pregeneric elements of literature"—the romantic, the tragic, the ironic or satiric, and the comic.[51] According to
Frye, each *mythos* corresponds to a season of the year's cycle—summer, autumn, winter, and spring respectively—and, taken together,
the *Mythoi* "may . . . be seen as four aspects of a central unifying
myth."[52]

> *Agon* or conflict is the basis or archetypal theme of romance, the
> radical of romance being a sequence of marvellous adventures.
> *Pathos* or catastrophe, whether in triumph or in defeat, is the
> archetypal theme of tragedy. *Sparagmos*, or the sense that heroism
> and effective action are absent, disorganized or foredoomed to
> defeat, and that confusion and anarchy reign over the world, is the

archetypal theme of irony and satire. *Anagnorisis,* or recognition of a newborn society rising in triumph around a still somewhat mysterious hero and his bride, is the archetypal theme of comedy.

My contention is that Melville's early career—from the "Fragment" in which the phylogenetic Hero is born, to *White-Jacket* in which he is reborn—prepares the way for the unfolding of this "quest-myth" and that the four prose monuments of Melville's middle and late career, three of which are major *termini,* exemplify the cyclic order Frye describes.

Moby-Dick represents "The Mythos of Summer: Romance," a tale of marvellous adventures, a "romance-anatomy"; Frye concentrates on the protagonist's conflict with Leviathan and the death and re-birth of the hero. *Pierre* represents "The Mythos of Autumn: Trag-edy," Melville's attempt at an American tragedy; Frye notes that "Pierre opens with a sardonic parody" of romance—it closes with the catastrophe *Moby-Dick* avoids. *The Confidence-Man* represents "The Mythos of Winter: Irony," and it is, in fact, a viciously ironic view of Man, foredoomed to defeat, stupidly imagining he can yet be saved. *Billy Budd* represents "The Mythos of Spring: Comedy," for "If we are right in our suggestion," says Frye, "that romance, tragedy, irony, and comedy are all episodes in a total quest-myth [the myth I have identified with the evolution of Melville's career], we can see how it is that comedy can contain a potential tragedy within itself."[53]

> In myth, the hero is god, and hence he does not die, but dies and rises again. The ritual pattern behind the catharsis of comedy is the resurrection that follows the death, the epiphany or manifes-tation of the risen hero. . . . Christianity . . . sees tragedy as an episode in the divine comedy, the larger scheme of redemption and resurrection. The sense of tragedy as a prelude to comedy seems almost inseparable from anything explicitly Christian. The serenity of the final double chorus in the St. Matthew Passion would hardly be attainable if composer and audience did not know that there was more to the story. Nor would the death of Samson lead to "calm of mind, all passion spent," if Samson were not a prototype of the rising Christ, associated at the appropriate moment with the phoenix.

And if we "stand back" from the texts, as Frye urges us to do, we shall also discover, in the passionless Passion of Billy's death, the final expression of a mythic order.

Melville's pilgrimage, in other words, carried him to Hell before it bore him to Heaven. In the midway of his life he endured the spiritual desolation of *The Confidence-Man*, and it was only "Toward the end," as W. H. Auden has finely said, that "he sailed into an extraordinary mildness," into that final harmony toward which the exercise of faith and the urge to individuation alike intend: the mergence of Man and God, the emergence of the Self.

> Instead of to knowledge through thought, essentially strange to faith, the individuation process leads to knowledge through inner experience, whose vitality and reality are lived out and thus grow into an unshakable certainty. . . . The religious unbeliever . . . who will not believe or, in spite of all his craving for a faith, cannot win it by an act of will or cognition, at least will be led on his way within to a real *experience* of the eternal principles of his being and perhaps will come in this way through his struggle to the charisma of faith.[54]

Billy Budd records that ultimate hour for one who long struggled with unbelief. For as Vere embraces Billy in the privacy of his state-room—an embrace more sacred than Melville can say or words can know—so fuse the opposites they represent: the Head and the Heart, the Male and the Female, Reason and Faith, Consciousness and the Unconscious, God and Man (for do not "the mass of [sea]men fear . . . and at bottom dislike . . . [Vere] . . . because they rather distrust His heart, and fancy Him all brain like a watch")? Melville's synthesis is symbolized by the Christ incarnate, the still-living myth of our culture.

Nevertheless *Billy Budd* is not without latent discord, and it would be foolish to deny this discord in the interests of an unattainable symmetry. Billy may triumph in eternity but Claggart truimphs in time. Besides,

> The symmetry of form attainable in pure fiction cannot so readily be achieved in a narration essentially having less to do with fable than with fact. Truth uncompromisingly told will always

have its ragged edges; hence the conclusion of such a narration is apt to be less finished than an architectural finial.[55]

Billy Budd is unfinished in the same sense that Ishmael speaks of unfinished personality: "any human thing supposed to be complete, must for that very reason infallibly be faulty." For perfection in literature or life is an ideal category, and that is why the "truth" of *Billy Budd* is only primarily (not wholly) benedictive and why Melville's personal achievement is only a proximate (not an absolute) individuation.

The bachelor Vere, who may be mad, quests passively. And motherless Billy, more obviously effeminate than motherless Clarel, finds his voice only when he regressively denounces the oedipal struggle: "God bless Captain Vere." There is much anguish here, and one remembers that Melville outlived both his sons, neither of whom married: Malcolm, the more docile one, who died a suicide in Melville's own house in 1867 at twenty (Billy's age) and Stanwix, the rover, the more difficult son, who died alone in a San Francisco hospital in 1886 at thirty-five (Claggart's age). To what extent did Melville believe himself responsible for the deaths of his children? To what extent did he believe their deaths the sacrifice life exacted for his "completion," even as Captain Vere, responsible yet not entirely responsible for Billy's death, takes back from life what life has taken from his sons and is thereafter blessed. To an indeterminate extent life—not Herman Melville—prevented Malcolm from challenging the oedipal imperative just as Billy's manhood is not a gift bestowed on death, it is a sacrifice demanded by life. To be sure, the Risen Billy is "complete," but he, after all, is the god-man. What of the others? Red Whiskers hurts Billy, then loves him; the Dansker loves Billy, then lets him be hurt. Claggart wants to love Billy but also wants him killed; Vere loves Billy but also has him killed. How can the Truth with all its ragged edges ever be told about them? How ever about Melville?

And yet *Billy Budd* offers us a last tantalizing clue, for with it the cycle of a career wheeled full turn and reached that final readiness. White Jacket, encased in cloth, falls into the sea and is reborn; Billy Budd, encased in his "canvas coffin," falls into the sea and is resurrected. And as the *oeuvre* is made whole, so, as nearly as one can say, is the personality of its maker:

> . . . as the aim of depth-psychology is the making conscious of what is unconscious [in Melville's case, through "the archetypal situation," not artificially through analysis], and the aim of individuation, in particular, is the making conscious of the 'self' —our own individual way of being whole—their aim is in fact that of human life generally, namely death, for it is death which, in one way or another, finishes and completes us; and the dread of death—the 'sickness unto death' of which Kierkegaard wrote so movingly and so profoundly, and which so often lurks behind our trivial but agonizing phobias—is the dread of our failure to become 'finished' personalities.[56]

Victor White, whose words these are, continues by quoting C. G. Jung:

> Death is the great Finisher (*Vollender*). . . . In death, supremely, is completion attained—in one way or another. Death is the end of the empirical, and the goal of the spiritual, man. . . . Everyone who is not yet where he should be, and has not yet brought to pass what should have been brought to pass, experiences dread (*Angst*) about his end, his final account. Man evades so long as he can becoming conscious of those things which are still wanting to his completion, and so hinders becoming conscious of his true 'self,' and thereby his readiness for death.

But the author of *Billy Budd* was ready. His Self realized, his work finished, he had engaged the great law of mythic, psychic, and biologic necessity: *Birth* ("I am like one of those seeds taken out of the Egyptian Pyramids, which after being three thousands years a seed and nothing but a seed, being planted in English soil, it developed itself. . . ."), *Maturity* ("But I feel that now I come to the inmost leaf of the bulb. . . ."), *Death* (". . . shortly the flower must fall to the mould. . . ."), *New Life* ("yet later spontaneous after-growth.")[57] The empirical man died not six months after *Billy Budd* was done. The spiritual man was ready.

M elville pasted this admonition inside his writing box where *Billy Budd* and his earliest juvenilia were posthumously discovered: "Keep true to the dreams of thy youth." He told Hawthorne one of those dreams long before: "I stand for the heart. To the dogs with the head! I had rather be a fool with a heart than Jupiter Olympus with his head." Near the end he dedicated the story of Billy Budd to the sailor-hero of his youth, "that great heart." At the end his physician "diagnosed his trouble as an enlargement of the heart," the final constellation of his fate.[58] Melville compelled art into life, and fulfillment of prophecy. He compelled life into art, the experience of myth. Myth and prophecy compelled him into pattern, the growth of soul. This pattern we are just beginning to understand.

Appendix: *Melville Before The Mast*

"The Death Craft"[1]

A calm prevailed over the waters. The ocean lay gently heaving in long regular undulations like the bosom of Beauty in slumbers. Pouring forth a heat only known in torrid climes, the sun rode the firmament like some fiery messenger of ill. No cloud disturbed the serenity of the heavens, which of the palest blue seemed withered of their brilliancy by the scorching influence of his rays. A silence, nowhere to be experienced but at sea and which seemed preliminary to some horrible convulsion of nature, hushed the universal waste.

I stood upon our ship's forecastle. The heavy stillness lay upon my soul with the weight of death. I gazed aloft, the sails hung idly from the yards, ever and anon flapping their broad surfaces against the masts. Their snowy whiteness dazzled my eyes.

The heat grew more intense, drops of tar fell heavily from the rigging, the pitch oozed slowly forth from the seams of the ship, the stays relaxed, and the planks under my feet were like glowing bricks.

I cast my eyes over the deck: it was deserted. The officers had retired into the cuddy, and the crew, worn out with the busy watches of the preceding night, were slumbering below.

. . . .

My senses ached; a sharp ringing sound was in my ears—my eyes felt as though coals of fire were in their sockets—vivid lightnings seemed darting through my veins—a feeling of unutterable misery was upon me. I lifted my hand and prayed the God of the Winds to send them over the bosom of the deep. Vain prayer! The sound of my voice pierced my brain and reeling for a moment in agony, I sank upon the deck.

I recovered and, rising with difficulty, tottered towards the cabin; as I passed under the helm, my eyes fell upon the helmsman lying athwartships abaft the wheel. The glazed eye, the distended jaw, the clammy hand were not enough to assure my stupified senses. I stooped over the body—Oh God! It exhaled the odor of the dead—and there, banqueting on the putrifying corpse, were the crawling denizens of the tomb! I watched their loathesome motions; the spell was upon me; I could not shut out the horrid vision: I saw them devour—Oh God! how greedily—their human meal!

A heavy hand was laid upon my shoulders—a loud laugh rang in my ear; it was the Mate. "See, see! THE DEATH CRAFT!" He sprang away from me with one giant bound, and with a long, long, shriek, that even now haunts me, wildly flung himself into the sea.

Great God! There she lay, covered with barnacles, the formation of years —her sails unbent—a blood-red flag streaming from her masthead— at her jib-boom-end hanging suspended by its long, dark hair, a human head covered with conjulated gore, and firmly gripping between its teeth a rusty cutlass! Her yards were painted black, and at each of their arms hung dangling a human skeleton, whiter than polished ivory and glistening in the fierce rays of the sun!

I shrieked aloud: "Blast—blast my vision, Oh God! Blast it ere I rave." I buried my face in my hands—I pressed them wildly against my eyes; for a moment I was calm—I had been wandering—it was some awful dream. I looked up—the ghastly appendage at the jib-boom seemed fixing its ghastly eye-balls on me—each chalky remnant of mortality seemed beckoning me toward it! I fancied them clutching me in their wild embrace—I saw them begin their infernal orgies; the flesh crisped upon my fingers, my heart grew icy cold, and, faint with terror and despair, I lay prostrate on the deck.

How long that trance endured, I know not; but at length I revived. The wind howled angrily around me; the thunder boomed over the surface of the deep; the rain fell in torrents, and the lightning, as it flashed along the sky, showed the full horrors of the storm. Wave after wave came thundering against the ship's counter over which I lay and flung themselves in showering seas over our devoted barque. Sailors were continually hurrying by me; in vain I implored them to carry me below; they heard me not. Some were aloft taking in sail—four were in the main-top-gallant-yard-arm. A squall quick as lightning struck the vessel took her all aback, whipping the canvas into ribbands, and with a loud crash sending overboard the mainmast. I heard the shrieks of those dying wretches, saw them clinging for a moment to the spar, then struggling for an instant with the waters, when an enormous wave bounding towards them, with its milk-white crest tossed high in the air, obscured them from my view. They were seen no more; they fed the finny tribes.

The ship with her hull high out of the water, her bowsprit almost perpendicular, and her taffrail wholly immersed in the sea, drove for a moment stern-foremast through the waters, when the wind shifting in an instant to the starboard quarter, she made a tremendous lurch to port and lay trembling on her beam-ends. That moment decided our fate.

"Keep her before the wind!" thundered the Captain.

"Aye, aye, Sir!"

And docile as the managed steed, she swerved aside, and once more sent the spray heaving from her bows! 'Twas an awful hour. Had the ship hesitated a second—aye, the fraction of one, in obeying her helm—she would have gone to fill the rapacious maw of the deep. As it was, with her larboard side encumbered with the wreck of the mainmast, her coursers rent into a thousand tatters, her sheets and clew lines flying in the wind which ran whistling and roaring through her rigging, she seemed rushing forward to swift destruction.

I looked forward; in the chains were stationed men standing by to part the lanyards; while with axe uplifted stood an aged seaman prepared at an instant's warning to cut away the foremast.

"Cut away," vociferated the skipper. The axe descended with the speed of thought—the shroud sprang violently up, till the lofty mast, yielding like some tall hemlock to the woodsman, fell heavily by the board. The ship eased, still driving with fearful velocity before the wind. "Where's the Mate?" hoarsely inquired the Captain. No one answered, no one knew but *me*. At that moment I lay clinging to one of the spare yards that were lashed around the deck. With a preternatural effort, I raised myself, and pointing to the foaming surface of the deep, I shrieked, "There—there!" The frightful apparition I had witnessed now flashed across my mind, and once more with a laugh of wild delirium I rolled upon the deck.

.   .   .   .

A gentle breeze lifted the locks from my brow; a delicious sensation thrilled through my veins; my eyes opened—the glorious main lay expanding before me, bright and beautiful and blue! I strove to speak: a rosy finger was laid upon my lips—a form as of an angel hovered over me. I yielded to the sweet injunction; a delightful languor stole over my senses; visions of heavenly beauty danced around me, and I peacefully slumbered.

.   .   .   .

Again I awoke. My God! Did I dream? Was this my own fair room? Were these the scenes of my youth? No, no! They were far away across the bounding deep. The horrors I had witnessed had distracted my brain; I closed my eyes; I tried to regain my thoughts, to recollect myself. Once more the same sweet objects were before me—something flitted before me; two lovely eyes were upon me, and the fond young girl, whom twelve months ago I had left a disconsolate bride, lay weeping in my arms!

Harry the Reefer.

What particularly invites our attention to this sketch are certain symbolic images of nightmarish intensity, the most important of which is the Death Craft itself, the Great Mother in her Terrible aspect, as hideous surely as the leprous Life-in-Death of "The Rime of the Ancient Mariner":

There she lay, covered with barnacles, the formation of years—her sails unbent—a blood-red flag streaming from her masthead—at her jib-boom-end hanging suspended by its long, dark hair, a human head covered with conjulated gore, and firmly gripping between its teeth a rusty cutlass! Her yards were painted black, and at each of their arms hung dangling a human skeleton. . . .

"Blood," as Erich Neumann tells us,

plays a decisive part in feminine taboos, which from earliest times until far into the patriarchal cultures and religions have caused men to turn away from all feminine matters as though from something numinous. The blood of menstruation, defloration, and birth proves to men that women have a natural connection with this sphere. But in the background there is a dim knowledge of the blood affinity of the Great Mother who, as chthonic mistress of life and death, demands blood and appears to be dependent upon the shedding of blood.[2]

The blood-red flag, in other words, is the flag of her own disposition. At her jib-boom-end hangs a human head covered with "conjulated gore" (a neologism probably meaning "congealed" but including an echo of "conjugated"): it is the Gorgon's head with a phallic cutlass between her castrating teeth. (We remember Pierre's encounter with Gorgon, and Taji's use of the phallic cutlass.) From the arms of her yards "hung dangling" human skeletons, and now we recall the probably castrated-cannibalized skeleton of Don Alexandro Aranda and the dangling, desexed Billy Budd.

On seeing the Death Craft, the young man shrieks, "Blast—blast my vision, Oh God! Blast it ere I rave." Terrified of the Terrible Mother, he unconsciously invokes the Oedipal punishment—blindness—the symbolic castration Ahab claims to suffer at the end of *Moby-Dick*, in lieu of its alternative—madness. The maddened man is, as we have seen, a standard figure in the Melville *oeuvre*, but the "raver" seems to belong to a special subclass, and it is significant that his disorder and early sorrow are nowhere better documented than in *Pierre*, Melville's major imaginative investigation of his youth and familial relations. (See below, pp. 272-273, ftnt. 61) The Mate, on the other hand, who lays a heavy hand on the young man's shoulder, chooses suicide, beyond maiming or mere aberration; his last shriek "even now haunts" the dreamer, and it is difficult not to suppose that Melville was at least unconsciously adverting to the raving death of his own father, his mother's mate.

After pressing his hands "wildly against . . . [his] eyes"—thereby calming himself but also, quite specifically I think, assuring himself that he has not lost his sight—he feels "for a moment" relieved. But then he fancies the Gorgon head "fixing its ghastly eye-balls" on him and the skeletons clutching him in their "wild embrace." Like Mow-Mow, Hautia, Jackson, Bland, and Cadwallader Cuticle, the Evil Eye'd Gorgon hypnotically clutches the eyes of its victim. And what do the skeletons clutch in their "infernal orgies" above their prostrate form? As above, so below. The threat of blindness and the threat of castration are everpresent and monumentally terrifying.

Reviving from a trance induced by this anxiety, the young man begs sailors nearby to carry him beneath decks: not that he has been physically struck or wounded but that, like Ishmael unable to move his hand in his dream, like Billy unable to speak after being accused by Claggart, the dreamer is momentarily paralyzed, rendered impotent. And he remains so—as the storm increases and men are driven overboard—until the Captain orders the mast cut down in order to save the ship: only then—after the phallus is once more sacrificed to the insatiable blood lust of the Terrible Mother—is "The ship eased." And only after the Terrible Mother is placated by blood sacrifice, can the paralyzed young man, "With a preternatural effort," manage to "raise" himself (ie. his sex; regain his potency). In answer to the Captain's question, "Where's the Mate?" he alone answers, for he alone knows that the Mate leaped overboard, shrieking in order to avoid confronting the Terrible Mother, just as Melville himself may have believed, in the fantasy of an adolescent's unconscious, that his father Allan, died a maddened conjugal sacrifice to his mother, Maria.

The "frightful apparition" of the dying Mate plunges the youth into delirium, but after his dream re-commences, he finds to his delight that the Terrible Mother, temporarily exorcised, has been replaced by the other half of the Great Mother archetype, the Good Mother angelically lavishing affection. One recalls how in "The Symphony" chapter of *Moby-Dick* the cruel stepmother world is also temporarily replaced by the gentle mother of the air who "now threw affectionate arms round . . . [Ahab's] stubborn neck, and did seem to joyously sob over him. . . ."[3] Responding to the mild breeze, Ahab thinks of the "girl-wife" he deserted and how he "sailed for Cape Horn the next day, leaving but one dent in . . . [his] marriage pillow";[4] the young man, waking at last, discovers "the fond young girl, whom twelve months ago I had left a disconsolate bride . . . weeping in my arms." She is the pure maiden we meet so often in Melville's books, and she is crying because she knows or intuits that, despite their marriage, she does not really possess her husband. The young man may well lie with her, but he too—like the Mate whose son, psychologically speaking, he is—still owes his primary allegiance to the maternal archetype. But unlike the Mate, he possesses potency: despite all, he neither commits suicide nor is castrated. Indeed, he finally "raises" himself, a "preternatural" act premonitory and symbolic, for, in retrospect, we realize that it is just this divinely inexplicable urge to differentiation and selfhood which distinguishes the Melvillean Quester and allows his ultimate release from the Great Mother.

"The Death Craft," then, records that transitional phase between intrauterine life and birth into consciousness. Unlike the Youth of the second "Fragment," the young man here confusedly glides from the womb of the unconscious, a real phylogenetic advance; but, at the same time, only a slight advance, because the world of dream and nightmare is still for him the real one and the waking world of pure love still an idle dream. Only with *Typee* did Melville begin to make those dreams come true.

Notes on the Text

CHAPTER ONE

1 *The Letters of Herman Melville*, eds. Merrell R. Davis and Willliam H. Gilman (New Haven, 1960), p. 129 (to Hawthorne).

2 James Baird, *Ishmael* (Baltimore, 1956), p. 56 (italics removed).

3 *Ibid.*, p. 16 (italics removed).

4 Newton Arvin, *Herman Melville* (New York, 1950), p. 32.

5 John Locke, *Works* (12th ed.), VI, p. 135. Alexander Pope, *An Essay on Man*, Epistle I, 1. 6. Pope had originally written "a mighty maze of walks without a plan"—that he could so easily reverse himself indicates not cynicism as much as enormous confidence in the revealed order of things. For Melville's use of the metaphor of the maze in a relevant context, see below, Chapter 3.

6 *Letters*, p. 129.

7 William Wordsworth, "Lines," 11. 95–96.

8 Samuel Taylor Coleridge, *Biographia Literaria*, Chap. xiii.

9 Baird, pp. 3, 15 (italics removed), 55 (italics removed).

10 *Ibid.*, pp. xiv, 18 (italics removed), 52.

11 *Ibid.*, pp. 18 (italics removed), 16, 28–29.

12 This correlation has never been examined in any depth. See Lewis Mumford, *Herman Melville* (New York, 1929), p. 220; Richard Chase, *Herman Melville* (New York, 1949), p. 163; Milton Stern, *The Fine Hammered Steel of Herman Melville* (Urbana, 1957), p. 165; Robert Shulman, "The Serious Function of Melville's Phallic Jokes," *AL*, XXXIII (May, 1961), 186.

13 Melville's choice of madness may possibly reflect his own uncertain feelings. "Allan Melvill [sic] was delirious for more than two weeks before he died," and even if, as Dr. Murray supposes, he suffered from a "temporary toxic psychosis," and not a more permanent mental illness, Herman, who was only twelve, must have been indelibly impressed. If the "evidence" of the quasi-autobiographical *Pierre* is to be trusted, Melville was to feel, years later on other occasions, "presentiments concerning his own fate—his own hereditary liability to madness." See *Pierre or, The Ambiguities*, ed. Henry

A. Murray (New York, 1949), pp. 454, 338. But even if we discount this remark, we cannot disregard a comment in one of Melville's letters about the minor poet Charles Fenno Hoffman:

This going mad of a friend or acquaintance comes straight home to every man who feels his soul in him,—which but few men do. For in all of us lodges the same fuel to light the same fire. And he who has never felt, momentarily, what madness is has but a mouthful of brains. What sort of sensation permanent madness is may be very well imagined—just as we imagine how we felt when we were infants, tho' we can not recall it.

See *Letters* (to Evert Duyckinck), p. 83.

[14] H. J. C. Grierson, quoted in *Romanticism*, eds. Robert F. Gleckner and Gerald E. Enscoe (Englewood Cliffs, 1962), p. 24.

[15] Quoted by Charles Feidelson, Jr. in *Symbolism and American Literature* (Chicago, 1953), p. 168.

[16] Examples of barrier or concealment imagery that Melville's contemporaries used, in order to symbolize the separation of Sacred from Secular Reality include Shelley's translucent "dome of many-colored glass [which],/Stains the white radiance of Eternity,/Until Death tramples it to fragments," ("Adonais," III) and Coleridge's opaque "mist, that stands 'twixt God and thee," but which, fortunately, "Defecates to a pure transparency,/That intercepts no light and adds no stain," revealing Reason. ("Reason," 11. 1–4.). Among the Americans one might cite is the transcendentalist Emerson, who, unlike Melville, found no unchallengeable barrier between himself and the divine:

. . . as there is no screen or ceiling between our heads and the infinite heavens, so is there no bar or wall in the soul, where man, the effect, ceases, and God, the cause, begins. The walls are taken away. ("The Over-Soul.")

as well as those who describe Death as the other side of the barrier—Oliver Wendell Homes, for instance. The snakes' eyes

. . . were of a pale golden, or straw colour, horrible to look into, with their stony calmness, their pitiless indifference, hardly enlivened by the almost imperceptible vertical slit of the pupil, through which Death seemed to be looking out like the archer behind the long narrow loop-hole in a blank turret wall. (*Elsie Venner*, chap. xv).

Or those who describe the barrier as conquerable only in death—for example, Emily Dickinson:

Our lives are Swiss—
So still—so cool—
Till some odd afternoon
The Alps neglect their Curtains
And we look farther on!

Italy stands on the other side!

While like a guard between—
The solemn Alps—
The siren Alps
Forever intervene!
(*The Poems of Emily Dickinson*, ed. Thomas Johnson [Cambridge, 1955],
I, 65.)
We do not mean of course that this kind of imagery has never been noticed
in Melville but rather that its extent and symbolic significance has never been
sufficiently demonstrated. Critics (aside from Charles Feidelson, noted
above) who, in one way or another, have touched on the subject include
Dorothee Metlitsky Finkelstein, *Melville's Orienda* (New Haven, 1961),
pp. 139ff; Tyrus Hillway, "Taji's Abdication in Herman Melville's *Mardi*,"
AL, XVI (November, 1944), 204–7; Leon Howard, *Herman Melville*
(University of Minnesota Pamphlet, no. 13; Minneapolis, 1961), p. 25;
Leo Marx, "Melville's Parable of the Walls," *SR*, LXI (Autumn, 1953),
602–7; Arthur Sale, "The Glass Ship: A Recurrent Image in Melville,"
MLQ, XVII (June, 1956), 118–27; Walter Weber, "Some Characteristic
Symbols of Herman Melville's Works," *ES*, XXX (October, 1949), 221;
and Nathalia Wright, *Melville's Use of the Bible* (Durham, 1949), pp.
187–88.
The "romantic" imagery of the double world is not, of course, confined
to nineteenth-century Romantic literature: for instance, one finds similar patterns in Auden ("The Labyrinth"); Arnold ("Thyrsis," 11. 144–47), and
Donne ("Third Satire," 11. 79–82). And Spenser (*The Faerie Queene*, Bk.
I, VI, iii–v), metaphorizes Sansloy's attempt to rape Una, in allegory his assault on Truth, as an attempt to ransack her fort.

17 Hoxie Fairchild, *Religious Trends in English Poetry* (New York, 1949), III,
3; David Perkins, *The Quest for Permanence* (Cambridge, Mass., 1959).

18 Fairchild, *The Romantic Quest* (New York, 1931), pp. 251 (italics removed), p. 256.

19 *Religious Trends . . .* , III, p. 505.

20 Ernst Curtius, *European Literature and the Latin Middle Ages*, trans. from
the German by Williard R. Trask (New York, 1953), pp. 195ff. See also
J. A. W. Bennett, *"The Parlement of Foules": An Interpretation* (Oxford,
1957), pp. 62–63, 70–71.

21 Feidelson, p. 165.

22 Finkelstein, p. 136.

23 Josef Goldbrunner, *Individuation*, trans. from the German by Stanley God-
man (Notre Dame, 1964), p. 70.

24 Mircea Eliade, *The Sacred and the Profane*, trans. from the French by Williard R. Trask (New York: Harper Torchbook, 1961), p. 20.

[25] Mircea Eliade, *Cosmos and History* (originally entitled *The Myth of the Eternal Return*), trans. from the French by Williard R. Trask (New York: Harper Torchbook, 1959), pp. 12, 17–18.

[26] Mircea Eliade, *Patterns in Comparative Religion*, trans. from the French by Rosemary Sheed (Cleveland: Meridian Paperback, 1958), pp. 233, 31.

[27] *Cosmos and History*, p. 18.

[28] *The Sacred and the Profane*, pp. 184, 135–36.

[29] *Patterns in Comparative Religion*, p. 193.

[30] H. Bruce Franklin, *The Wake of the God* (Stanford, 1963), p. 71. Franklin cites the bibliographic reference (p. 211) for these European and Asiatic analogues.

[31] *The Sacred and the Profane*, p. 130.

[32] *Ibid.*, pp. 32ff.

[33] Erich Neumann, *The Origins and History of Consciousness*, trans. from the German by R. F. C. Hull (New York: Harper Torchbook, 1962), I, 125.

[34] Neumann, I, 5, 8, 10, 11, 14.

[35] In *The Melville Log* (New York, 1951), p. 97 Jay Leyda tentatively attributed this sketch to Melville, and since documentary proof of authorship is still lacking, I have not used "The Death Craft" to elaborate my argument. Nevertheless, I am convinced it is Melville's and, therefore, have decided to print it in full (for the first time since its original publication) in an appendix, to interpret it in the context of my argument, and to let the reader decide for himself whether or not it belongs in the canon.

[36] Neumann, I, 39, 40, 39, 94.

[37] Neumann, I, 36.

[38] Goldbrunner, p. 132.

[39] *Ibid.*, p. 134.

[40] Quoted by Eleanor Melville Metcalf in *Herman Melville* (Cambridge, Mass., 1953), pp. 92–93.

[41] Metcalf, p. 161.

[42] C. G. Jung, *Two Essays on Analytical Psychology*, trans. from the German by R. F. C. Hull (Cleveland: Meridian Paperback, 1956), pp. 182–83. Reprinted as Vol. 7 of *The Collected Works of C. G. Jung*.

[43] Jolande Jacobi, *The Psychology of C. G. Jung*, trans. from the German by K. W. Bash (5th ed., London, 1951), pp. 126, 145 (italics removed), 129.

[44] Jung, quoted by Jacobi, p. 130.

[45] Neuman, I, 198.

[46] Jacobi, pp. 131, 141.

[47] C. G. Jung, "The Stages of Life," *Modern Man in Search of a Soul*, trans. from the German by W. S. Dell and Cary F. Baynes, (New York, 1933), pp. 104ff. Reprinted in Vol. 8 of *The Collected Works of C. G. Jung*.

[48] Letters, p. 130 (to Hawthorne).

[49] Arvin, pp. 195–96.

[50] Jacobi, pp. 141–42.

[51] Quoted from Jung in Jacobi, p. 148.

[52] Jung, *Two Essays...*, pp. 250, 252.

[53] Jacobi, p. 154 (italics removed).

[54] Jung, *Two Essays ...*, p. 250.

[55] *Moby-Dick*, ed. Charles Feidelson, Jr. (New York, 1964), pp. 498–99.

[56] Jung, "Psychology and Literature," *Modern Man ...*, p. 154. Reprinted in Vol. 15 of *The Collected Works of C. G. Jung*.

[57] Jacobi, pp. 143, 142 (italics removed).

[58] Baird, p. 309.

[59] C. G. Jung, "Commentary on *The Secret of the Golden Flower*," trans. from the German by Cary F. Baynes, reprinted in *Psyche and Symbol*, ed. Violet S. de Laszlo (New York: Doubleday Anchor Paperback, 1958), p. 340. Reprinted in Vol. 13 of *The Collected Works of C. G. Jung*.

[60] William Braswell, *Melville's Religious Thought* (Durham, 1943), p. 124.

[61] Neumann, II, 414.

[62] *Patterns in Comparative Religion*, pp. 421, 419.

[63] C. G. Jung, *Aion: Contributions to the Symbolism of the Self*, trans. from the German by R. F. C. Hull, as reprinted in *Psyche and Symbol*, pp. 52, 35–36. Reprinted in Vol. 9, Part II, of *The Collected Works of C. G. Jung*.

[64] Jung, *Psyche and Symbol*, p. 38.

[65] Jung, "The Stages of Life," *Modern Man ...*, p. 110.

[66] Maud Bodkin, *Archetypal Patterns in Poetry* (Oxford, 1934), pp. 23, 60, 23–24.

[67] *Moby-Dick*, p. 641.

[68] Bodkin, p. 60.

[69] *Billy Budd, Sailor*, eds. Harrison Hayford and Merton M. Sealts, Jr. (Chicago, 1962), p. 129.

[70] Jolando Jacobi, "The Process of Individuation," *Journal of Analytical Psychology*, III (1958), 105.

[71] *Moby-Dick*, p. 181.

CHAPTER TWO

[1] The only full and corrected versions of the second "Fragment" is printed in *Melville's Early Life and Redburn* by William Gilman (New York, 1951), pp. 265–71.

[2] All page references to Melville's novels noted in the text of this chapter are to volume and page of the Constable Edition of Melville's *Works* (London, 1922–1924).

[3] Gilman, pp. 194–95.

[4] Gilman, p. 120.

[5] Donald Houghton, "The Incredible Ending of Melville's *Typee*," *ESQ*, No. 22 [1961], pp. 28–31.

[6] D. H. Lawrence, *Studies in Classic American Literature* (New York, 1923), p. 146. Lawrence was the first to recognize the unconscious implications in *Typee*. Amplifications of Lawrence's birth-myth theory may be found in Richard Chase, *Herman Melville* (New York, 1949), pp. 9–15; and in Helen Petrullo, "The Neurotic Hero of *Typee*," *American Imago*, XII (Winter, 1955), 317–23.

[7] Lawrence, p. 152.

[8] As a conservative in socio-cultural affairs, Babbalanja often stands in opposition to the more radical Taji (see pp. 60-61 for Babbalanja's opinions). I do not mean to diminish this aspect of Melville—indeed, it becomes more important as his career proceeds—but in this discussion of *Mardi* I shall concentrate on Taji because it is with him, after all, that the chartless voyage begins and ends.

[9] Milton Stern, *The Fine Hammered Steel of Herman Melville* (Urbana, 1957), p. 129.

[10] F. O. Matthiessen, *American Renaissance* (New York, 1941), p. 384.

[11] Chase, p. 34.

[12] James E. Miller, *A Reader's Guide to Herman Melville* (New York, 1962), p. xiii.

[13] Dorothee Metlitsky Finkelstein, *Melville's Orienda* (New Haven, 1961), p. 221.

[14] Erich Neumannn, *The Origins and History of Consciousness*, trans. from the German by R. F. C. Hull (New York: Harper Torchbook, 1962), I, 154, 156.

[15] Merrell R. Davis, *Melville's Mardi: A Chartless Voyage* (New York, 1952), p. 147, fn. 6. Davis notes that the name "Donjalolo" may be derived from the island Du Djailolo. Davis' book is the definitive account of the development of *Mardi* through successive versions, its satire and political allegory.

[16] Lawrence Thompson, *Melville's Quarrel with God* (Princeton, 1952), p. 67.

[17] Nathaniel Hawthorne, *English Note-Books*, 30 November 1856.

[18] Tyrus Hillway, "Taji's Abdication in Herman Melville's *Mardi*," *AL*, XVI (November, 1944), 206.

[19] William Gilman, *Melville's Early Life and Redburn*, fully discusses the relationship between the facts of Melville's biography and their imaginative projection in *Redburn*.

[20] *Redburn*, V, 321; *Pierre*, IX, 147. For other similarities between Redburn and Isabel, see p. 108.

[21] Howard Vincent, " 'White-Jacket': An Essay in Interpretation," *NEQ*, XXII (September, 1949), 314.

[22] Leslie Fiedler, *Love and Death in the American Novel* (New York, 1960), p. 523.

[23] George Stewart, "The Two Moby-Dicks," *AL*, XXV (January, 1954), 417ff.

[24] *The Letters of Herman Melville*, eds. Merrell R. Davis and William H. Gilman (New Haven, 1960), p. 117.

[25] *Letters*, p. 142.

[26] *Letters*, p. 146.

CHAPTER THREE

[1] Although most critics agree that the Whale is symbolic, a tiny minority dissents. See, for instance, E. E. Stoll, "Symbolism in *Moby-Dick*," *JHI*, XII (June, 1951), 450. "Of ambiguity, to be sure, there is plenty—contradiction and paradox, dualism and antinomy," but no symbolism.

[2] These points of view are respectively propounded by: [Evil] Yvor Winters, *Maule's Curse* as reprinted in *In Defense of Reason* (Denver, 1947), p. 201; thus Winters echoes Ahab, *Moby-Dick*, ed. Charles Feidelson, Jr. (New York, 1964), p. 247; all quotations from *Moby-Dick* in this chapter are from this edition. [Energies of Existence] Lewis Mumford, *Herman Melville* (New York, 1929), p. 184. [Phallic Being] D. H. Lawrence, *Studies in Classic American Literature* (New York, 1923), p. 173. [Freudian Super-Ego] Henry A. Murray, "In Nomine Diaboli," *Discussion of Moby Dick*, ed. Milton R. Stern (Boston, 1960), p. 29; reprinted from *NEQ*, XXIV (December, 1951), 432–52. [Parent] Newton Arvin, *Herman Melville* (New York, 1950), p. 173. [Life] Howard P. Vincent, *The Trying-Out of Moby Dick* (Boston, 1959), p. 180. [God] As God, Moby Dick has been characterized in three principal ways: as *Good* by Marius Bewley, *The Eccentric Design* (New York, 1959), p. 201; as a "Satan-God" with

Evil evidently predominant by Lawrance Thompson, *Melville's Quarrel with God* (Princeton, 1952), p. 171; and as *Indifferent* by, among others, Newton Arvin, p. 189.

[3] Again, identifying these points of view as they are stated in the text: [endlessly suggestive . . .] Richard Chase, *The American Novel and Its Tradition* (New York, 1957), p. 110. [essential of all meanings . . .] R. E. Watters, *Discussions*, p. 83; article reprinted from *UTQ*, XX (January, 1951), 155–68 "with a few changes by the author." [irreducible symbol . . .] Harry Levin, *The Power of Blackness* (New York, 1958), p. 233. [convincement . . .] Daniel Hoffman, *Form and Fable in American Fiction* (New York, 1961), p. 271.

[4] Treasure-hunting is particularly relevant in *Moby-Dick* because it strengthens the link between Ahab and the Germanic Epic Hero who, as in *Beowulf*, battles a dragon protecting a trove. Ishmael, we recall, following Isaiah, identifies dragons with whales. Note the following passage as well in which Stubb and his crew hunt gold:

[Stubb's] . . . crew were all in high excitement, eagerly helping their chief, and looking as anxious as gold-hunters. . . .
'I have it, I have it,' cried Stubb, with delight, striking something in the subterranean regions, 'a purse! a purse!!' (522)

[5] Watters, *Discussions*, p. 83.

[6] Geoffrey Stone in "Herman Melville: Loyalty to the Heart," *American Classics Reconsidered*, ed. Harold Gardiner, S.J. (New York, 1958), p. 223.

[7] The passivity of Queequeg, the archetypal sage, is best explicated by James Baird, *Ishmael* (Baltimore, 1956), pp. 226–55.

[8] See, for instance, Hoffman, *Form and Fable* . . . , p. 256: "The cannibal-bedmate is that part of Ishmael's own primeval self which asserts his love of life, as Ahab objectifies his primordial urge toward suicide."

[9] Hoffman, p. 270.

[10] The words are quoted by Perry Miller in *Consciousness at Concord* (Boston, 1958), p. 35.

[11] Chase, *The American Novel* . . . , p. 107.

[12] Hoffman, p. 258.

[13] An argument for Ahab as a tragic hero is made by Vincent in *The Trying-Out* . . . , pp. 109–17.

[14] William Ellery Sedgwick, *Herman Melville* (Cambridge, 1944), p. 97. See also Mumford, p. 189: "[Ahab] . . . stands for human purpose in its highest expression."

[15] Hoffman, p. 234. See also Henry F. Pommer, *Milton and Melville* (Pittsburgh, 1950), p. 98: Pommer notes how Ahab assumes the role of God and appropriates His function in "overcoming the devil. . . ."

16 R. W. Short, "Melville as Symbolist," *UKCR*, XV (Autumn, 1958), 45.

17 C. G. Jung, "Commentary on *The Secret of the Golden Flower*," trans. from the German by Cary F. Baynes, reprinted in *Psyche and Symbol*, ed. Violet S. de Laszlo (New York: Doubleday Anchor Paperback, 1958), pp. 321–22.

18 Jung, "Concerning Mandala Symbolism," from Vol. 9, Part I, *The Collected Works of C. G. Jung*, trans. from the German by R. F. C. Hull (Bollingen Series XX; New York, 1953-   ), p. 384.

19 Jolande Jacobi, *The Psychology of C. G. Jung*, trans. from the German by K. W. Bash (5th ed.; London, 1951), p. 158.

20 John Halverson, "The Shadow in *Moby-Dick*," *AQ*, XV (Fall, 1963), p. 440. Halverson is in part preceded by Dr. James Kirsch in "The Enigma of *Moby-Dick*," *Journal of Analytical Psychology*, III (1958), 135: Ishmael's marriage to Queequeg indicates "his union with the shadow and his beginning descent into the dark recesses of the collective unconscious."

21 Jung, "The Syzygy: Aniam and Animus," from *Aion*, reprinted in *Psyche and Symbol*, p. 21.

22 Jacobi, p. 131.

23 Jung, "Concerning Mandala Symbolism," p. 384.

24 Halverson, p. 445.

25 For a Freudian analysis of their love, see Leslie Fiedler, *Love and Death in the American Novel* (New York, 1960), pp. 531–39.

26 Arvin, p. 173; Murray, "In Nomine Diaboli," p. 30. See also the psychoanalysts, Edmund Bergler, "A Note on Herman Melville," *Am Imago*, XI (1954), 387; and Charles Kligerman, "The Psychology of Melville," *Psychoanalytic Review*, XL (April, 1953), 135.

27 W. H. Auden, *The Enchafèd Flood* (New York, 1950), pp. 148–49, 139.

28 Harry Slochower, "Freudian Motifs in *Moby-Dick*," *Complex*, III (Fall, 1950), 24.

29 Harry Slochower, "*Moby-Dick*," *AQ*, II (Fall, 1950), p. 264, fn. 6; reprinted in *Discussions*, pp. 45–51.

30 Robert Shulman, "The Serious Function of Melville's Phallic Jokes," *AL*, XXXIII (May, 1961), 192 notes that "The image of the 'ravished Europa' [midway through 'The Chase—First Day'] is basic to much of what follows, since at one—perhaps unconscious—level, the imagery in the remainder of the narrative is that of rape, of primal sexual assault." Of the "jokes" in *Moby-Dick* Shulman specifies the "phallic inneudo" implicit in "horn" imagery: Sir Martin Frobisher "on bended knee . . . presented [Queen Elizabeth with] . . . a prodigious long horn of the Narwhale, which for a long period after hung in the castle at Windsor" (18). Of particular interest is that Melville double-puns on "horn." Here it refers to the whale's "black

limber bone"; in "The Paradise of Bachelors," to the musical instrument. In both instances, the pun is phallic.

[31] Erich Neumann, *The Origins and History of Consciousness*, trans. from the German by R. F. C. Hull (New York: Harper Torchbook, 1962), I, 163.

[32] Neumann, I, 163.

[33] *Ibid.*, 152.

[34] *Ibid.*, 153.

[35] *Ibid.*, 165.

[36] *Ibid.*, 195.

[37] D. H. Lawrence, pp. 62–64.

[38] Herman Melville, *Pierre or, The Ambiguities*, ed. Henry A. Murray (New York, 1949), p. xiii. All quotations from *Pierre* in this chapter are from this edition.

[39] Newton Arvin, *Herman Melville* (New York, 1950), p. 218.

[40] Murray, p. xiv.

[41] See R. P. Blackmur, *The Expense of Greatness* (New York, 1940), p. 165. *Pierre* is a failure "because of [Melville's] . . . radical inability to master a technique—that of the novel—radically foreign to his sensibility."

[42] Rendered in psychoanalytic terms, this explanation runs as follows: [Melville's] . . . "destructive attack on the symbolic mother-image [in *Moby-Dick*] only worsened his position in relation to the punitive, maternal superego, and the conflict raged on with continued fury. But now [during the writing of *Pierre*, which was not the case during the writing of *Moby-Dick*] Melville lacked the support of Hawthorne [a "Good Father" figure] and faced his new tasks with a decompensating ego so that the fantasies emerged in much less disguised form. . . ." (138). "Too much was required [of Melville] in the desperate defensive struggle to maintain ego integrity . . . therefore . . . much of what is projected [in *Pierre*] attains a reality of its own and is no longer subject to the control of the ego" (140). See Charles Kligerman, "The Psychology of Melville," *Psychoanalytic Review*, XL (April, 1953), 125–43.

[43] George C. Homans, "The Dark Angel: The Tragedy of Herman Melville," *NEQ*, V (October, 1932), 699, 729. Homans, anticipating both Willard Thorp and Ellery Sedgwick notes that *Mardi*, *Moby-Dick*, and *Pierre* form "a tragedy in three acts," "the tragedy of the mind refusing to admit its limits."

[44] *The Letters of Herman Melville*, eds. Merrell R. Davis and William H. Gilman (New Hoven, 1960), p. 142.

[45] For the identification of Plinlimmon with Hawthorne, see Murray, p. lxxviii–lxxix.

46 Leon Howard, *Herman Melville: A Biography* (Berkeley, 1951), p. 236.

47 Howard, p. 313.

48 *Collected Poems of Herman Melville*, ed. Howard P. Vincent (Chicago, 1947), pp. 229–29.

49 Richard Chase, *Herman Melville* (New York, 1949), pp. 114–15.

50 It is also called the Memnon Stone, and Melville notes that Memnon—who is a kind of prefiguration of the later Pierre—died before the walls of Troy. H. Bruce Franklin, *The Wake of the Gods* (Stanford, 1963), p. 118, tells us that the Testing has Druidic antecedents, and that, by crawling beneath the Stone, Pierre "relives a primitive Druidic ritual."

51 Murray, pp. 475–76. For amplification of Murray's thesis, see William Van O'Connor's "Plotinus Plinlimmon and the Principle of Name Giving," in *The Grotesque* (Carbondale, 1962), pp. 92–97.

52 Merlin Bowen, *The Long Encounter* (Chicago, 1960), p. 112 regards Plinlimmon as a "dramatic prefiguration" of a "withdrawn and self-absorbed diety. . . ."

53 Murray, p. lxiii.

54 Walls also invade Delly Ulver's rhetoric. Like Father Mapple praying in the belly of a whale, Delly, another believer, prays for salvation through a wall: 'God that made me, and that wast not so hard to me as wicked Delly deserved,—God that made me, I pray to thee! ward it [sin] off from me, if it be coming to me. Be not deaf to me; these stony walls—Thou canst hear through them.' (378). But there is no evidence that the God who responds to Father Mapple ever hears poor Delly, another instance of the corrosive irony of *Pierre*.

55 Marius Bewley, *The Eccentric Design* (New York, 1957), p. 219.

56 Ulalume is buried in a "misty mid region," near a "dank tarn," in a "ghoul-haunted woodland," and her tomb is visited when "the leaves . . . [are] withering and sere" and 'the skies . . . ashen and sober." Similarly, Isabel lives in a "wet and misty" region (128), near a silent lake surrounded by "mysterious mountain masses," and she too is visited "at fall of eve" beneath "the unfeatured heavens" (128), when from out "the depths of caves and rotted leaves . . . of those profoundest forests came," among other sounds, the devilish gibberish of the forest—ghouls" (129).

57 Murray, p. li.

58 Leslie Fiedler, *Love and Death in the American Novel* (New York, 1960), p. 535.

59 *Directionary of American Slang*, comp. and ed. by Harold Wentworth and Stuart Berg Flexner (New York, 1960). Although the editors cite only twentieth-century examples for the sexual meanings of "lay" and "screw,"

they do comment further as follows: "Even though taboo ['lay'] . . . is so common as to be colloq. The ety. may be the lit. one, to 'lay' a woman down for sexual purposes. However, the psychological relationship between taking or stealing and sex, as shown in several other sl. words, points to an obvious relation between the two . . . meanings. Thus 'lay' = coitus prob. grew out of 'lay' = robbery, or fig. taking or stealing sexual pleasure from a woman. Unfortunately, most dictionaries and researchers ignore such taboo words; thus it is difficult to establish a first date for this use, *but it is old.*" (Definition 2, p. 313). (Italics removed throughout except for the last clause.) The editors derive "screw" "from the taboo but *too old and well known* to be sl. v.i., v.t. 'to screw' = to have . . . sexual satisfaction through sexual intercourse. . . ." (Definition 7, p. 452.) (Italics added.)

60 ". . . the sweet unconditional thought of Lucy slid wholly into his soul, dislodging thence all such phantom inhabitants," a clear allusion to Isabel (57); and, "For an instant, the fond, all-understood blue eyes of Lucy displaced the as tender, but mournful and inscrutable dark glance of Isabel" (515).

61 Milton Stern, *The Fine Hammered Steel of Herman Melville* (Urbana, 1957), p. 176, fn. 12. Other instances of such use of language unnoted by Stern but which provide useful insights into the text are these (1)–Isabel's letter to Pierre warns him that if he tries to rescue her, the world will call him "fool, fool, fool!" (74); this is precisely what he imagines Plinlimmon calls him (345), the prophecy come true. (2)–Lucy tells Pierre that, as lovers, they must not keep secrets from one another so that "when I walk the streets, and meet thy friends, I must still be laughing and hugging to myself the thought,—They know him not. . . ." (43); the last spoken words in the book are Isabel's to Charlie Millthorpe in allusion to Pierre, " 'All's o'er, and ye know him not!'" (427). (3)–Speculating on the personality of Pierre's father on the basis of his bachelor portrait, Melville tells us that he was "a very little bladish perhaps" (85), but the word assumes a more sinister connotation when we learn that several young men at Glen Stanly's party also have "bladish voices" (279). (4)–We should also observe the many ironic turns taken by the word "rave": first Mrs. Glendinning advises her son, "Never rave, Pierre; and never rant. Your father never did either. . . ." (20); then, in the belief that the unacknowledged Isabel is his sister, Pierre cries, "I will be a raver, and none shall stay me!" (76); third, in recollection of his father's death, Pierre thinks, "Mince the matter how his family would, had not his father died a raver? [A refutation of his mother's statement]. Whence that raving, following so prosperous a life? Whence, but from the cruellest compunctions?" (209). Melville of course well remembered that his own father had died mad after a prosperous life before meeting business disaster. Fourth, in a passage previously quoted, Isabel tells Pierre (who has just voiced, however elliptically, the realization of his incestuous desires)

that "this is some incomprehensible raving" (321); and finally, at the news of his mother's death, Pierre "wept, he raved, at the bitter loss of his parent" (336). Other ravers in Melville include Taji, Ahab, and the peg-legged cynic in *The Confidence Man*.

[62] For other similarities and differences, see Mary Dichmann, "Absolutism in Melville's *Pierre*," *PMLA*, LXVII (September, 1952), 702–15. Although it may be argued that "Saddle Meadows and the Apostles' are but differing manifestations of the same social system, their seeming dichotomy . . . in reality an example of the simultaneity of all human experience," I should rather argue that if these societies are coincidentally alike in that each collaborates in crushing Pierre, that tells us more about the constancy of Pierre's behavior than about the societies'.

[63] William Ellery Sedgwick, *Herman Melville* (Cambridge, 1944), p. 145.

[64] Murray, p. lxiii.

[65] His entrance into New York City is, nonetheless, described in images from the Inferno. See Howard H. Schless, "Flaxman, Dante, and Melville's *Pierre*," *BNYPL*, LXIV (February, 1960), 74ff.

[66] One should observe the nearness of Charlie's oratorical tendency and political opinions to those of Melville's own older brother, Gansevoort, who was a hard-working orator in Polk's campaign for the Presidency in 1844 and who once observed in a private communication to the candidate:

First, the Texas question has not been argued before the people on the stump as it should have been fully, boldly, and directly. In the 10 or 12 mass meetings which I talked to in this state from the Ohio river to Lake Erie I found it to be universally the case that the people listened to a manly discussion of that issue with interest and even astonishment pictured in their faces and fairly with their mouths open—

(See Jay Leyda, *The Melville Log* [New York, 1951], p. 185.) That Herman would subject Gansevoort to worse than ridicule, even long after his death, is certain from an analysis of "Timoleon" (c. 1877), (see p. 219); that he would parody Gansevoort's ideas in *Pierre* and calumniate his "brilliant" brother as the witless Millthorpe seems evident from the synonymity of their names: as *Pierre* is to *Stanly*, so (as Mr. Harry de Puy once observed in conversation) is Mel-*ville* to Mill-*thorpe*. That *Pierre* is, in fact, a sardonic, even vicious, *roman à clef* is clear from Dr. Murray's skillful demonstration (see *Pierre*, ed. Murray, p. xxiiff.)

[67] Chase, p. 120.

[68] Erich Neumann, *The Origins and History of Consciousness*, trans. from the German by R. F. S. Hull (New York: Harper Torchbook, 1962), I, 88ff.

[69] Neumann, I, 88.

[70] Murray, p. liii.

[71] Neumann, I, 198.

[72] *Ibid.*

[73] Murray, p. xliv.

[74] Neumann, I, 202–3.

[75] *Ibid.*, 204.

[76] *Ibid.*, 198.

[77] Sigmund Freud, "Medusa's Head," trans. from the German by James Strachey, reprinted in *Collected Papers*, ed. James Strachey (New York: Basic Books, 1959), V, 105–6.

[78] Neumann, I, 214.

[79] Richard Chase, *Herman Melville* (New York, 1949), pp. 143ff. All page references in the text are to the *Selected Writings of Herman Melville* (New York: Modern Library Giant, 1952). This edition reproduces Jay Leyda's text of *The Complete Stories of Herman Melville* (New York, 1949).

[80] Richard Fogle, *Melville's Shorter Tales* (Norman, 1960), p. 18.

[81] Kingsley Widmer, "The Negative Affirmation: Melville's 'Bartleby,' *MFS*, VIII (Autumn, 1962), 282 also notes this "Cain-and-Abel motif." Widemer's final judgment is that "Bartleby" is a "sardonic existential comedy in which the rebellious negation is Melville's real affirmation" (p. 286, fn. 16).

[82] Mordecai Marcus, "Melville's 'Bartleby' as a Psychological Double," *CE*, XIII (February, 1962), 367. Marcus also suggests that "the wall may . . . symbolize those limitations which give every individual his personal identity. . . ." (367) and "the human condition in the society within which Bartleby feels trapped, and by extension the burden of his own identity within the limitations of such a society" (368).

[83] Leo Marx also makes this point in "Mellville's Parable of the Walls," *SR*, LXI (Autumn, 1953), 605–7.

[84] Milton Stern, *The Fine Hammered Steel of Herman Melville* (Urbana, 1957), p. 198.

[85] Quoted by Wylie Sypher, "Our New Sense of the Comic,' 'in *Comedy* (New York, 1956), pp. 196–97.

[86] *Ibid.*, p. 197.

[87] *Ibid.*, p. 198.

CHAPTER FOUR

[1] All quotations in the text from the short stories are from the *Selected Writings of Herman Melville* (New York: Modern Library Giant, 1952). Although I follow the general sequence in which these tales were written, I do

not discuss them in the strictest chronological order. Rather I am guided by patterns of theme, motif, etc. As a consequence, for instance, I discuss "The Bell-Tower" and "Jimmy Rose" before "Benito Cereno," although Melville probably wrote them after. *Pierre* quotations from the Murray edition (New York, 1949).

2 It should be noted, however, that in certain respects they are vastly dissimilar. See Richard H. Fogle, *Melville's Shorter Tales* (Norman, 1960), pp. 32–33.

3 For interpretations of the other names in "The Fiddler"—Hautboy, Helmstone, and Standard—see Richard Chase, *Herman Melville* (New York, 1949), p. 175, fn.*; and W. R. Thompson, "Melville's 'The Fiddler': A Study in Dissolution," *TSLL*, II (1961), 495ff.

4 James Baird, *Ishmael* (Baltimore, 1956), p. 341.

5 Like the Lightning-Rod Man, the Happy Failure is also something of a Confidence Man *before* he gives up the quest. He inveigles his nephew into rowing ten miles upstream in the blazing sun with the heavy mechanism aboard: "Now then, if you don't want to share in the glory of my experiment; if you are wholly indifferent to halving its immortal renown; I say, sir, if you care not to be present at the first trial of my Great Hydraulic-Hydrostatis Apparatus [cf. The Confidence Man's Omni-Balsamic Reinvigorator] for draining swamps and marshes, and converting them, at the rate of one acre the hour, into fields and more fertile than those of the Genessee [sic]; if you care not, I repeat, to have this proud thing to tell—in far future days, when poor old I shall have been long dead and gone, boy—to your children and your children's children; in that case, sir, you are free to land forthwith." (224–25)

6 Chase, p. 168.

7 "Cultural failure"—Baird, p. 399; "castration"—Chase, pp. 124–25.

8 Johann Sebastian Bach's own nickname was "Old Wig."

9 References to the notoriously sexual "The Tartarus of Maids" have ranged from E. H. Eby's pioneering and hence rather primitive reading to William Bysshe Stein's quite sophisticated analysis. [See Eby, "Herman Melville's 'Tartarus of Maids,' " *MLQ*, I (1940), 95–100; and Stein, "Melville's Eros," *TSLL*, III (1961), 297–308, an article which discusses both halves of the diptych.]

10 My reading, although different in detail and emphasis, is substantially the same as Professor Fogle's. See Fogle, pp. 36ff.

11 The presence of Thoreau in Melville's work seems to confine itself to just those Berkshire years between 1853 and 1857. Thoreau is most notably present, as Egbert, in *The Confidence-Man* [see Egbert S. Oliver, "Melville's Pictures of Emerson and Thoreau in *The Confidence-Man*," *CE*, VIII

(1946), 61–72]; and least probably an influence on that tale of another
solitary dissenter, "Bartleby" [although Oliver makes a try: see "A Second
Look at 'Bartleby,' " *CE*, VI (May, 1945), 431–39.] On somewhat safer
ground Oliver tries to demonstrate how Melville satirically uses *A Week*
in " 'Cock-a-Doodle-Doo!' and Transcendental Hocus-Pocus," *NEQ*, XXI
(June, 1948), 204–16; and William Bysshe Stein in "Melville Roasts
Thoreau's Cock," *MLN*, LXXIV (March, 1959), 218–19 does demonstrate
Melville's parodic use of Thoreau's "Walking" essay in "Cock-A-Doodle-
Doo!" Melville also took some of the details for his "The Apple-Tree
Table" from *Walden* [see Frank Davidson, "Melville, Thoreau, and 'The
Apple-Tree Table,' " *AL*, XXV (January, 1954), 479–88]. In short, Mel-
ville seems to have maintained an unspoken dialogue with Thoreau just as
he had with Emerson.

[12] Richard Fogle notes the parallelism of these scenes but does not comment
on it. Fogle, p. 16.

[13] Sidney Kaplan, "Herman Melville and the American National Sin: The
Meaning of 'Benito Cereno,' " *JNH*, XLI (1956), 311–38, and XLII
(1957), 11–37. The quoted phrase is from XLI, 330. William Bysshe Stein
regards the shaving scene as "a rite of castration" and Max Putzel recognizes
the implications of castration therein; "threatened castration" would be more
precise. See Stein, "The Moral Axis of 'Benito Cereno,' " *Accent*, XV
(1955), 221–33; and Putzel, "The Source and the Symbols of Melville's
'Benito Cereno,' " *AL*, XXXIV (1962), 191–206.

[14] Quotations from *Israel Potter* are to *His Fifty Years of Exile (Israel Potter)*,
(New York: American Century Series, 1957).

[15] John T. Frederick, "Symbol and Theme in Melville's *Israel Potter*," *MFS*,
VIII, iii, [1962], 266, 268, and 272 respectively.

[16] Quoted by Howard C. Horsford, *Melville's Journal of A Visit to Europe
and the Levant, October 11, 1856–May 6, 1857* (Princeton, 1955), p. 19.

[17] In reading *The Confidence-Man* as a Hindu myth, H. Bruce Franklin has
traveled a road as far apart from mine as is possible, and yet we have arrived
at similar conclusions: "Melville made the shape-shifting struggles and the
ultimate identity of Vishnu [the Preserver] and Siva [the Destroyer] into
the central structural fact of *The Confidence-Man*. Confidence and distrust,
tame animals and wild animals, love and hate—all become indistinguishable
in a universe in which black is only another appearance of white." See Franklin, *The Wake of the Gods* (Stanford, 1963), p. 187. Quotations from *The
Confidence-Man* are to the Grove Press edition (New York, 1949).

[18] Daniel Hoffman, "Melville's 'Story of China Aster,' " *AL*, XXII (May,
1950), 146 for translation of Orchis; John W. Schroeder, "Sources and
Symbols for Melville's *Confidence-Man*," *PMLA*, LXVI (June, 1951),

363–80 notes seven instances in which the Con Man is spoken of in snake imagery.

[19] Lewis Leary, Introduction to *His Fifty Years of Exile*, p. viii.

[20] Newton Arvin, *Herman Melville* (New York, 1950), p. 249.

[21] This quotation is taken from John D. Seelye's adaptation of Appendix I in the Hendricks House edition of *The Confidence-Man*, ed. Elizabeth S. Foster (New York, 1954), pp. 379–90. It clearly illustrates the kind of prose Melville apparently wrote for, but ultimately eliminated from, *The Confidence-Man*:

Above the Falls of St. Anthony for the most part he [The Mississippi] winds evenly in between banks of flags or through tracts of pine over marbled sands in waters so clear that the deepest fish have the visible flight of the bird. Undisturbed as the lonely life in this bosom feeds the lonely life on its shores, the coronetted elk and the deer, while in the watery form of some mossy crouched rock in the channel, furred over with moss, the furred bear on the marge seems to eye his amphibious brother. Wood and wave wed, man is remote. The Unsung Time, the Golden Age of the billow.

By his Fall, though he rise not again, the unhumbled river ennobles himself, now deepens, now purely expands, now first forms his character and begins that career whose majestic serenity, if not overborne by fierce onsets of torrents, shall end only with ocean.

Like a larger Susquehanna, like a long-drawn bison herd, he hurries on through the prairie, here and there expanding into archipelagoes cycladean in beauty, while fissured and verdant, a long China Wall, the bluffs sweep bluely away. Glad and content the sacred river glides on.

But at St. Louis the course of this dream is run. Down on it like a Pawnee from ambush foams the yellow-jacket Missouri. The calm is gone, the grouped isles disappear, the shores are ragged and rent, the hue of the water is clayed, the before moderate current is rapid and vexed. The peace of the Upper River seems broken in the Lower, nor [is it] ever renewed.

The Missouri sends rather a hostile element than a filial flow. Longer, stronger than the father of waters, like Jupiter he dethrones his sire and reigns in his stead. Under the benign name Mississippi, it is in short the Missouri that now rolls to the Gulf, the Missouri that with the snows from his solitudes freezes the warmth of the genial zones, the Missouri that by open assault or artful sap sweeps away fruit and field, graveyard and barn, the Missouri, that not a tributary but an outlaw enters the sea, long disdaining to yield his white wave to the blue.

See "Timothy Flint's 'Wicked River' and *The Confidence-Man*," *PMLA*, LXXVIII (March, 1963), 75. The sweeping rhythms and ornate effects of this passage are peculiar to the author of "The Piazza."

[22] Merton M. Sealts, Jr., *Melville as Lecturer* (Cambridge, Mass., 1957), p. 136, fn. 13.

[23] Richard Fogle is also impressed by this quality, calling it "archly ornate" and "dangerously overwrought," p. 85.

[24] William Ellery Sedgwick, *Herman Melville* (Cambridge, Mass., 1944), p. 194.

[25] Henry E. Pommer, *Milton and Melville* (Pittsburgh, 1950), p. 33.

[26] Merton M. Sealts, Jr., "Herman Melville's 'I and My Chimney,' " *AI*, XIII (1941), 150.

[27] Chase, pp. 170, 171.

[28] As a symbol the chimney has been interpreted in various ways other than as Secular Reality and the Masculine Phallus. I have already noted the opinions of Sedgwick and Chase. Sealts asserts (147) that it represents Melville's "heart and soul," and he might have added sciatic spine; Stuart C. Woodruff regards it as "an emblem of the empirical reality of time." [His argument is much more convincing than this bare statement allows: see Woodruff, "Melville and His Chimney," *PMLA*, LXXV (June, 1960), 285.] In short, like the White Whale, the Chimney is a rich enough symbol to permit divergent explications and, to some degree, to accommodate them all.

[29] Another pun, obscene and not very funny, concerns the "ash-hole" (401) at the base of the chimney.

[30] E. Hale Chatfield, "Levels of Meaning in Melville's 'I and My Chimney,' " *AI*, XIX, (1962), 168. For other evidence identifying the chimney with the phallus, see p. 167.

[31] Frank Davidson, p. 487.

[32] Horsford, *Journal*, p. 167.

[33] *The Letters of Herman Melville*, eds. Merrell R. Davis and William H. Gilman (New Haven, 1960), p. 129 (to Hawthorne).

[34] *Journal of a Visit to London and the Continent by Herman Melville*, ed. Eleanor Melville Metcalf (Cambridge, Mass., 1948), p. 18. *Letters*, p. 199 (to Allan Melville).

[35] *Letters*, p. 96 (to Evert Duyckinck).

[36] *Letters*, p. 143 (to Hawthorne).

[37] *Collected Poems of Herman Melville*, ed. Howard P. Vincent (Chicago, 1947); poems quoted in this section are from this edition. Hennig Cohen reminds us that a source for "Pausilippo" was the imprisonment of the Italian dramatist Sylvio Pellico (1789–1854) for "revolutionary activities." Melville apparently saw his own plight mirrored therein, and dramatized Pellico's fate to suit his own purposes. See *Selected Poems of Herman Melville*, ed. Hennig Cohen (New York: Doubleday Anchor Paperback, 1964), p. 203.

[38] Horsford, *Journal*, pp. 141–42.

39 Dorothee Metlitsky Finkelstein, *Melville's Orienda* (New Haven, 1961), p. 224.

40 Leon Howard, *Herman Melville: A Biography* (Berkeley, 1951), p. 140.

41 *Ibid.*, p. 155.

42 *Ibid.*, p. 267.

43 Horsford, *Journal*, pp. 187–88.

CHAPTER FIVE

1 Leon Howard, *Herman Melville: A Biography* (Berkeley, 1951), p. 281.

2 *The Letters of Herman Melville*, eds. Merrell R. Davis and William H. Gilman (New Haven, 1960), p. 199 (to Allan Melville).

3 All quotations from Melville's poetry in the text of this chapter (with the exception of those from *Clarel*) are taken from the *Collected Poems of Herman Melville*, ed. Howard P. Vincent (Chicago, 1947). Hereafter cited as *Collected Poems*.

4 Robert Penn Warren, "Melville the Poet," *KR*, VIII (Spring, 1946), 218ff.

5 *Selected Poems of Herman Melville*, ed. Hennig Cohen (New York: Doubleday Anchor Paperback, 1964), p. 183.

6 *Melville's Journal of a Visit to Europe and the Levant, October 11, 1856– May 6, 1857*, ed. Howard C. Horsford (Princeton, 1955), p. 132.

7 Mircea Eliade, *The Sacred and the Profane*, trans. from the French by Williard R. Trask (New York: Harper Torchbook Paperback, 1961), pp. 43, 45.

8 Horsford, *Journal*, p. 149.

9 From the Introduction to *Clarel: A Poem and Pilgrimage in the Holy Land*, ed. Walter E. Bezanson (New York, 1960), pp. lxxxiv–lxxxv. All quotations in the text are to this edition.

10 Bezanson, p. 580.

11 Bezanson, pp. lxix, lxx.

12 C. G. Jung, "Yoga and the West," from Vol. 11, *The Collected Works of C. G. Jung*, p. 535.

13 C. G. Jung, "Commentary on *The Secret of the Golden Flower*," trans. from the German by Cary F. Baynes, reprinted in *Psyche and Symbol*, ed. Violet S. de Laszlo (New York: Doubleday Anchor Paperback, 1958), p. 340.

14 James Baird, *Ishmael* (Baltimore, 1956), p. 422.

15 Baird, p. 422.

16 Bezanson, p. 640.

[17] Bezanson, p. 640.

[18] *Ibid.*, p. cxvii, fn. 105.

[19] Bezanson, p. 640.

[20] *Moby-Dick*, ed. Charles Feidelson, Jr. (New York, 1964), p. 364.

[21] From "In a Bye-Canal" in the *Collected Poems*, p. 240.

[22] William Bysshe Stein, "Melville's Poetry: Its Symbols of Individuation," *L&P*, VII (May, 1957), 21.

[23] C. G. Jung, *Answer to Job*, trans. from the German by R. F. C. Hull (Cleveland: Meridian Paperback, 1960), p. 181.

[24] Howard, p. 334.

[25] Walter Sutton, "Melville's 'Pleasure Party' and the Art of Concealment," *PQ*, XXX (July, 1951), 326.

[26] *Letters*, p. 121 (to Evert Duyckinck).

[27] For additional resemblances and evidence of dating, see Merton M. Sealts, Jr., "Melville's Burgundy Club Sketches," *HLB*, XII (Winter, 1958), 253–67.

[28] Quotations by members of the "coterie" are taken from Eleanor Melville Metcalf, *Herman Melville* (Cambridge, 1953), pp. 267, 278, 276, 274 respectively.

[29] Jay Leyda, *The Melville Log* (New York, 1951), p. 378.

[30] *The Works of Herman Melville*, ed. Raymond W. Weaver (London, 1922–1924), XIII [*Billy Budd and Other Prose Pieces*], pp. 339–45.

[31] Dorothee Metlitsky Finkelstein, *Melville's Orienda* (New Haven, 1961), p. 110.

[32] *Ibid.*, p. 112.

[33] *Billy Budd and Other Prose Pieces*, pp. 117–22.

[34] William Braswell, *Melville's Religious Thought* (Durham, 1943), p. 125.

[35] Metcalf, p. xvi.

[36] Leyda, p. 359.

[37] *Pierre*, ed. Murray, p. 16.

[38] F. O. Matthiessen, *American Renaissance* (New York, 1941), p. 509.

[39] *Answer to Job*, p. 197.

[40] The novel "which sheds most light on *Billy Budd* is, as one might expect, *White-Jacket*" says Leonard Casper in "The Case against Captain Vere," *Per*, V (Summer, 1952), 147. Many of the resemblances in language and idea have been pointed to by Harrison Hayford and Merton M. Sealts, Jr. in their definitive edition [see *Billy Budd, Sailor* (Chicago, 1962)], and here are cited only the most important affinities between these two works.

Melville himself draws the first connection by dedicating *Billy Budd* to Jack Chase, the Handsome Sailor of *White-Jacket*. Both books describe "The World in a Man-of-War"—the *Neversink* and the *Indomitable* (an earlier name for the ship eventually renamed the *Bellipotent*). Aboard each, naval inhumanity is ironically afforded legal and Christian sanction, and it has even been suggested that Article XIV of the Articles of War as printed in *White-Jacket* "contains what is, probably, the germ of *Billy Budd*": see Arthur Sale, "Captain Vere's Reasons," *Cambridge Journal*, V (October, 1951), 6.

All the major characters and several of the minor ones in *Billy Budd* are drawn, to one degree or another, from *White-Jacket*. The insidious Bland has long been recognized as the prototype of Claggart, and Hayford and Sealts note that as one of Claggarts corporals is nicknamed "Squeak," so when "Bland is suspended from his office, a suspected informer called 'Sneak' takes his place. . . ." (167). The cold-blooded surgeon Cadwallader Cuticle seems to have sat for the heartless Surgeon in *Billy Budd* who hurriedly leaves the mess to return to the sick bay; and Norman Holmes Pearson observes that "In the crew of the *Neversink* was the physical duplicate of the aged Dansker, the mainmastman who served as Billy's 'Delphic counsellor . . .' ": see "*Billy Budd*: 'The King's Yarn,'" *AQ*, III (Summer, 1951), 102.

According to James E. Miller, Jack Chase derives from the same stock as Captain Vere: both are men of "moderation with heart and intellect in ideal balance"; both add "to an instinctive wisdom the wisdom of books"; both are "without a trace of deception." See *A Reader's Guide to Herman Melville* (New York, 1962), pp. 225–26. But Charles Anderson draws an equally cogent parallel between Jack Chase and Billy Budd, and, therefore it would appear that Chase served as a portrait for both the young Handsome Sailor and the older Good Administrator (in Milton Stern's phrase); Anderson associates

their common possession of high health and fine looks, their frankness and candor, their free and easy but courteous manners, their good hearts which made them loved by the men, and their excellent seamanship which made them admired by the officers. More specifically, in both cases their masculine beauty was marred by a single defect, Chase by the loss of a finger, Budd by a tendency to stammer; and, again, though both were of obscure origin, they were obviously gentlemen and, it is hinted, 'by blows' of some nobleman.

See Charles R. Anderson, "The Genesis of *Billy Budd*," AL, XII (November, 1940), 344.

Finally, we should note that White Jacket, as well as Jack Chase, contributes to the character of Billy. Arthur Sale (in an article cited above) suggests that the incident in which White Jacket is almost flogged,

whether personal experience or not, must have remained unhealed in
Melville's mind, for, half a century later, he makes Billy Budd so horrified
to see a man flogged for the same minor fault of which White Jacket is
accused that the young sailor binds himself never to 'make himself liable
to such a visitation.' (6)

The fact is that both men are originally innocent and do not "fall" until
innocence is violently wrestled from them.

41 John B. Noone, Jr., "*Billy Budd*: Two Concepts of Nature," *AL*, XXIX
   (November, 1957), p. 249.

42 E. L. Grant Watson, "Melville's Testament of Acceptance," *NEQ*, VI (June,
   1933), 324–25.

43 C. G. Jung, *Aion: Contributions to the Symbolism of the Self*, trans. from
   the German by R. F. C. Hull, reprinted in *Psyche and Symbol*, p. 39.

44 W. H. Auden, *The Enchafèd Flood* (New York, 1950), pp. 148–49.

45 Captain Vere, as he exists in Melville's "unfinished" manuscript, has been
   subject to extraordinarily diverse interpretation by many reputable critics; in
   this respect he is like the Whale about whom there is also neither agreement
   nor a moratorium on criticism in sight. A tactful introduction to the problem may be found in Hayford and Sealts, *Billy Budd, Sailor*, pp. 24–39.

46 Eleanor M. Tilton, "Melville's 'Rammon': A Text and Commentary," *HLB*,
   XIII (Winter, 1959), 62.

47 Hayford and Sealts, pp. 31–32.

48 Watson, pp. 324–25.

49 Richard Chase, *Herman Melville* (New York, 1949), p. 275.

50 Milton R. Stern, *The Fine Hammered Steel of Herman Melville* (Urbana,
   1957), p. 220.

51 Northrop Frye, *Anatomy of Criticism* (Princeton, 1957), p. 162.

52 *Ibid.*, p. 192.

53 *Ibid.*, p. 215.

54 Jolande Jacobi, *The Psychology of C. G. Jung*, trans. from the German by
   K. W. Bash (5th ed., London, 1951), p. 169.

55 *Billy Budd, Sailor*, p. 128.

56 Victor White, O. P., *Soul and Psyche: An Enquiry into the Relationship of
   Psychotherapy and Religion* (New York, 1960), p. 181.

57 *Letters*, p. 130; *Collected Poems*, p. 482.

APPENDIX

1 Published in *The Democratic Press and Lansingburgh Advertiser* for 16 No-

vember 1839—the relevant issue is housed in the Public Library in Troy, New York—Melville undoubtedly wrote "The Death Craft" soon after returning from his voyage to Liverpool that summer. Certainly the nautical language is deliberately technical, as if, by using a terminology too complex for ordinary landlubbers to fathom, the pseudonymous author were parading his own seaworthiness—not to say his newly acquired vocabulary.

In transcribing this sketch I have regularized the spelling and punctuation, although I have not in general tampered with Melville's melodramatic dashes and exclamation points.

[2] Erich Neumann, *The Origins and History of Consciousness*, trans. from the German by R.F.C. Hull (New York: Harper Torchbook, 1962), I, 57.

[3] *Moby-Dick*, ed. Charles Feidelson, Jr. (New York, 1964), p. 682.

[4] *Ibid.*, p. 683.

Index to the Text